REALITY Quest

The Doctrines of God, the Bible, Man, Sin, Salvation, Christ, the Holy Spirit, Christian Living, the Church, Spirit Beings and Future Events

Student Edition

Authors
Sharon R. Berry, Ph.D.
Ollie E. Gibbs, Ed.D.

LifeWay

LifeWay.

Published by
LifeWay Christian School Resources
Nashville, Tennessee

Created and Developed by
Christian Academic Publications and Services, Inc.
Birmingham, Alabama

ISBN: 978-1-4158-3483-1
Item Number: 005035295
Dewey Decimal Classification: 248.82
Subject Heading: TEENAGERS / CHRISTIAN LIFE--TEXTS / BIBLE--TEXTS / DOCTRINE

RealityQuest, Student Edition, Revised

Printed in the United States of America.

For ordering or inquiries visit *www.lifeway.com*, or write LifeWay Church Resources Customer Service, One LifeWay Plaza, Nashville, TN 37234-0113.

RealityQuest
Table of Contents

RealityQuest
Table of Contents

The Doctrine of the Holy Spirit

The Doctrine of Christian Living

The Doctrine of the Church

The Doctrine of Spirit Beings

The Doctrine of Future Events

RealityQuest
Introduction

In previous *QUEST* courses, students have studied the Bible in chronological order or have studied portions of Scripture in depth. With this background you are now ready to begin one of the most fascinating studies of Scripture—that of seeing how various portions of Scripture, written over about 1600 years, all blend together to cohesively present the truths of God. These truths are called doctrines, simply meaning "the teachings."

In each unit you will study various passages related to a single subject, such as God, the Bible, mankind, sin, Christ, salvation, Christian living, church, angels, Satan, hell, Heaven and future events. You will have the opportunity to discover exactly what the Bible, as a whole, teaches about a particular topic. For example, for the Doctrine of Man: Where did mankind come from? What accounts for mankind's tremendous abilities and potential? What happened to destroy mankind's original purpose? What accounts for mankind's inherent nature? How can mankind live successfully? What will the future be for mankind?

As always, you will not just be learning lots of information for the sake of knowledge. The principle of Bible study is to learn so as to do. Therefore, you will have lots of opportunities to put into practice what you study. The ultimate objective of this course is the application of Scriptural principles to life's everyday challenges. Because the course is more topical in design, you may find it challenging. However, the truths you learn this year will give you a solid foundation for the future.

You will encounter several unique features in the course. First, each unit relates to a setting where young adults are conducting research, either to fulfill assignments or to satisfy their own quest for answers. Their experiences are similar to those you are likely to encounter in the future. Their questions, their findings, and their conclusions provide a real-life context for the truths you will study.

A second feature is your challenge to develop a set of good notes that logically and clearly present the topic being addressed in each unit. From these, you will write your own summaries so that you will have a ready reference for future studies. Be conscientious in keeping a notebook for the material presented and in completing each assignment, entitled QuestNote, presented in your book.

A constant feature in all *QUEST* courses is the opportunity you have to study God's Word for yourself, share what you learn with your friends, then apply the truths to your life. You will participate in a variety of classroom activities, with one day seldom being the same as another. Your instructor will provide a number of handouts, outlines, quotes, and reaction sessions. The course can be challenging, but fun and beneficial.

Note the words in the last sentence. "Can be" implies a future potential. Only you can make that potential a reality.

God relates to individuals. His desire is to draw you into a personal relationship with Himself. Studying the Bible without a commitment to your own quest for truth would be a waste of time and effort. In fact, the Bible teaches that knowledge alone leads to pride and antagonistic disputes. It is only through God's Spirit that knowledge provides skills for successful living.

God has promised that through the Holy Spirit, believers can know the truth, and the truth will set them free. "Free from what?" you might ask. The truth, especially about God, provides a foundation from which you can confidently express your thoughts and govern your actions. Thus, you are free from insecurities, misguided advice, cult pressures, and evil deceptions in the world. Knowing the truth helps you step out of the darkness into His glorious light, then helps you to walk in the light. For this reason, the year could be one of the most important ones of your life.

The possibilities are endless as you determine to conscientiously take ownership over what you learn—not to just earn a grade, but to gain truth that will be meaningful for the rest of your life. The real value of the course is what you put into it and what you personally accomplish through it. That depends on you. God will do His part if you will commit to yours—a mind open to His teachings, a heart's desire to honor His name, and actions based on obedience.

Will you embark on your own quest for truth? That's the challenge and desire of the authors. May you be blessed as you consider week by week the wonderful words and works of God.

Blessings!
The authors

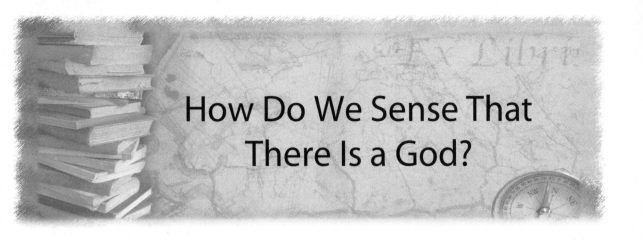

How Do We Sense That There Is a God?

"Welcome back!" Kelly shouted across the room. "I didn't expect to see you for at least another week. Sydney, down in the research library, told me that you had gotten home safely. It's good to see you again. I'm relieved that you survived the island!"

"Survived the island," Ryan thought to himself. "She doesn't have the slightest idea what it was like to live on that island for six months. If I had known before what I know now, I would've never volunteered for that particular assignment."

Ever since high school Ryan had wanted to do history research. So when he landed the job with JDR Publications right out of college, it was a dream come true. JDR was one of the most respected publishers of historical research in the country. They published magazines, books and, of course, the prestigious *History Journal*.

One of Ryan's many responsibilities was to propose articles for future editions of the journal. Along with the rest of his writing team, he had to prepare months in advance to research the various articles for an issue.

The island idea all began about a year ago as Ryan and several of his colleagues discussed future issues of *History Journal*. As the team sat around the conference table discussing potential articles, their conversation shifted to a discussion of the nominees for "Best Picture" at the upcoming Academy Awards. One thing led to another, and soon they were discussing the genre of shows that had recently become very popular both in theaters and on television.

Questions to consider:

1. Where did it all
   come from?

2. Why are we here?

3. How do we know
   ...what is right
   and wrong?
   ...what is beauti-
   ful?
   ...that life is more
   than what we can
   see?

4. What is the nature
   of the Force/Being
   behind everything?

5. What does He
   expect from us?
   How can we know
   what He wants?

6. How are we to
   relate to this
   Force? How are we
   to relate to each
   other?

Ryan couldn't remember who first came up with the idea, but he thought it was brilliant. The public loved shows that focused on the difficulties of survival. Why not conduct actual research on what it's like to be a castaway on a deserted island?

The level of excitement in the room started to rise as the team continued to brainstorm. They saw the potential of a whole series of articles that would explore every aspect of the experience. The team even envisioned the possibility of an award they might receive someday. It was a great idea! They couldn't believe that no one had thought of it previously.

Before he knew it, Ryan found himself volunteering for the assignment. The planning was intense. Every potential hazard had to be identified. Although he would be alone on the island, the publisher wanted assurances that emergency contact with him would be possible at all times. His safety was their greatest concern.

The weeks of planning flew by, leading to the chartered flight and months alone on the island. Now it was over. He was back and had an unbelievable story to tell. Actually, he had more to report than he'd bargained for—those solitary, endless days on the island.

Suddenly, he was brought back to reality by a familiar voice.

"Welcome back, my friend. I'm sure you have a story that we all want to hear."

Ryan turned his head and saw Dr. Mitchell walk through the door. It wasn't often that the president of the company walked into his office. But this was no ordinary occasion—he was now a celebrity. He had communicated with the outside world only twice during that entire time. He had a lot to say, and this was the person he needed to talk with first.

"It is good to see you again, sir," Ryan responded. "I'm glad you stopped by. I have my research notes with me. Or I could show you the highlights from the journal I kept. Either will give you a good idea of what happened during the entire six months."

Taking a seat at the small table in Ryan's office, Dr. Mitchell slowly shook his head. "No, Ryan. I'm not interested in either your notes or your journal right now. I want to know how you're doing. You've been on quite an adventure. I'm sure that there are a lot of things running through your mind. Let's start there."

That was not the question Ryan had expected. He wasn't really prepared to talk about his personal feelings from the ordeal, although he really wanted to. His trip to the island had been more than a research project. It had been a personal journey. His time on the island had raised many questions in his mind—questions for which he had no answers. Is this what Dr. Mitchell wanted to hear? Maybe, maybe not. But he knew he had to tell him. This was the man who sponsored the trip. He had a right to know.

"Well, sir," Ryan slowly began, "I would like to talk with you about some things."

The next time he looked at his watch, almost two hours had passed. Ryan apologized for taking up so much of Dr. Mitchell's time, but it seemed that he was in no hurry. He was intrigued by the personal—and spiritual—issues that Ryan had struggled with while on the island.

More questions:

7. What will happen to everything in the future?

8. Where can I find the truth?

For since the creation of the world His invisible attributes are clearly seen, being understood by the things that are made, even His eternal power and Godhead, so that they are without excuse . . . who exchanged the truth of God for the lie, and worshiped and served the creature rather than the Creator, who is blessed forever. Amen.

Romans 1:20, 25

Arguments of Logic:
(External)

1. Cosmology: the
study (ology) of
the natural world
(cosmos) as argu-
ments for the exis-
tence of God

2. Teleology: the
study (ology) of the
design and final
purpose (teleos) for
all created things
as an argument for
the existence of God

"Ryan, before you begin your journal articles I want to give you another assignment. I want you to record the thoughts and conclusions that you've just shared with me. I also want you to research the answers to your questions. Take all the time you need. These questions need to be settled in your mind before you come back to work. Send your reports directly to my attention so I can keep up with your progress."

Dr. Mitchell left, and Ryan was once again alone in his office. How would he even begin to make sense of the thoughts, fears and questions that he had faced while on the island? He began to reflect on how it all had started. After about three weeks on the island, everything became rather routine. The excitement had passed, and then each day was spent conducting his assigned research. He remembered a night that he couldn't sleep. The moon was so bright that he decided to take a walk along the beach.

For some reason he started thinking about the Sakuddeis. During his college days he had conducted research on this isolated Indonesian tribe that was on the verge of extinction. How strange that he would think about them in the middle of the night on that island. Stranger still, he couldn't believe how much he remembered.

The Sakuddei tribe lives on the island Siberut, an atoll formed by volcanoes on the Pacific Rim. It has no valuable resources; and because no important sea routes pass it, Siberut has almost no contact with the outside world. As a result, life on the island has remained virtually unchanged for centuries.

Like many other primitive tribes, the Sakuddeis have developed a lifestyle that respects and worships nature. For example, it is natural for a Sakuddei to apologize to an animal before he kills it for sacrifice. They believe that nature is full of spirits. If humans fail to cooperate or show a lack of respect to them, everyone on the island is threatened.

A good example of this is when Aman Laut-Lau, the leader of the tribe, took his pig for a walk three times around the building so that he was sure its spirit would find its way back. He believed he had to make the pig understand that the sacrifice of its life provided food for the coming feast. He then killed the pig by cutting its throat. After that he removed the pig's intestines and saved them to be used by the spiritual shaman, the Kerei, to foretell the future.

Ryan realized that his profound, transcendent spiritual quest all began with his memory of the Sakuddeis and the pig sacrifice. Although he considered himself religious, he wasn't a very consistent church-goer.

Maybe his questions could have been answered sitting in a pew. He'd never know for sure. But what he did know was that being alone on the island, and the memories of the Sakuddeis, had focused his thoughts on God.

If there is a God, he thought, surely He would not reside in the spirit of a pig. In fact, Ryan did not understand how any group of people could have developed such a concept. It was then that he started to wonder about his own beliefs about God. That first question opened the door of his mind to many others. Why do I have this yearning for God? How do I know that God exists?

Arguments of Logic:
(Internal)

3. Ontology: the study (ology) of existence (ontos) as proof of God as the Supreme Being

4. Anthropology: the study (ology) of human (anthropo) nature, especially the presence of the conscience as the judge of good and evil, as a logical argument for the existence of God

Is there any way that I can find out what God is like?

This would be his starting point for his report to Dr. Mitchell. He was accustomed to difficult research, but this might be the toughest assignment he had ever accepted. He knew that his research would have deep personal implications for his own life.

Nature is "before our eyes as a most beautiful book in which all created things, whether great or small, are as letters showing the invisible things of God to us."
Belgian Confession
1561

This most beautiful system of sun, planets and comets could only proceed from the counsel and dominion of an intelligent and powerful Being.
—Isaac Newton
Father of Modern Mathematics
1642 – 1727

QuestNote 1.1
Arguments for the Existence of God

Summarize the four logical arguments for the existence of God.

Cosmological

Teleological

Ontological

Anthropological

QuestNote 1.2
Notes from Romans 1

Read Romans 1:18–25 and summarize your answers.

1. Why is God angry at the wicked?

2. What has been plainly revealed to them?

3. How have these been revealed?

4. What happened to their thinking?

5. What did they seek in place of the invisible God?

6. What differences in their behavior resulted?

How Has God Revealed Himself?

JDR Publications had developed an incredible library. No university library anywhere in the country matched the extensive collection of books on history and archeology. Prior to the assignment Dr. Mitchell gave him, Ryan had spent only a few hours at a time in this particular library. Yet each time he came, he had always felt comfortable in its surroundings. He even had a special place to sit and conduct his research.

But for some strange reason, this time he was uncomfortable amidst the shelves of books. His uneasiness was not due to any physical change in the library. Matter of fact, not one single piece of furniture had been moved in the entire time he had been with the company. He was the one who had changed. Every other time he had come to the library, his research was part of his job. This time, however, he was on a personal quest. He had thought about a lot of things while on the island. But his questions about God continued to haunt him.

In the week since his meeting with Dr. Mitchell, he had made considerable progress in his research. But, interestingly enough, in spite of all he had learned, it had only revealed the unfathomable mysteries of his subject. There was so much more he wanted to know.

"How's it going, Ryan?" Sandy asked as she pulled up a chair to the table. Sandy was the member of his writing team who had originally suggested his six-month island experience.

"Pretty good," Ryan replied. "I have studied both the ancient cultures and the contemporary tribes, and it is obvious that a belief in gods or a Supreme Being is universal. All these people have sensed that there is more to life than what they can see."

God is . . .

Eternal - timeless, everlasting, without beginning or end, infinite in time, endless duration

Immutable - incapable of change, everlastingly the same

Omnipotent - all powerful, almighty; unlimited authority, force, energy and strength; infinite ability to act

Omnipresent - everywhere present; existing in all places and at all times

Omniscient - having all knowledge; knowing both the actual as well as all possibilities; infinite in perception, awareness, understanding, wisdom

For the next forty minutes Ryan shared his research with Sandy. She was particularly interested in the many different concepts of God throughout history. However, what surprised her the most was the consistency between many of these beliefs and the concept of God taught in the Bible.

Of course, there was no way that Sandy considered herself a Bible scholar. When she was younger she had attended church regularly. And even while in college she had found time to go at least occasionally. Although she didn't have a detailed knowledge of the Bible, she had a general understanding of what it said.

"Tell me again what you said about the Baha'i concept of God," Sandy asked as she moved from the table to sit on the windowsill. "Some of their ideas about deity sure sound a lot like what I learned in Sunday School years ago."

After finding the right page in his notes, Ryan read what he had recorded. "The Baha'i belief in one God means that the universe and all creatures and forces within it have been created by a single supernatural Being. This Being has absolute control over His creation (omnipotence) as well as perfect and complete knowledge of it (omniscience). According to Baha'i teachings, God is so far beyond His creation that, throughout all eternity, human beings will never be able to formulate any clear image of Him. They can only gain a remote appreciation of His superior nature."

Ryan looked up from his notes to see if Sandy wanted to hear more. He could tell by the look on her face that she was deep in thought. "Here, let me read one of my conclusions. I want your opinion on what I've written."

She watched as he carefully turned the pages in a spiral notebook. She immediately knew why this notebook was so important. It contained his personal observations and conclusions from his study during the past week. She couldn't believe how much he had already written.

"Here it is," he said. "Tell me what you think of this conclusion." Ryan leaned back in his chair and read slowly enough for Sandy to gain a full appreciation of his words. "Even if we say that God is all-powerful, all-loving, infinitely just, such terms are derived from a very limited human experience of power, love or justice. Indeed, our knowledge of anything is limited to our experience with those attributes and the qualities perceptible to us."

"Let me get this straight," Sandy began as she slowly walked around the room. "Are you trying to say that there is a God out there somewhere, but that it is impossible to really know Him? That doesn't even make 'walking-around sense' to me. I can't believe that the God who created the whole universe doesn't want to be known by His own creation."

"She has a point," Ryan thought to himself. Before he had time to respond, Sandy picked up her briefcase from the table.

"I've got to go," she said. "I've got a 5:00 deadline this afternoon. Let's get together for lunch this weekend. I want to hear some of your other conclusions."

Ryan was once again alone. He couldn't get her expression "walking-around sense" out of his mind. That was one of Sandy's favorite sayings. She was right. It just doesn't make any sense for a supernatural Being to

God is . . .

self-existent - having life within Himself, Being; infinite, eternal procession of God's essence, nature and personality; the meaning of I AM WHO I AM; self-sustaining, dependent on no one and nothing, autonomous, independent, free

sovereign - supreme authority and power to rule all aspects of nature and life; sustained control and direction of the creation; having ability to accomplish God's divine Will

spirit - without body, incorporeal; a supernatural being or essence; unbounded by human flesh; quality that gives life and vitality

go to all of the trouble to create this universe but then not care enough to reveal Himself to His creation.

It was then that he remembered something he had read at the beginning of the week. Although it was only six days ago, it seemed like months. He fumbled through the stacks of books surrounding him until he found the one he was looking for. Turning to the authors' opening comments in Chapter Two, he read the following:

> "The existence of a personal, moral God is fundamental to all that Christians believe. If there is no moral God, there is no moral being against whom we have sinned; therefore, salvation is not needed. So the first question that must be addressed is, 'Does God exist?' The second question is very closely related to the first: 'If God exists, what kind of God is He?'"

The authors of this book had it exactly right. Ryan realized that the first step was to determine whether or not God even exists. Once he had carefully reviewed the arguments for the existence of God, he would be better able to describe what God is like. His research had taken on an entirely new focus. He pushed aside the sociology and anthropology books and stacked the theology books right in front of him. It was time to do some serious reading!

The hours passed quickly. Ryan didn't realize how late it was until the night watchman told him that he had to leave the building. Although he didn't want to stop, he knew that he needed some rest. He was making progress in his research now—real progress.

If there is no moral God, there is no moral being against whom we have sinned; therefore, salvation is not needed. So the first question that must be addressed is, "Does God exist?"

—Norman Geisler

On his way back to the library the next morning, Ryan stopped by the office to check his messages. Most of them weren't too important, but the one from Dr. Mitchell caught his attention. Actually, he wasn't surprised to hear from him. He knew that his boss would want an update on the progress of his research. But, by noon today! Ryan couldn't believe his eyes. Dr. Mitchell wanted to meet for lunch to discuss his findings.

It was a frantic morning, but Ryan arrived at the restaurant on time. As always, Dr. Mitchell was punctual and prepared. After a few moments of pleasantries, Dr. Mitchell got right to the point. "Tell me what you've learned so far," he said. "I don't want all of the details just yet. But I do want to know the direction your research is taking you."

Ryan began by reviewing what he had learned from other cultures. First, it seemed that every culture had some belief in a Supreme Being. While supernatural power was attributed to these gods, they were all represented by some natural phenomena. Second, he found it very interesting that the supernatural characteristics and powers attributed to these gods were often similar to the way in which the God of the Bible was described.

"So, what do you conclude about the concept of God?" Dr. Mitchell asked.

"While there may be others, I believe that there is one obvious conclusion. It is clear that mankind is different from every other creature on earth. Part of this difference is our realization that there is more to life and to this world than what we see around us. As a result, we want to know how we got here, why we are here and where we are going. That forces us to think in terms of the supernatural. We are looking for some Supreme Being who will provide answers to these questions."

As you have given Him authority over all flesh, that He should give eternal life to as many as you have given Him. And this is eternal life, that they may know You, the only true God, and Jesus Christ whom You have sent.

John 17:2–3

To know more about God I must . . .

• accept the Bible as His revealed Truth.

• be an honest seeker. God reveals His truths to those who open their hearts and minds to His teaching.

Noting Dr. Mitchell's satisfaction with that response, Ryan proceeded to explain that before he could determine what God was like, he had to answer the question "Does God exist?" He took out his spiral notebook and laid out the four arguments for the existence of God that he had identified. The terms "cosmological," "teleological," "anthropological" and "ontological" were not new to Dr. Mitchell. But he admitted that it had been a long time since he'd heard those words.

The lunch crowd had disappeared and the two men were pretty much alone in the restaurant. "I'm impressed," Dr. Mitchell said at the end of Ryan's presentation. "But you still have more work to do. You've made a powerful case for the existence of the God of the Bible. But I want to know what He's like. Rather than studying the religious beliefs of other cultures, I now want you to focus on how the Bible describes God. We'll meet here again next week, and you can tell me what you've learned."

Driving back to his office, Ryan was pleased that Dr. Mitchell had been impressed with the research he had completed. It's always good to be appreciated by your boss. But he knew his biggest test was yet to come. There were hundreds, if not thousands, of volumes written on the subject of God. How would he summarize that information in a way that he could present it clearly to Dr. Mitchell?

As he turned into the company's parking garage, all he could think about was getting to the library. He had a lot of work to do in a very short amount of time. He wondered if the night watchman would let him stay later in the evenings. "It wouldn't hurt to ask," he thought.

QuestNote 2.1
Natural Attributes of God

Read the verses, then provide answers.

1

Scriptural Background: Exodus 3:13–14; John 5:26; Genesis 1:1a; Romans 1:19–20; Revelation 4:11; Isaiah 40:21–22, 25–26, 28.

These verses best relate to the following attribute of God: (Circle one.)

              loving   **self-existent**   **omniscient**

The definition (description) of this attribute:

_____

Why would people, in general, resist a God with this attribute?

_____

What encouragement does this attribute provide to believers?

_____

_____

2

Scriptural Background: Psalm 102:27; Malachi 3:6; James 1:17.

These verses best relate to the following attribute of God: (Circle one.)

              merciful   **self-existent**   **immutable**

The definition (description) of this attribute:

_____

Why would people, in general, resist a God with this attribute?

_____

What encouragement does this attribute provide to believers?

_____

QuestNote 2.1
Natural Attributes of God

Scriptural Background: Genesis 21:33; Psalm 90:1–2; Psalm 102:12, 24–27; Habakkuk 1:12; Ephesians 3:21; Revelation 1:8; 22:13.

These verses best relate to the following attribute of God: (Circle one.)

eternal   omnipotent   holy

The definition (description) of this attribute:

_____

Why would people, in general, resist a God with this attribute?

_____

What encouragement does this attribute provide to believers?

_____
_____

Scriptural Background: Genesis 18:14; Job 42:2; Psalm 107:25–29; Jeremiah 32:17; Luke 1:37; Matthew 19:26; Acts 17:24–28; Ephesians 1:18–21; 3:20.

These verses best relate to the following attribute of God: (Circle one.)

omnipotent   omniscient   omnipresent

The definition (description) of this attribute:

_____

Why would people, in general, resist a God with this attribute?

_____

What encouragement does this attribute provide to believers?

_____

QuestNote 2.1
Natural Attributes of God

5

Scriptural Background: Psalm 139:7–12; Hebrews 4:12–13; Jeremiah 23:23–24.

These verses best relate to the following attribute of God: (Circle one.)

omnipotent   omnipresent   omniscient

The definition (description) of this attribute:

Why would people, in general, resist a God with this attribute?

What encouragement does this attribute provide to believers?

6

Scriptural Background: Psalm 139:1–6; Proverbs 5:21; 15:3; Job 11:7–8; Isaiah 40:28; 46:9–10; Job 37:16; Psalm 147:5; 1 John 3:20; Romans 11:33; Matthew 10:29–30; Acts 15:18.

These verses best relate to the following attribute of God: (Circle one.)

omnipotent   omnipresent   omniscient

The definition (description) of this attribute:

Why would people, in general, resist a God with this attribute?

What encouragement does this attribute provide to believers?

QuestNote 2.1
Natural Attributes of God

7

Scriptural Background: Deuteronomy 4:39; 1 Chronicles 29:11–12; Job 12:9–10; Psalm 24:1; 50:10; Proverbs 16:9; Isaiah 14:24, 27; 46:10; Daniel 6:26; John 10:29; Ephesians 1:11, 22; Revelation 19:6.

These verses best relate to the following attribute of God: (Circle one.)

merciful   holy   sovereign

The definition (description) of this attribute:

_____

Why would people, in general, resist a God with this attribute?

_____

What encouragement does this attribute provide to believers?

_____

_____

8

Scriptural Background: John 4:24; Acts 7:48; 17:25; 1 Kings 8:27; Luke 24:39; Colossians 1:15; 1 Timothy 1:17; John 1:18.

These verses best relate to the following attribute of God: (Circle one.)

spirit   bountiful   loving

The definition (description) of this attribute:

_____

Why would people, in general, resist a God with this attribute?

_____

What encouragement does this attribute provide to believers?

_____

_____

What Kind of God
Is He?

Ryan settled into his chair with the stack of theology books staring him in the face. He sat puzzled, not knowing which book to pick up first. Then he remembered what one of his college professors had said about research, "The best place to begin is at the beginning." If he was going to use theology books in his research, he needed to make sure that he knew what the word "theology" meant. While he was at it, there were some other terms that he needed to check as well.

He soon learned that the word "theology" was the combination of two Greek words, *theos* (God) and *logos* (word). "Theology can't mean 'Word of God'," he thought. "That's what the Bible has been called." As he dug a little deeper, he realized that the word "*logos*" also means "rational expression." That made more sense. The study of theology was the rational study of God. In other words, it is the study of who God is and how He relates to mankind and nature.

After looking up the word "religion," he realized that religion and theology were not synonymous. Derived from the Latin *religare*, which means "to bind fast," religion refers to a set of beliefs, attitudes or practices that binds someone to something which is supreme. He also learned that the words "worship" and "religion" are often used together. Worship is an Anglo-Saxon word derived from "worthship." It describes a prescribed set of activities by which supreme worth (value) is attributed to someone or something.

Although the study of religion and worship might be fascinating, his focus was on theology. That was not only the reason for most of his questions, it was also the assignment that Dr. Mitchell had given him. He needed to learn what God is like through a systematic study of His attributes—those qualities that make Him uniquely God.

God is . . .

Unity in Trinity - There is one God, supreme creator and ruler of the universe, who manifests Himself in three persons—God the Father, God the Son and God the Holy Spirit.

Holy - God is infinitely above and beyond His creation. God is perfect and complete. God is sinless. There is nothing morally impure, defiling, evil or wrong in God's nature.

Good - God works to benefit His creation. He is benevolent and bountiful. He both cares and provides for our needs.

As before, the night watchman reminded Ryan that the library would close in a few minutes. "Are you sure I can't stay a little longer, Ernest?" Ryan asked as he looked up from his books. After spending so many days in the library, Ryan and Ernest were now on a first-name basis. In fact, Ernest seemed to have an innate understanding of the questions Ryan was struggling with.

"Ryan, I knew you would ask me that. So I came prepared. I talked with my supervisor, and he said I could give you this." Ernest reached into his pocket and pulled out a magnetic key. "Dr. Mitchell already arranged approval with my supervisor. He said to give you this. It will open or lock any part of the building. It's been activated for one week, then you'll have to give it back."

"Thanks," Ryan responded in disbelief. "I never thought you'd even let me stay in the building, let alone give me a key to every room in the place."

"You must be doing some mighty important research for Dr. Mitchell. In all the years I've worked here, we've never loaned one of these keys to anyone." Ernest started to walk away, but then changed his mind. As he approached the table, he could see that Ryan was already busy recording his thoughts. "Ryan, what exactly are you doing? Is it too secret to tell me?"

Ryan looked up and almost laughed out loud. "No, of course not," he said. He then told Ernest about his research on the island, the things he had thought about, his meetings with Dr. Mitchell and his impending deadline.

"Ah . . . now I understand why you've been in here so much. Listen, when you're finished with your research, will you tell me what you've learned about God? I've had some of the same questions you have."

Ryan nodded and agreed to sit down with him again. His curiosity satisfied, Ernest continued his nightly rounds.

The days passed quickly and Ryan amassed a wealth of information. He was surprised at how easy it had been to organize his research. Like the theology books, he organized the material according to God's attributes (characteristics). As he reviewed his work, he realized that for each of the attributes, he had begun with the words "God is."

"God is . . . Spirit." He found it interesting that the Bible never tried to define God. The closest thing to a definition of God he could find was when Jesus was speaking to the woman at the well in John 4:24. "God is Spirit, and those who worship Him must worship in spirit and truth."

"God is . . . Immutable." After this description, Ryan wrote the word "changeless." God does not change. Malachi 3:6 says, "For I am the Lord, I do not change." The writer of Hebrews expressed it with these words, "Jesus Christ is the same yesterday, today, and forever" (13:8).

"God is . . . Eternal." Ryan remembered asking himself, while he was on the island, "I wonder who created God?" Now he knew that the answer is "no one." Because God is eternal, He never had a beginning and will never have an end. Although there were

---

God is . . .

Loving - God did not withhold even His own Son, but sacrificed Him as a means of restoring us to fellowship with Him. This word of action includes terms such as grace, mercy, patience and kindness.

True - God has veracity, truth, reality, acts according to facts, total honesty, sincerity. God cannot lie; it is in opposition to His nature.

Just - God must act in judgment and retribution against all that opposes His innate nature of righteousness (holiness).

many verses of Scripture that identified this attribute of God, Ryan wrote Isaiah 57:15, Deuteronomy 33:27, and Psalm 90:2 in his notes.

"God is . . . Infinite." This means that God is not limited by or confined to the universe. He is entirely independent of finite (limited, measurable) things and beings. The Psalmist declared that no matter where he went, God was present (Psalm 139:7–12). Paul's statement in Acts 17:24–25 points out that God does not dwell in man-made shrines, because He is the Lord of Heaven and earth.

"God is . . . Omnipotent, Omnipresent, Omniscient." These were easy to remember because they all began with the prefix "omni" meaning all. God is all-powerful (Acts 17:26), present everywhere at the same time (Jeremiah 23:23), and all-knowing (Psalm 147:5).

"God is . . . Love." After studying this attribute of God, Ryan couldn't help but think how much he had misunderstood this word. The only way he could think of love was in the context of emotions. However, God's nature exhibits love as a fundamental characteristic of who He is. Everything that God does, including judgment and discipline, is based upon His love for us (1 John 4:8).

"God is . . . Righteous." Ryan noted that this attribute and the next one involved God's law (something he would need to study in more detail later). The righteousness of God means that God commands only what is right. But it also means that His actions are in accord with the law He Himself has established (Genesis 18:25; Jeremiah 9:24).

The Apostles' Creed

I believe in God, the Father Almighty, Creator of Heaven and earth.

I believe in Jesus Christ, His only Son, our Lord. He was conceived by the power of the Holy Spirit and born of the Virgin Mary. He suffered under Pontius Pilate, was crucified, died and was buried. He descended to the dead. On the third day He rose again. He ascended into Heaven and is seated at the right hand of the Father. He will come again to judge the living and dead.

(Continued)

"God is . . . Just." Not only does God Himself act in conformity with His law (righteousness), but He also administers His kingdom in accordance with it (justice). For example, the justice of God requires that sin be punished (Romans 6:23). Because God is just, He administers His law fairly, not showing favoritism or partiality (Deuteronomy 32:4).

"God is . . . Holy." It was God's holiness that had the most profound impact upon Ryan. After all, it is the most-mentioned attribute in Scripture. Although he knew it was not possible for God to be more of one attribute than another, it seemed that God's holiness was the most comprehensive of all of His attributes. As holy, God is the absolute standard of perfection. Holiness describes God's moral perfection, His inability to even look upon evil (Habakkuk 1:13).

Ryan realized that this characteristic had enormous implications for conscientious believers. Both Paul and Peter urge us to make holiness (perfection) our goal. Yet he knew so many people who attended church but had a very casual attitude toward a sinful lifestyle. He felt preplexed by this inconsistency.

Ryan closed his notebook and once again leaned back in his chair. He had learned so much, but it seemed as if he had only "scratched the surface." His experience on the island had surely taken him in a direction that he hadn't expected. God had been the farthest thing from his mind when he first stepped onto that island. Now, He was all Ryan could think about.

Before filing his report with Dr. Mitchell, he knew there was at least one more aspect of God's nature that had to be addressed. As he began to write the word "Trinity" in his notebook, he saw Sandy coming through the door.

I believe in the Holy Spirit, the holy catholic Church, the communion of the saints, the forgiveness of sins, the resurrection of the body, and the life everlasting. Amen

c 400 A.D.

TRINITY TRUTHS

Statement 1: There is one living and true God who exists in three Persons: God the Father, God the Son and God the Holy Spirit.

Statement 2: Jesus Christ, the Son of God and the second Person of the Trinity, is fully divine and yet became fully man without sin.

Statement 3: The Holy Spirit, the third Person of the Trinity, is fully divine.

Statement 4: Although each member of the Trinity is fully divine, as members of the Godhead there are some differences in their work.

Statement 5: As the one living and true God, the members of the Godhead work together in absolute unity.

"Hey, Ryan, how's it going?" she asked as she approached his desk.

"Everything is going well, but do you have a few minutes to talk? I'd like to tell you what I've learned about the Trinity. Talking it over with you will help me when I write my report for Dr. Mitchell."

Sandy hadn't expected a theology lesson but agreed to listen. Once again, she took her place on the windowsill.

Ryan began by telling her that although the word "Trinity" is never mentioned in the Bible, the idea of a triune God is consistently taught from Genesis through Revelation. He even told her how some people have so much difficulty understanding how God can be both one and three at the same time that they actually deny the doctrine altogether.

Ryan illustrated the Trinity by comparing the Persons of the Godhead to light, heat and air. He explained that if you hold your hand out and look at it, each of these three things is present. There is light, because it is only by light that you can see your hand. There is heat, which can be easily proved by holding a thermometer in your hand. There is air, because you can blow on your hand and feel it. The point is that each of these three—light, heat and air—is distinct. They act independently but, at the same time, in total unity. It is not possible to have one without the other. Together, they make up our environment.

"I've tried to summarize my research about the Trinity in five statements. Tell me what you think." Ryan began to read once again from his special notebook.

24

"Very well-written," Sandy replied as she hopped down from the windowsill. "I'm extremely impressed with all you've accomplished in such a short period of time. I sure hope you'll let me read your final report to Dr. Mitchell. In fact, everyone in the office would like a copy when you're done."

"No problem," Ryan said as he reached for another book on the table. "I have something else I want you to hear. Do you have time?"

"Sorry, Ryan, I've got to go. But I have a couple of questions for you. What are you going to do with all this information? Is it just going to sit on the shelf like some of our other research studies? This study seems so different from all the rest."

Ryan could see that Sandy was dead serious about what she had said. She just stood there and looked at him. He didn't know how to respond. As she walked away, he knew he had to answer her questions.

Strangely, his mind once again went back to the months he spent on the island. It almost seemed as if God had used that experience as a wake-up call for his life. God had turned his physical journey to the island into a spiritual quest. It had now become his life aim to know the truth about God.

But why was God taking him on this journey? Would he end up putting these theological studies on the shelf when his report was complete? Or, would this be just one more step?

He picked up the Bible that had been lying on the desk among the theology books. He wasn't quite sure where to start but decided to turn to the book of

Psalm 100

1. Make a joyful shout to the Lord, all you lands!

2. Serve the Lord with gladness; come before His presence with singing.

3. Know that the Lord, He is God; it is He who has made us, and not we ourselves; we are His people and the sheep of His pasture.

4. Enter into His gates with thanksgiving, and into His courts with praise. Be thankful to Him, and bless His name.

5. For the Lord is good; His mercy is everlasting, and His truth endures to all generations.

Thinking about God

- How does nature witness to God's existence?
- How do human thoughts, feelings and conscience witness to God's existence?
- Why must the Bible ultimately be our source of information about God?
- What natural attributes of God does the Bible present?
- What moral attributes of God does the Bible present?
- Why are these attributes important?
- What response should a person make to these truths?

Romans. From his research he knew that Romans was probably the most systematic, theological book in the Bible. Maybe he could find the answers to his questions there.

By the time he had reached the sixth chapter, he was beginning to realize what his quest was all about. Paul laid it out so clearly in Romans—sin had separated mankind from God. As a result, we were all condemned. Yet God acted to restore our relationship with Himself.

Now it was all beginning to make sense. The same God who had created the universe and provided a way of salvation for mankind had been with him on the island. Although Ryan had learned a lot about God, he still did not personally know God. That's what the research was all about. It was a pathway to an intimate relationship with God.

Up until now his report was a logical presentation of the information he had learned about God. Now it would take on a different direction. God is not some abstract concept or supernatural grandfather. While He is the Creator God of the universe, He is also a personal God. Ryan found it hard to fathom that this God would care so much about him, but he knew it was true.

He couldn't wait to write his report for Dr. Mitchell. But first he had to talk to Sandy and Ernest. He wanted them to be the first to know what he had discovered.

QuestNote 3.1
Moral Attributes of God

Read the verses, then provide answers.

1

Scriptural Background: (A) Deuteronomy 6:4; Isaiah 44:6–8; 45:5; 1 Timothy 2:5; 1 Corinthians 8:4; (B) Genesis 1:1–2 and 26; Isaiah 6:8; Matthew 28:19; 2 Corinthians 13:14; note who is God in Romans 1:7; Hebrews 1:8 and Acts 5:3–4.

These verses best relate to the following attribute of God: (Circle one.)

polytheism   **unity in Trinity**   **atheism**

The definition (description) of this attribute:

_____

Why would people, in general, resist a God with this attribute?

_____

What encouragement does this attribute provide to believers?

_____

2

Scriptural Background: Exodus 15:11; Job 34:10; Psalm 30:4; 99:9; 145:17; Isaiah 6:3-5; 57:15; Jeremiah 12:1; Habakkuk 1:13; Luke 1:49; 1 Peter 1:15–16; Revelation 15:4.

These verses best relate to the following attribute of God: (Circle one.)

loving   **holy**   **sovereign**

The definition (description) of this attribute:

_____

Why would people, in general, resist a God with this attribute?

_____

What encouragement does this attribute provide to believers?

_____

QuestNote 3.1
Moral Attributes of God

3

Scriptural Background: Psalm 35:6; 104:21; 145:8–9, 16, 18–20; Matthew 5:45; 6:26; Acts 14:17.

These verses best relate to the following attribute of God: (Circle one.)

just	**sovereign**	**good**

The definition (description) of this attribute:

_____

Why would people, in general, resist a God with this attribute?

_____

What encouragement does this attribute provide to believers?

_____

_____

4

Scriptural Background: John 3:16; 16:27; Romans 5:8; 8:35–39;1 John 4:8–10, 16; Ephesians 2:4–5; Isaiah 63:7; Psalm 63:3; 86:15; Deuteronomy 4:31; Luke 6:36; Isaiah 55:7; 2 Peter 3:9; 2 Thessalonians 2:16.

These verses best relate to the following attribute of God: (Circle one.)

holy	**loving**	**sovereign**

The definition (description) of this attribute:

_____

Why would people, in general, resist a God with this attribute?

_____

What encouragement does this attribute provide to believers?

_____

QuestNote 3.1
Moral Attributes of God

5

Scriptural Background: Numbers 23:19; 1 Corinthians 1:9; 2 Timothy 2:13; Hebrews 6:17; 10:23.

These verses best relate to the following attribute of God: (Circle one.)

infinite	self-existent	true

The definition (description) of this attribute:

Why would people, in general, resist a God with this attribute?

What encouragement does this attribute provide to believers?

6

Scriptural Background: Psalm 99:4; 145:17; Isaiah 45:21; Romans 1:32; 2:9; 12:19; Acts 17:31; Deuteronomy 7:9, 12–13; Hebrews 2:2; 11:26; 2 Thessalonians 1:5–8.

These verses best relate to the following attribute of God: (Circle one.)

just	immense	merciful

The definition (description) of this attribute:

Why would people, in general, resist a God with this attribute?

What encouragement does this attribute provide to believers?

QuestNote 3.2
The Doctrine of God

Write an essay that summarizes the truths related to the existence and nature of God. The essay should reflect your best thinking, and should be well organized and written.

The outline can generally follow these questions:
- How does nature witness to God's existence?
- How do human thoughts, feelings and conscience witness to God's existence?
- Why must the Bible ultimately be our source of information about God?
- What natural attributes of God does the Bible present?
- What moral attributes of God does the Bible present?
- Why are these attributes important?
- What response should a person make to these truths?

As often as possible, include Scripture references that support the statements you make. Also use the vocabulary you are learning that describes the various concepts. The length of your essay should be at least one-and-a-half to two pages.

_____

_____

_____

_____

_____

_____

_____

_____

_____

_____

_____

QuestNote 3.2
The Doctrine of God

_____
_____
_____
_____
_____
_____
_____
_____
_____
_____
_____
_____
_____
_____
_____
_____
_____
_____
_____
_____
_____
_____
_____
_____

A Written Record Was Needed

1 "Denise, do we have to get here so early? I'm sure we won't be fighting the crowds to get in."

The walk along the sidewalk was exhilarating. It was a typical, cold November morning in Washington, D.C. Ann had heard on the news that it might snow that night. But it wasn't just the weather that made the walk exciting. They had been given permission to conduct their latest research project in the Library of Congress. In just a few minutes they would be ushered into parts of the library where only a select few are allowed access.

"Pick up the pace, Ann," Denise said as they turned the corner. "I want to be there when they open the doors. Did you know that the Library of Congress is the largest library in the world, with more than 120 million items displayed on almost 530 miles of bookshelves?"

"Here she goes again," Ann said to herself. "Ever since we got permission to conduct our research in the library, she's been memorizing facts about the place. I wonder what else she's going to tell me this time."

2 "The library collections include more than 18 million books, 2.5 million recordings, 12 million photographs, 4.5 million maps, and 54 million manuscripts," Denise continued. "It's those manuscripts I want to see!"

"I hope you don't plan on looking at all 54 million. I've got a date Saturday night," Ann joked with a hint of concern in her voice. "Are you serious? Are there really 54 million manuscripts in this library?"

All Scripture is given by inspiration of God, and is profitable for doctrine, for reproof, for correction, for instruction in righteousness.

2 Timothy 3:16

For prophecy never came by the will of man, but holy men of God spoke as they were moved by the Holy Spirit.

2 Peter 1:21

"Absolutely! Did you know that the oldest written material in the library is a cuneiform tablet dating from 2040 B.C.? I just can't believe that we've been given permission to work in the rare books and manuscripts section of the library for the next three weeks."

"All right. We're here!" Ann exclaimed as she reached out to open the door. Her tug on the door handle nearly pulled her off her feet. It was still locked! No wonder there were no crowds. The library wasn't scheduled to open for another 45 minutes. "I told you we were early," Ann said as she looked for a place to get out of the cold.

"Come on, let's go to the coffee shop," Denise said as she started back down the steps. Fortunately, the coffee shop was in the James Madison building, the same building in which the office of Research Guidance was located. Denise and Ann had to check in there before they could even begin.

Ann wasn't a real fan of coffee, but it was nice to escape the cold. She was also glad for the opportunity to review their plan for the day. They only had a three-week window of time to complete their research. Every minute had to be used wisely.

As they sipped their coffee (Denise had a donut), they reminisced about their work together over the last seven months and what they had gone through to gain approval to continue their research in the Library of Congress. Although the young women had many things in common, they were also quite different.

Both were graduate students conducting research for their master's theses. Denise was in the history department. Her particular passion was ancient forms of communication. Ann, on the other hand, was earning her master's in English. Her focus was on the role that the Bible played as literature throughout the centuries. They had met while attending a seminar a year earlier. One conversation led to another, and they soon decided to work together on the research phase of their respective theses. Now they were about to enter the most famous research library in the world.

Denise had promised to help Ann for the first few days because Ann was not as experienced in working with ancient manuscripts. Later, Ann would assist Denise in the structure of her arguments to support her research topic. Both had areas of expertise not possessed by the other. For now, they would locate the manuscripts that Ann needed first.

In preparation for their research, each had written a series of questions to guide their work. Although Ann's list of questions was short, it was by no means a simple list.

- Why does the Bible claim to be the Word of God?
- What is the purpose of the Bible?
- Why did God choose this method of communication?
- What is so special about this book?
- Did God actually "write" this book?
- Is this book finished?

While Ann's research would not be conducted exclusively in the rare books and manuscripts section, that is where she had to begin. She wanted to know more about various writings of Scripture such as the Masoretic Text, the Septuagint, the Dead Sea Scrolls, the various New Testament manuscripts, and how the information in these texts was passed from one generation to the next.

The Old Testament

- *39 books*

- *written over 1540 years*

- *Hebrew language except for a few Aramaic passages*

- *Structure of books:*
Law	*5*
History	*12*
Poetry	*5*
Prophecy	
– Major	*5*
– Minor	*12*

The New Testament

- 27 books

- written from about 35 A.D. to 95 A.D.

- about 10 authors

- Greek language, common throughout the Roman Empire

- Structure of books:

Gospels	4
History	1
Paul's epistles	
to churches	9
to individuals	4
General Epistles	8
Prophecy	1

"Okay, Ann," Denise said as she reached for another cup of coffee, "Let's go over what we know so far about the manuscripts of the Bible. Also, tell me again what you've already learned about how these manuscripts were transmitted over the centuries."

By the time Denise had finished her sentence, Ann was prepared to review her notes. She began by reminding Denise that the books of the Old Testament were written over a period of about 1,540 years in the Hebrew language, except for a few selected passages which were written in Aramaic. The total time period over which the New Testament was written was approximately 60 years. It was originally written in Greek.

Beginning with the Old Testament, Ann reminded Denise that the stories of the patriarchs were passed from generation to generation by word of mouth, in an oral tradition, before they were actually written. This was also true of the messages of the prophets. Even the narratives of the life of Jesus Christ were repeated orally for probably 30 years.

The first person in the Bible to have written anything down for sure was Moses. From the time of Moses to the end of the New Testament period, the books and letters that comprise the Bible continued to be written. However, none of the original Biblical documents, called the "original autographs," has survived. What we have today are copies of the original manuscripts. Today's translations of the Bible are based on these copies.

"That's right. The older, handwritten copies of the Bible texts are called manuscripts," Denise interrupted as Ann broached her field of expertise. "The early manuscripts of the Bible were usually written on either papyrus or animal skins. Papyrus was a type of paper made from a reed plant. Although inexpensive, papyrus rotted quickly when exposed to dampness. The skins of animals were much better than the papyrus. Did you know that parchment is the result of a special refining process for an animal skin?"

"Yes, I did," Ann replied, trying not to sound impatient. "Listen, the library is going to open in a few minutes. We need to review the rest of this information before we get started."

Ann turned to the page in her notes entitled "Ancient Versions." She had learned that the oldest Bible translation in the world was made in Alexandria, Egypt, where the Old Testament was translated from Hebrew into Greek. Evidently, there was a Greek-speaking Jewish community in Alexandria around 250 B.C. They needed the Hebrew Scriptures translated into the only language they knew—Greek. This version was called the Septuagint.

The Septuagint actually became the Scriptures used by the Christians in the first century. It could be understood by the Greek-speaking Jews and also the Gentiles. Most of the Old Testament quotations in the New Testament are taken from this Greek text. The Septuagint became the "official version" for the early church.

The writers of the New Testament completed their manuscripts within about 65 years after Jesus' crucifixion. At the time the New Testament was written,

Bible

≈ *1600 years*
40+ authors
66 books
1 message

God's Plan of Redemption

- *The Need*

- *The Nation*

- *The Person*

- *The Explanation*

- *The End*

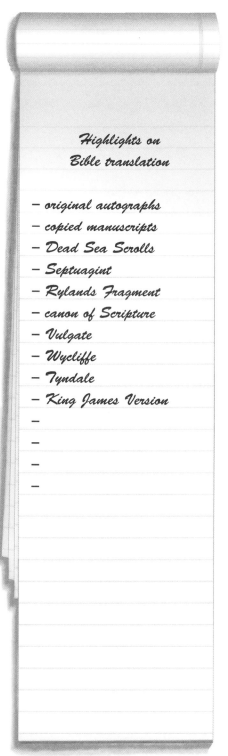

literature and scholarship flourished throughout the known world. As a result, copies of the New Testament text were constantly being produced. Today we have approximately 15,000 complete manuscripts and quotations of the New Testament extending back to the second century. The most complete copy is the *Codex Sinaiticus* which dates to the fourth century. During this time, the leaf-book (*codex*) form of books appeared because scrolls were so difficult to handle.

Some fragments of the New Testament text were written on *ostraka* (scraps of pottery that early writers used as a cheap form of stationery) and talismans (pendants, bracelets, and other objects worn to ward off evil spirits). However, the papyrus manuscripts provide us with the most complete record of the New Testament writings.

"I've read a lot about those papyrus manuscripts," Denise once again interrupted. "The earliest known fragment of a New Testament papyrus manuscript dates from about 125 A.D., commonly called the Rylands Fragment because it is housed in the John Rylands Library of Manchester, England. Although it is only 6 centimeters by 9 centimeters (2.5 inches by 3.25 inches), the fragment contains a portion of John 18:31–38."

"Yes, I already know that, too. I've seen a number of very good photographs of the Rylands Fragment," Ann replied in a matter-of-fact manner. "Listen, the library will be open in just a couple of minutes. After we get checked in, I want to start researching the purpose of the Bible. Actually, I want to understand why God chose this method of communication. That's why I'm so interested in the manuscripts. I believe that most people don't realize that the Bible is actually ancient literature. Unless I understand how ancient communication occurred, I won't be able to fully understand how we got the Bible we have today."

Denise downed her last swallow of coffee and began to pick up the trash on the table. At the same time, Ann gathered her notes. The time had come, and they were certainly ready. Conducting research in the Library of Congress was a dream come true. However, neither of them was fully prepared for what they would soon encounter.

Facts about the Bible

- *In six words: God, man, sin, redemption, justification, sanctification*
- *In two words: grace, glory*
- *In one word: Jesus*
- *Number of verses: 31,102*
- *Number of words: 775,693 (KJV)*
- *Longest chapter: Psalm 119*
- *Shortest chapter: Psalm 117*
- *Longest verse: Esther 8:9*
- *Shortest verse: John 11:35*
- *Longest book in Old Testament: Psalms*
- *Longest book in New Testament: Luke*
- *Shortest book in OT: Haggai*
- *Shortest book in NT: 3 John*

Harold Willmington

QuestNote 4.1
The Bible Is the Word of God

Summarize why we believe the Bible is the Word of God.

Revelation

1. Why is special revelation necessary for us to know God?

_____

_____

2. What are the true means of special revelation?

_____

_____

• •

Unity of Scripture

1. Describe the historical development of the Bible (time, authors, number of books, etc.).

_____

_____

2. Why is the unity of the Bible evidence of God's control of the process? _____

_____

3. What is the unifying theme of the Bible? _____

4. Outline the five sections of the Bible related to this theme.

Topic	Reference
1. _____	_____
2. _____	_____
3. _____	_____
4. _____	_____
5. _____	_____

QuestNote 4.1
The Bible Is the Word of God

Preservation of Scripture

1. How were the books of the Old Testament developed and preserved?

2. When was the canon of the Old Testament established?

3. What is the Septuagint?

4. How were the books of the New Testament developed?

5. What is the *Codex Sinaiticus*?

6. When was the canon of the New Testament established?

7. What challenges were faced by early translators?

8. What effect did the Reformation have on the availability of God's Word?

9. How does the preservation and spread of Scripture offer evidence that it is God's Word?

QuestNote 4.1
The Bible Is the Word of God

Terms to Define or Describe

1. Bible

2. Septuagint

3. *Codex Sinaiticus*

4. Rylands Fragment

5. Vulgate

6. Revelation

7. canon

8. Apocrypha

9. John Wycliffe

10. William Tyndale

The Authority of
God's Word

"Would you look at that," Denise said in awe as the curator led the two young researchers into the room housing the rare and special book collection. "I have never seen so many old books in all my life. They are just beautiful!"

Ann had to admit that it was an awesome sight. For the first time a true feeling of excitement came over her. To her left she saw the collection of Biblical texts and associated materials. She was now only half-listening to the curator's orientation. She knew what she wanted to look at first. But for now she needed to at least act like she was interested in the guide's description of the holdings in this room.

Finally, the orientation was finished. Turning to leave, the curator spoke to them one last time. "Well, that does it. Be sure to keep your pass with you at all times. It will allow you to enter any of the rooms that I've shown you. Remember, the pass is only good for the next three weeks. If you have any questions or problems, let me know."

Denise and Ann looked at each other and then slowly gazed around the room. It was huge! Even though other people were in the room, they felt as if they had the entire place to themselves. The two small desks and large table, located in the far corner of the room, would be a perfect place to work. They carefully laid their briefcases on their respective desks. It was now time to get started.

The morning passed quickly. It was actually Denise who first felt hunger pains. "Let's take a break and get something to eat," she said as she rose from the table. "We can leave our books and papers here while we're gone. I'm sure they'll be safe."

Revelation

General :
- *Nature, the Creation*
- *Original knowledge, history*
- *Conscience*

Special:
- *God's written Word — the Bible*
- *God's Living Word — His Son Jesus Christ*
- *The Holy Spirit*

As they left the Thomas Jefferson building, the cold wind reminded them that it was still November in Washington. They walked quickly back to the James Madison building. The curator had told them that the cafeteria on the sixth floor was a great place for lunch.

Finding a small table by the window, they placed their trays opposite each other. They had hardly begun eating when Denise asked a totally unexpected question. "Tell me, Ann, why did you choose the Bible as the focal point for your research?"

"It all has to do with authority," Ann replied. "When I was an undergraduate student I took a philosophy class. Throughout the semester, the professor kept talking about what he called the "ultimate questions." He was referring to questions about existence, truth, meaning and destiny. Every time a student gave an answer to one of the ultimate questions, the professor would ask, 'Upon what authority do you make that statement?' That class really made me think about the importance of ultimate authority."

In spite of the fact that her lunch was getting cold, Ann felt that she needed to provide a more detailed explanation. She began by reminding Denise that the source of ultimate authority had to reside either within humanity or within some Supreme Being higher than humanity. She knew that mankind couldn't be the ultimate authority. Her knowledge of history and current events had convinced her of that. Mankind certainly did not have the answers to the ultimate questions.

She concluded that ultimate authority had to reside in a Supreme Being who was higher than humans and

44

everything else that had been created. As a result, this Supreme Being has the right to establish a standard for belief and practice.

At this point, Ann began to reveal a very personal struggle that she had faced earlier in her life. She knew there had to be a God but was confused by various religions all claiming that their god was the true God. So she determined to learn all she could about the various religions. She went right to the source and studied the claims and teachings of these gods as revealed in their religious books and documents.

Ann then told Denise that as a result of her study of the Bible, she had become a Christian during her senior year. She had realized that God not only revealed Himself in His creation, but also through a book—the Bible. Because the Bible reveals His message, it carries the same weight as if God Himself were speaking to us personally.

While Ann started on her salad, Denise continued to ask questions about her struggle of faith and her belief in the authority of the Bible.

"So, why do you believe that the Bible is more authoritative than other religious books or documents? I've read parts of the Bible and found it very interesting. But I've never considered it more authoritative than the *Qur'an* or the *Bhagavad Gita*. What convinced you of its authenticity?"

The questions and doubts that Denise expressed did not surprise Ann. She had felt the same way years before. That's why her struggle had been so difficult.

God, who at various times and in various ways spoke in time past to the fathers by the prophets, has in these last days spoken to us by His Son, whom He has appointed heir of all things, through whom also He made the worlds.

Hebrews 1:1-2

Reasons to Believe the Bible
is God's Word

1. Its unity in presenting
   one central message—
   God's Plan of
   Redemption

2. Its miraculous preservation throughout history

3. Its fulfilled prophecy

4. Its accuracy and integrity

But she was now confident in her faith and more than happy to share with her friend what she had learned.

"Do you really want to know?" Ann asked, excited that she had the opportunity to share so freely. "I know you're in a hurry to get back to work. But if you really want to know, I can give you a quick synopsis of what I've learned. I promise that it will only take a few minutes."

Denise agreed and Ann began outlining the evidences that convinced her that the Bible was the authoritative Word of God. First, there was the claim of the Scriptures themselves. The writers of the books of the Bible clearly claimed that what they had written was the Word of God. While this is certainly not a proof in itself, it did raise an interesting question. "How can books that seem to be right in every other way, be wrong at the crucial point of their self-awareness?" In Ann's mind, that was strong evidence for the authenticity of the Bible.

Second, there was the testimony of Jesus who taught that the Bible was God's Word. Even if you believed that Jesus was only a great teacher, you could not ignore His testimony about the Bible. If He was mistaken on this issue, by what authority could you believe His other teachings?

Before continuing, Ann clearly stated her belief that Jesus Christ was not only the Son of God but was also her Savior. For the next couple of minutes, Ann told the story of her salvation experience. She then continued to list the evidences that convinced her of the authenticity of the Bible.

Next, there is the ethical superiority of the Bible. No other religious book maintains such a high moral standard. For example, the Bible places a high value on life—even for those who are disabled or have serious diseases. Even unbelievers acknowledge the Bible's superiority in areas of moral and ethical teachings.

A fourth reason for regarding the Bible as the Word of God is the extraordinary unity of the book. There are 66 books in the Bible, written over a period of approximately 1,600 years (from about 1450 B.C. to 95 A.D.) by more than 40 different authors. Interestingly, not only were these people from many different backgrounds, very few of them knew each other. Yet, the Bible reveals a single story of God's plan of redemption. The only way that this unity can be possible is that God guided the writers of the various books.

Another evidence of the Bible's authenticity is its accuracy. Stop and think about how often newspapers and other news media get the facts wrong on a story. We have the highest level of communication the world has ever known, yet even a simple thing, like the spelling of a name, is often inaccurately reported in the news media.

The Bible is filled with facts, names, titles and dates written over centuries by individuals who had little or no opportunity to communicate with each other. Yet the Bible has been proven time and time again to be accurate in its presentation of these details. This could only happen because the Bible is the revealed Word of God.

A sixth reason is fulfilled prophecy. There are more than twenty Old Testament predictions alone

5. Its moral excellence and wisdom

6. Jesus' confirmation

7. Its power to change lives

8. Its inspiration and thus its inerrancy

relating to the events surrounding the death of Jesus Christ—prophecies that were written centuries before His crucifixion. All of these events were fulfilled, just as they had been prophesied.

But the Bible contains more than just prophecies about Jesus Christ. There are also prophecies about the nation of Israel, as well as other nations and their capitals. These also came to pass. Fulfilled prophecies are clear evidences that the Bible is the Word of God.

Ann's seventh reason is how God has protected and preserved His Word throughout time so that it could be made available to all people. From the original autographs to the careful copying of manuscripts—even the invention of the moveable type printing press—show how God reveals Himself.

Ann paused, carefully choosing how she wanted to express this last evidence for the authenticity of the Bible. "Denise," Ann said, looking intently at her friend, "I believe the Bible is God's Word because it is a book that understands me."

Denise was quiet for what seemed like an eternity. Finally, she responded to Ann's statement. "I don't understand what you mean. I've spent my life trying to understand books. I've never known a book that tried to understand me."

"That's not quite what I mean," Ann replied. "When I read the Bible, it is not like any other book I've read. The words speak to me. Sometimes they point out my weaknesses and remind me that I'm not as smart as I think I am. Other times, they comfort me and give me peace. I don't know any other way to describe it. The Bible is the only book I've ever read that understands me."

"You really believe that God speaks to us through the Bible?" Denise asked.

"More than that," Ann explained. "I believe that all of the Bible was written by God as His way of communicating personally to us."

Denise reacted immediately to Ann's discussion. "There is no way that God could have written the Bible. You said yourself that people wrote it."

"Let's save that conversation for dinner tonight," Ann said as she got up from the table. "We've got a lot of work to do this afternoon before the library closes."

QuestNote 5.1
The Bible Is the Word of God

Summarize four of the arguments that the Bible is God's Word.

Its Fulfilled Prophecy

1. Regarding Christ:

2. Regarding other historical events:

• • • • • • • • • • • • • • • • • • • •

Its Accuracy and Integrity

1. Historical Proofs:

2. Archaeological Support:

3. Scientific Concerns:

QuestNote 5.1
The Bible Is the Word of God

Its Moral Excellence and Wisdom

• •

Jesus' Confirmation

1. Related to the Old Testament:

2. Related to the New Testament:

The Perfection of God's Word

Ann looked up from her books, took off her glasses and rubbed her eyes. For the past three and a half hours, her head had been buried in the stack of books on her desk. Although she and Denise had shared a couple of comments during the afternoon, there had been little talk between them since lunch. They both had work to do and were serious about getting it done.

Yet Ann could not help but think about their lunch conversation. It all began with Denise's question about the authority of the Bible. By the time lunch had ended, Ann had not only outlined several evidences for the Bible's authority, but had also shared her personal faith in Christ. She had known Denise for a long time. They had never had a conversation like this before.

Could it be that God was using her research project to open Denise's heart to His Word? If it wasn't happening right before her eyes, she wouldn't have believed it. Lunch had ended with Denise's declaration, "There is no way that God could have written the Bible." Did Denise say that because she truly believed it? Or was the conversation becoming too personal and she was looking for a way out? Regardless of the reason, Ann knew that she wanted to continue the discussion at dinner.

Ann put on her glasses again and resumed reading where she had left off. But she found it difficult to concentrate this time. Her mind was on Denise, their discussion at lunch and what she would say at dinner. Tonight's conversation might be the turning point in Denise's life. Ann began to structure the conversation in her mind.

She knew she wanted to explain the inspiration of the Bible. She remembered how difficult this concept was for her to grasp at first. Especially because most of the scholars she read seemed intent on proving that the Bible was not inspired. While some believed that the Bible contained words from God, the majority of them did not believe that the Bible was completely and totally inspired by God. Their disparaging remarks were hard to dismiss.

Finally, the reading of 2 Timothy 3:16 had caused her to carefully research the meaning of inspiration. Since she had a good understanding of New Testament Greek, she knew that the word *theopneusis*, translated as inspiration, literally means God-breathed. This was an important fact that she would be sure to share with Denise.

Ann now realized that she had become so focused on her dinner conversation with Denise that she had ignored the research task at hand. She tried to refocus her attention on the books in front of her, but to no avail. She could not ignore the possibility that God was using her to reach out to Denise. She had to outline the ideas she could share with Denise that evening. Turning the page on her notepad, she began to write.

Definition of inspiration – The supernatural influence of the Holy Spirit upon the Scripture writers which made their writings an accurate record of the revelation of God which resulted in what they wrote actually being the Word of God.

Reasons why I believe the Bible is inspired:

- *The authors of the New Testament believed in the inspiration of the Scriptures. Peter wrote "Knowing this first, that no prophecy of Scripture is of any private interpretation, for prophecy never came by the will of man, but holy men of God spoke as they were moved by the Holy Spirit"*

All Scripture is given by inspiration of God, and is profitable for doctrine, for reproof, for correction, for instruction in righteousness.
2 Timothy 3:16

For prophecy never came by the will of man, but holy men of God spoke as they were moved by the Holy Spirit.
2 Peter 1:21

For the word of God is living and powerful, and sharper than any two-edged sword, piercing even to the division of soul and spirit, and of joints and marrow, and is a discerner of the thoughts and intents of the heart.
Hebrews 4:12

(2 Peter 1:20–21). It is clear from these verses that Scripture is not of human origin, nor is it the result of human will. The Bible is not the product of human effort. Matter of fact, the prophets sometimes wrote what they could not fully understand (1 Peter 1:10–11) but were still faithful to write what God revealed to them.

- The authors of the Old Testament believed in the inspiration of the Scriptures. More than 3800 times the writers of the Old Testament introduced their messages with such statements as these: "The Lord spoke," "the Lord said," "the word of the Lord came." Repeatedly the Old Testament writers recorded that God commanded them to write and that they wrote what He told them (Exodus 17:14; 24:4; 34:27; Numbers 33:2; Deuteronomy 32:24; Jeremiah 30:1–2; 36:1–2, 4). In addition, Jesus recognized the Old Testament as fully inspired. Jesus said He came not to destroy either "the law or the prophets" (Matthew 5:17). This expression is often used for the entire Old Testament. In fact, the terms "God said" and "Scripture says" are used interchangeably throughout the Bible.

- The character of God requires a belief in inspiration. God is a Person—omnipotent, omniscient, omnipresent, perfect in holiness, righteousness and love. He is the Creator, Preserver and Governor of the universe. If all of these things are true about God—and they are!—then it is only logical to believe that God would want to reveal Himself to us. And, if God is who He says He is and has communicated to us by way of a book, it stands to reason that the contents of the book are true. If the contents are not God's words, exactly

Inspiration

The authors of the New Testament said it!
- Christ's confirmation
- Peter
- Paul

The authors of the Old Testament accepted it!
- God said . . . 3800xs
- quoted in NT

The character of God requires it!

as stated in the Bible, then that makes God a liar. It is not possible to hold a view of God's perfect character without also believing that His Word is perfect.

As Ann reviewed these last few comments, she was pleased with what she had written. She believed that this would be a good starting point for her conversation with Denise that evening. It would help Denise to understand the inspiration of Scripture. The fact that the Bible is God-breathed is fundamental to the Christian faith. If the Bible is not God's Word, then the claims it makes about the nature of God and the nature of man cannot be trusted.

Ann now realized that tonight's conversation had to go beyond just a discussion about inspiration. Even if Denise agreed that God inspired the writers of Scripture, she would still be very skeptical about the accuracy of the Bible we have today. After all, modern Bibles are translations of the original manuscripts copied over many centuries. Ann remembered her own initial skepticism.

"What are you so deep in thought about?" Denise whispered in Ann's ear. "I've been watching you for the last few minutes. It almost seems like you're in a trance. Is there a problem?"

Although startled at first, Ann regained her composure and smiled. "There's no problem. I was just thinking about some things that happened in my life a few years ago. I guess I lost track of time."

"Oh, is that all? I was getting a little concerned. Listen, I've got to go back to the curator's office before it closes. I need to ask him a couple questions before we return tomorrow. I'll meet you at O'Malley's for dinner at 6:30. Is that okay?"

Inerrancy

- Scripture comes from God through a human author.

- God directed the exact words used but allowed the experiences of the author to be reflected.

- Inspiration guarantees inerrancy.

54

"Sounds good to me," Ann replied.

Denise gathered her materials and headed for the door. Ann was glad that Denise had decided to meet with the curator before dinner. She needed a few more minutes to organize her thoughts for their discussion about inspiration and inerrancy. Inerrancy! That's the word she was trying to recall before Denise interrupted her train of thought.

She started to remember the questions she had once asked about the dependability of the Bible.

- If we don't have the original manuscripts of the Bible, how do we know the copies are accurate?

- How can we be certain that the writers of Scripture accurately recorded what God directed them to say?

- Doesn't the translation of the Bible into many different languages affect its accuracy?

Ann knew that Denise would have the same questions. She would also need to explain why the Bible is inerrant (meaning that there are no errors). As she had done before, Ann began to structure her response.

Reasons why I believe the Bible is inerrant:

- *While Scripture comes from God, a human author received the revelation and actively participated in its writing. God gave the revelation and oversaw the writing. As a result, the message is wholly from God, but the humanity of the writer has been reflected. Both the divine and human concur in the same words (1 Corinthians 2:13). The parallel is in the divine and human nature of Jesus Christ, the Living Word.*

Illumination

- *The Word of God is complete in the canon of Scripture.*

- *No one is to add or to take from its words.*

- *Therefore, revelation of new Scripture does not occur.*

- *Rather, the Holy Spirit illuminates Scripture to give us its meaning and application.*

- *Thus, we have the Word of God written by men chosen by God, inspired not only in its concepts, but in the exact words used to express those concepts. The human writers are not mere secretaries, but active agents who express their own experiences, thoughts and feelings in what they have written. It is God's message in written form (Hebrews 1:1; 2 Peter 1:21).*

- *If the Bible is the Word of God and God can only speak truth, then there is no way to avoid the conclusion that the Bible contains no errors. Inspiration guarantees inerrancy. This does not mean that the way we understand the Bible is perfectly true; it does mean that the Bible's truth can be understood correctly. Nor does it mean that everything in the Bible must be understood literally. Figures of speech are found throughout the Bible. There is a considerable difference between telling truth in a metaphor and telling mythical stories.*

Ann sat back in her chair and reviewed what she had written. Denise was sure to have many more questions, and Ann was uncertain of her ability to answer them. After all, she was no theologian! There were, of course, many scholars they could consult for answers. But Denise would have to earnestly want to know the truth, just as Ann had a few years earlier. Ann knew that God draws and reveals Himself to those who seek Him.

The lights began to dim in the room, indicating that it was almost time for the library to close. Ann gathered her materials and placed them securely in her briefcase. She would have to hurry or Denise would start wondering what happened to her. Although she was a little anxious about the evening, Ann firmly believed that God was using this research opportunity to reach Denise with the Gospel.

As she left the library and descended the steps, Ann saw that the sun was already beginning to set behind the Washington Monument. But she didn't notice the cold wind this time. Her thoughts were focused on the Bible. In her mind, she knew exactly how she would begin her conversation with Denise.

The Bible has many faces. It can be studied as literature and explored as a set of stories and poetic expressions, or viewed as history which tells us of the beginnings and growth of God's people. For some it is a guide to archeology, pointing the way to buried civilizations. There is a place and a purpose for each of those aspects. But at the basis of it all, the Bible is the Word of God. It is God's message to a rebelling world of how people can return to Him. The Bible is God's letter of love and hope to all of us.

QuestNote 6.1
The Bible Is the Word of God

Summarize two more reasons to conclude that the Bible is God's Word.

Its Power to Change Lives

• •

Its Inspiration, Thus Its Inerrancy

1. Facts Related to Inspiration

2. Facts Related to Inerrancy

QuestNote 6.2
The Bible Is . . .

Summarize your own beliefs (doctrine) about the Bible.

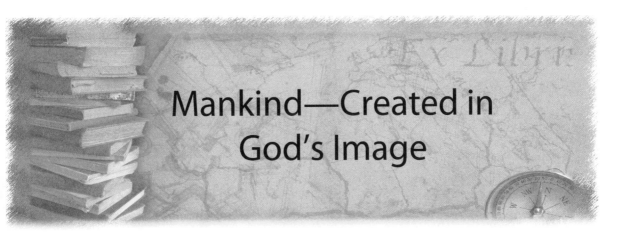

Mankind—Created in God's Image

"Where do you want to sit?" Cecelia asked as they entered the large auditorium. "It really doesn't make a lot of difference to me. I just want to make sure that there are enough chairs so that we can all sit together."

The five reporters moved slowly down the center aisle, looking for just the right place in the auditorium. They wanted to be near enough to the front that they could see the expression on the speaker's face. Yet they didn't want to sit so close that they would draw attention to themselves. After all, it isn't often that five journalists are assigned to cover one story. Of course, no conference like this had ever come to their city.

"Let's sit over there," Roger said as he pointed to the five seats, on the aisle, about half way back from the podium. "It'll give us a good view of the speaker, and we can observe the reaction of the audience."

As the group settled into their seats, a short video presentation describing the two-day conference was beginning on the center screen. In bold, bright red letters the title of the conference "Man – His Meaning and Destiny!" appeared on the screen. The title alone was adequate explanation for why so many reporters had been assigned to cover the event. The conference speakers were certain to generate considerable media interest because of the controversial topics they would be discussing.

"Does everyone have a conference program?" Jenna asked as she looked down the row. Jenna had been the fortunate one to get the seat on the aisle. But with the privilege came responsibility to pass out materials needed during the opening session. She moved quickly not wanting to miss the comments of the speaker and later, any opportunity to ask questions.

Something Like God

God is not something like us, only better.

Rather, we are something like God, only infinitely less.

With Jesus Christ as the central evidence and supreme manifestation of that "something like," this likeness is the most wonderful truth in the entire universe.

–Gardner Taylor

For the next few minutes, the five journalists studied the conference program. The title of the opening general session, Who Is Man?, was certain to provide some good quotes for their stories. Just the title alone would generate controversy. But actually, the title was tame compared to other topics to be covered during the workshop sessions.

As Kevin reviewed his program, he circled the workshops he wanted to attend.

Why Parents Kill Their Newborns
Are We Playing God?
Final Exit – The Benefits of Assisted Suicide
   for the Dying
If We Can Clone Sheep, Why Not People?

"I can't believe this stuff," Michelle said. "I've always considered myself pretty open-minded, but I think that some of this goes way too far. I don't know about you guys, but it's going to be hard for me to be objective. I have some pretty strong opinions about these subjects."

Just then the moderator stepped to the podium to welcome the delegates. For the next few minutes he reviewed the program and introduced the workshop leaders. He then gave each one the opportunity to highlight his or her workshop. Finally, the moderator thanked the delegates along with the corporate sponsors of the conference.

With the preliminaries completed, the moderator began his introduction of the keynote speaker. The person was obviously well qualified, holding graduate degrees from five universities on three different continents. He served on numerous human rights commissions and had authored more than 20 books. It would be interesting to see how he answered the question, Who Is Man?

The keynote speaker walked to the platform with a sense of confidence that was hard to describe. He launched immediately into his address. "Who am I? This piercing question of identity must be answered by every person in this room. Our answer, whether we realize it or not, has enormous influence upon our thoughts, actions, outlook, and life in general."

All five reporters were surprised by his forceful opening statement. They had heard many scholarly presentations, most of which were vague, impractical and boring. This speech was definitely going to be different. For the next 45 minutes, the journalists furiously took notes. They seemed to be most focused on his comments about the "images" of humankind. There were three particular images that interested them most. They carefully recorded his words.

Image 1: Man as a Machine

One common view of humans is in terms of what they are able to do. The employer, for example, is interested in the human being's strength and energy, the skills or capabilities he or she possesses. In a real sense, the employer "rents" the employee for a certain number of hours each day. Of course, we know that in some cases the employer actually believes that he owns the employee.

Imago Dei

- A sense of self-existence, of being

- An ability to envision higher purpose, order and God's plan

- A sense of life extending over great time and space

- An inherent perception of values, a judgment of right and wrong

- The ability to think rationally and logically

- An understanding that all truth ultimately relates to God

- An ability to make decisions based on consideration of the future

- An ability to relate to others and form strong bonds

- The experience of emotions

- Communication skills, including spoken and written words

- Self-governance of emotions and actions

According to this "image" of man, people are basically viewed as things—mere machines that engage in productivity, valuable only as long as they have usefulness. They are a means to an end rather than an end in themselves. They are replaceable as needed. Their death is simply disassembly with no eternal consideration.

Image 2 – Man as an Animal

This view is probably the most widely accepted view in our world. Matter of fact, most school children are taught from the day they enter school that they have evolved to be the highest form of animal life. As such, man is seen as a member of the animal kingdom. There is no qualitative difference between human beings and animals. The only difference is one of degree.

Do you see what this implies? First, motivation is understood primarily in terms of biological drives. Second, discernment is gained not through introspection, but by animal experimentation—simply the process of rewarding the behaviors desired. How many delegates are there in this room who view themselves as a highly evolved ape?

Image 3 – Man as a Pawn of the Universe

Many believe that mankind is at the mercy of whimsical forces in the environment that control their destiny but have no real concern for them. Consider all the people who daily study their horoscope in the newspaper or call a psychic hot-line to learn their fate. These people believe that there are forces over which they have no control that direct their destiny. This pessimistic view sees man as a victim trapped in a hostile world. This view leaves us with quite a sense of helplessness, doesn't it?

Albert Camus captured this view in his retelling of the classical Greek myth of Sisyphus. Sisyphus had died and gone to the nether world. However, he was given the opportunity to visit the natural world briefly. When he was recalled to the nether world, he refused to return. He was too attached to the pleasures of this world. As punishment he was brought back and sentenced to push a large rock up to the top of a hill. When he got the rock to the top of the hill; however, it would always roll back down. He would then have to descend to the bottom of the hill and push the rock up again. Of course, once he reached the top, the rock would roll back down to the bottom. He was doomed to repeat this process for eternity. In spite of all of his efforts, there was no way that he could escape his fate.

Many today—some of you right here in this room—hold this "image" of man. Some of you are afraid of dying. Others are worried about global warming and the destruction of our planet. And then there are those of you who constantly worry about terrorism, chemical warfare, famine or a nuclear holocaust. In many ways you feel like Sisyphus. You believe you are a pawn at the mercy of the universe. At times the sense of helplessness is overwhelming.

. . . .

The keynote address came to an end all too quickly. Not once during the entire 45-minute presentation did any of the reporters talk with each other. Engrossed in the speaker's comments, they were barely aware that they had come as a group to cover the conference. The speaker was able to make a personal connection with each of the journalists.

- Ability to act for the good of others rather than self

- An appreciation of beauty and grace

- Creativity, curiosity and generativity

- An understanding that eternal life follows earthly life

- A spiritual core that reflects these characteristics in acknowledgement that God is the center of the universe and that mankind must be rightly related to Him

Then God said, "Let Us make man in Our image, according to Our likeness; let them have dominion over the fish of the sea, over the birds of the air, and over the cattle, over all the earth and over every creeping thing that creeps on the earth." So God created man in His own image, in the image of God He created him; male and female He created them.

Genesis 1:26–27

The follow-up question-and-answer period was brief. It seemed that the speaker had to catch a flight to New York for an evening meeting. Although the reporters had no opportunity to personally ask questions, they were intrigued by the questions of other delegates.

One doctor wanted to know what the speaker thought of the comments of Peter Singer (bioethicist from Princeton University), who said, "Parents should have the option to kill disabled or unhealthy newborns up to 28 days after birth." Another doctor asked, "Why is such a large segment of our society, over 60% in some communities, enamored with the possibility of physician-assisted suicide?" The journalists all agreed that the questions were better than any they would have asked.

"Let's go to lunch," Michelle said when the session ended. "I'm starved!" Michelle was normally the quiet one in the group, except when she was hungry. "Wait a minute. The door is over there. Where are you going?"

"We don't have time to eat just yet," Kevin explained. "We should compare our notes first to see if we've missed anything. Let's head for that corner. It looks pretty quiet."

The reporters circled their chairs and got out their notes. Michelle wasn't very happy, but she knew that her job came before her growling hunger pains. For the next few minutes they compared notes. It was obvious that everyone had been paying attention. Their information seemed complete, accurate and quite detailed.

Roger was first to observe an interesting parallel drawn by the speaker. "Did you notice that he spent a lot of time talking about the 'images' of man? I don't think he was trying to be religious or anything. But image is the word that God uses in reference to mankind as well. According to the Bible, man is made 'in God's own image.'"

"But he didn't say anything about God in his speech, Roger," Kevin replied. "Do you think he was referring to the Bible?"

"I'm not suggesting that. I just find it interesting that he structured his speech around the word 'image,' and that's the same word used in the Bible." Roger had spent his first two years after high school at a Bible college. His coworkers knew him as a religious guy, even though he kept his faith pretty much to himself. Whenever any questions about the Bible or religion came up, they would go to him for the answers.

"The Christian view of humanity is that we are created by God, made in His image," Roger continued. "First of all, this means that mankind originated not through a chance process of evolution, but through a conscious, purposeful act by God. We are here because God wants us to be here. Second, the Bible also teaches that His 'image' in us is what makes us different from animals. Of all creation, we alone are capable of having a personal relationship with our Creator."

The other four members of the group sat quietly as Roger continued to explain what the "image of God" meant. They weren't taking notes this time. They were just listening. For most of them, Roger's explanation was the most detailed theological lesson they had ever heard.

"Can we please go to lunch now?" Michelle pleaded as soon as he finished. "If I don't eat soon, I'll be so weak that you guys will have to carry me."

"Okay," Cecelia agreed, "I guess we had better get going. The afternoon workshops will start soon. We certainly can't miss our assignments."

"I agree," Kevin chimed in. "But I do want to talk some more about this 'image of God' thing. Roger, can we get together this weekend at my house? The rest of you are welcome if you want to come."

As the group walked out of the conference room, Roger and Kevin compared calendars. The others were thinking seriously about joining them. In the space of just a few hours, their assignment to cover a conference had become a personal journey—a journey to understand themselves in an entirely new way.

QuestNote 7.1
The Creation of Mankind

Summarize what you have learned this week by answering the questions.

1. Briefly describe the creation of mankind.

_____

_____

_____

_____

2. Define and explain how to answer four arguments related to special creation versus evolution.

   1) spontaneous generation of DNA sequences

   _____

   _____

   2) the age of the earth and fossil records

   _____

   _____

   3) microevolution versus macroevolution

   _____

   _____

   4) intelligent design

   _____

   _____

QuestNote 7.1
The Creation of Mankind

3. Explain why it makes a difference whether a person believes that God created life or that life is not dependent on a God-directed process.

4. List five ways in which mankind is different from animals.

5. What two commands was mankind originally given?

6. Explain how mankind was created "in God's image."

QuestNote 7.1
The Creation of Mankind

7. Explain the nature of mankind in the original creation.

    1) Personality

        • mind _____

        _____

        • emotions _____

        _____

        • will _____

        _____

    2) Morality

    3) Spirituality

8. In relation to God, for what purpose was mankind created?

Mankind— His Sin and Fall

Michelle was the last to get in the car but the first to voice an opinion on the restaurant selected for lunch. "That was a great place to eat, Kevin. I had no idea that Thai food could be so good. When did that become your favorite?"

"While I was in Thailand," Kevin said. "I was in the Marines for four years. We stopped in Thailand for training on both of my deployments. Although we didn't have a lot of free time, we did have time to try some of the local cuisine. I thought the food was great!"

While Kevin and Michelle carried on their conversation, Roger, Cecelia and Jenna remained silent. They weren't as enthusiastic about Thai food as their colleagues. But, to spare Kevin's feelings, they decided it was best not to mention it.

Jenna looked at her watch. "We'd better hurry. The workshop sessions are due to start in less than twenty minutes."

Since they were only a few blocks from the conference center, they weren't really concerned about getting back in time. The group's real concern was locating the workshops they had selected and then getting a seat near the front. Since each member of the team planned to attend a different workshop, they were pretty much on their own when they got back to the center.

"See you later," Roger shouted as he jumped from the back seat of the car. "Let's meet in the lobby after the sessions this afternoon. We can choose a place for dinner and compare notes then."

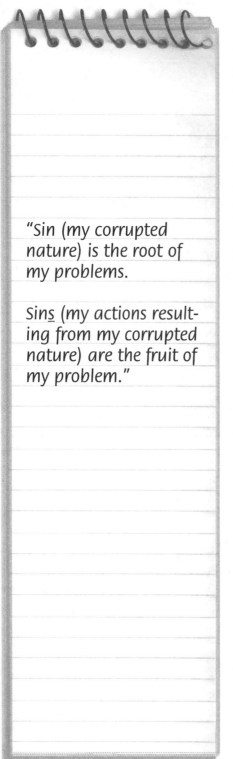

"Sin (my corrupted nature) is the root of my problems.

Sins (my actions resulting from my corrupted nature) are the fruit of my problem."

Each of the reporters voiced their agreement as they exited the vehicle and hurried off to their respective meeting rooms. Roger, Cecelia and Jenna were already thinking of AMERICAN places to suggest for dinner that evening.

Kevin had decided to attend the session entitled: Why Parents Kill Their Newborns. Of course, he knew that the topic was actually infanticide. The workshop leader began by telling two true stories. The first was about Amy Grossberg and Brian Peterson. These 18-year-old college sweethearts delivered their baby in a motel room and, according to prosecutors, killed him and left his body in a dumpster. The second story was about another 18-year-old, Melissa Drexler, who arrived at her high-school prom, went into labor, locked herself in a bathroom stall, gave birth to a baby boy, then left him dead in a garbage can. Afterward she touched up her makeup and returned to the dance floor.

Kevin noted that the speaker was visibly repulsed by these stories. But then he went on to remind his audience that while most people would describe these acts as murder, many of these same people would justify killing an unborn child who had some kind of mental or physical problem.

For the next hour Kevin listened to the brutal facts surrounding the rampant increase of infanticide in our nation. He remembered his experience in Thailand, where children with disabilities were thought to reflect the gods' displeasure with the parents. These children were often abandoned to die, expecting that their next reincarnated life would be an improvement. He thought of his heartbreak while visiting an orphanage housing 700 such disabled children.

Are We Playing God? was the session that Jenna decided to attend. The speaker began by asking a very controversial question, "Is it wrong to combine genes from different species?" She went on to answer her own question by explaining that one gene does not define a species. Bacteria, for example, are composed of thousands of genes; and it is estimated that humans possess as many as 100,000 genes. Therefore, transferring one gene from one organism to another does not create a hybrid in the traditional sense. Genes, she reminded her audience, are composed of DNA. DNA is a molecule; it is not living in and of itself.

But then she explained how genetic engineering was different. Through genetic engineering, DNA material is added to a cell that will change its composition, possibly for as long as it lives, and potentially can be passed on to future generations. Through genetic technology, mankind possesses a power never before imagined—the ability to intentionally design or create a new variety of organism by altering its genetic structure. Such research using embryonic stem cells could offer cures for debilitating diseases or paralysis resulting from spinal cord injuries. It could offer great hope for the future.

Jenna was fascinated by the idea of designing a new organism but was bothered by the term "embryonic stem cells." Then the speaker started explaining how genetic technology might some day be used to learn, only hours after conception, if a baby has birth defects. Using this technology, the speaker explained, the parents could then make a decision whether or not to abort the baby. Although genetic technology has the potential of providing many positive benefits for mankind, the opportunities for using the same technology for evil were frightening to Jenna.

As it is written: "There is none righteous, no, not one; there is none who understands; there is none who seeks after God. They have all turned aside; they have together become unprofitable; there is none who does good, no, not one.

Romans 3:10–12

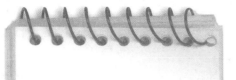

Perspectives on Sin

1) Some say discussion of sin is too negative.

2) Evidences of sin are everywhere.

3) Sin is more than wrong acts; it is the state of sinfulness.

4) Sin is the failure to live up to the standard that God expects of us in the areas of our actions and our thoughts.

5) Failure to believe the truth presented to us is rebellion.

6) Sin spiritually disables us.

Cecelia was the only one who had expressed interest in attending: Final Exit—The Benefits of Assisted Suicide. Among other things, she learned the distinction between mercy-killing and what some call mercy-dying. Purposefully ending a human life is not the same as allowing nature to take its course when a terminally ill patient dies. The former is immoral (even criminal), while the latter is not. But she also learned that drawing a clear distinction between these two categories is not as easy as it used to be. Modern medical technology has significantly blurred the line between hastening death and allowing nature to take its course.

For almost an hour Cecelia listened to the defenses for euthanasia. Yet she was troubled by what she heard. While physician-assisted suicide seemed compassionate on the surface, it also appeared that the patient was being abandoned in favor of the convenience and financial considerations of the family and society. Besides, where would it all end? Once a right to physician-assisted suicide is established, it soon degenerates into others having the power to make the decision for you.

Later that afternoon the five journalists realized how personally involved they had become in the workshops they had attended. Matter of fact, Roger had even started an argument with the professor conducting the workshop he attended.

"Listen to us," Michelle said in disbelief. "We're acting more like college freshman than journalists. What happened to our objectivity? Why have these workshops upset us so much?"

"I just can't believe that we, human beings that is, have become so callous about life," Kevin answered.

"I don't want you to think I'm a fanatic or anything, but there's something wrong when we use the scientific advances from genetic engineering to determine whether or not we are going to abort a baby because it's not the gender we want."

"I couldn't agree more," Jenna chimed in. "Some of the things I heard today were frightening. Yet the delegates in my session seemed to be in full agreement with everything that was said. I knew that these issues existed, because I've read about them. But I had no idea that they were so widely accepted among scientific and medical communities. There are so many things I heard today that just seem so . . . so . . . wrong!"

"They are wrong," Roger said, realizing that now was probably the time for him to speak up. "What you heard today was a clear illustration of the effects of sin."

The rest of the group was surprised at Roger's bold statement. For sure, he was religious, but they also knew he was pretty level-headed as well. Besides, they were all upset with what they had heard in their workshops. Maybe what he was saying had some truth in it.

"Do you remember what I said about mankind being made in the image of God?" Roger continued. "When Adam and Eve disobeyed God and sinned, the relationship between mankind and God was broken. Additionally, mankind's sin affected every part of life."

Roger began by explaining that as important as the doctrine of sin is, it is not an easy topic to discuss in today's society. Like death, sin is not a popular topic. Besides, people don't like to think of themselves as bad or evil. Even though they admit mistakes, the discussion of sin seems too negative. However, even though

7) When we sin, the image of God, in which we were created, is distorted.

8) When we place something else, anything, in the supreme place which belongs to God, it is sin.

9) We do and say wrong things because we have a sinful nature.

10) Because we are sinners, we need a Savior.

The real problem is in the hearts and minds of men. It is not a problem of physics but of ethics.

It is easier to denature plutonium than to denature the evil spirit of man.

–Albert Einstein
Physicist

many people are ignorant of, and uncomfortable with, the topic of sin, it is a truth that cannot be ignored. Its evidences are everywhere.

Roger continued by helping his friends understand the nature of sin. He first explained that sin is an inward inclination. Sin is more than just wrong acts, it is the state of sinfulness. It is an inner disposition that motivates us to commit wrong acts. That's why Jesus condemned anger and lust just as strongly as He did murder and adultery (Matthew 5:21–22, 27–28). Sin is the failure to live up to the standard that God expects of us in our actions and our thoughts.

Next, Roger explained that sin is rebellion and disobedience. Whether through natural or special revelation, the truth of God has been revealed to all people. Paul, for example, notes that this includes even the Gentiles, who, though they do not have God's special revelation, have the law of God written on their hearts (Romans 2:14–15). Failure to believe the truth that is presented to us is rebellion. Adam and Eve, for instance, were told not to eat of the tree of the knowledge of good and evil (Genesis 2:16–17). But they rebelled against God's authority and disobeyed Him.

Roger surprised the group with his next characteristic of the nature of sin. He noted that sin spiritually disables us. The reporters certainly knew a lot about people with disabilities, but they had never thought about a spiritual disability. Roger explained that sin alters our inner condition, our character. When we sin, the image of God, in which we were created, is distorted. Paul describes this process in Romans 1 when he refers to the sinner's mind as darkened (v. 21) and debased (v. 28). Simply said, we sin because we are sinners. Because we are sinners, we need a Savior.

Finally, Roger explained that sin is the displacement of God from His rightful place in our life. When we put something else, anything, in the supreme place which belongs to God, it is sin. The Ten Commandments begin with the command to give God His proper place. "You shall have no other gods before Me" (Exodus 20:3). Similarly, Jesus reminded His disciples of the first and greatest commandment: "And you shall love the Lord your God with all your heart, with all your soul, with all your mind, and with all your strength" (Mark 12:30).

Jenna was the first to respond to Roger's mini-lecture on sin. "Maybe you have a point. It's obvious that the problems we face in our society are not the result of limited education, poverty or difficult circumstances. I know people who have very little education, and a lot of people who aren't very rich, who try to live honestly and do what's right. On the other hand, I know some very intelligent and rich people who do very bad things. The problem doesn't seem to be our circumstances or environment; the problem seems to be us."

"That's exactly right," Roger replied. We do and say wrong things because we have a sinful nature."

"So how can that be changed?" Cecelia asked.

"I don't think we have time for that right now," Kevin interrupted. "If we don't get busy on our stories, we will miss our deadlines. Listen, why don't you guys join me at Roger's house for a cookout next week? I know we all have lots of questions. Besides, that will give us time to digest these things some more."

Cecelia spoke up, "Sounds good to me. I'll be there."

"Me too," Jenna said.

Michelle had to check her schedule, but said that she would do her best to be there.

As the journalists left the conference center, they were each contemplating how they were going to report what they had observed. For sure, the day had ended differently from how it began.

QuestNote 8.1
The Nature of Sin

Answer the questions as a review of the nature of sin.

1. Explain how sin was first committed by Adam and Eve.

2. Explain the consequences of their sin on . . .

   1) the world in general.

   2) Adam and Eve's physical, mental, emotional and social condition.

   3) Adam and Eve's spiritual condition.

3. How was the slaying of animals a picture of Christ's future death on the cross?

QuestNote 8.1
The Nature of Sin

4. Why does God declare that every human being is guilty based on Adam's sin?

5. What is meant by the phrase "We sin because we are sinners"?

6. Because all have sinned, all are under the penalty of death. Explain the three meanings for the word "death" in Scripture.

1) spiritual

2) physical

3) eternal

QuestNote 8.1
The Nature of Sin

7. Write a definition of sin that encompasses its various aspects.

8. Explain the difference between temptation and sin.

9. Explain the progression of temptation becoming sin, based on James 1:14–15.

10. Explain the avenues to temptation, based on 1 John 2:16. How do these apply to teens?

11. Explain how the world, in general, explains mankind's propensity to do evil.

QuestNote 8.1
The Nature of Sin

12. Explain how a false view of mankind results in accepting practices such as assisted suicide, euthanasia, abortion, etc.

13. Counter these claims:

1) Through science, economic conditions and education, people are becoming better.

2) I'm better than a lot of people I know. If I do my best, God won't punish me.

3) Surely, young innocent children are not sinners.

QuestNote 8.1
The Nature of Sin

14. Explain how we are affected by sin in . . .

1) Our relationship with God _____

_____

_____

2) Our relationship within ourselves _____

_____

_____

3) Our relationship with others _____

_____

_____

15. What is the only cure for sin?

_____

_____

_____

_____

_____

_____

_____

_____

_____

_____

Overcoming the Sin Nature

"C'mon in," Roger yelled when he heard the doorbell. "It's unlocked."

By the time Roger had made his way to the living room, all four of his friends were seated comfortably. He was a little bit surprised to see Michelle since she had not called to confirm that she was coming. But he was glad to see her just the same.

It had been more than two weeks since they were together at the conference center. At the time, they seemed very interested in spiritual matters. That's why they agreed to meet with Roger at his home. They hoped he could answer some of their questions. But, quite frankly, Roger thought they would get "cold feet" and politely back out of their promise to get together. He was pleasantly surprised when they all showed up.

"I hear we're going to cook out later," Michelle said with a hopeful look in her eyes. "Whatever you're cooking, I like mine medium rare."

Laughing, Jenna teased, "You're always concerned about what's to eat. I believe that for every 100 words that come out of your mouth, 75 of them have to do with food."

"Not true," Kevin interrupted. "I believe it's more like 85 words per 100!"

Everyone laughed, as they also looked forward to grilled steaks. Michelle headed for the refrigerator to get something cold for everyone to drink. Roger had bowls of chips and salsa already strategically positioned around the living room. While everyone was getting settled, he brought out a tray of fruit and several bowls of assorted nuts. Although not much of a cook, Roger did enjoy having friends over to talk.

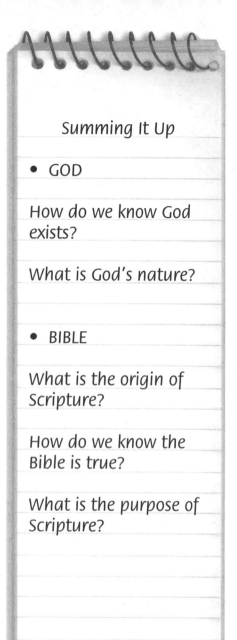

Summing It Up

- GOD

How do we know God exists?

What is God's nature?

- BIBLE

What is the origin of Scripture?

How do we know the Bible is true?

What is the purpose of Scripture?

After a few minutes of pleasantries, Kevin decided to get down to business. "Do you guys remember what happened that brings us together tonight?" he asked. As he looked around the room, it looked like Jenna wanted to answer his question but didn't know whether or not she should. "Go on, Jenna," Kevin said, "tell us what happened as the conference came to an end."

Not all of her memories of that day were perfectly clear, but Jenna did remember that it was her statement that caused everyone to stop and think. "I remember that we were pretty upset after the workshops. None of us could believe the terrible things that humans are doing to each other. Then I said that the problem doesn't seem to be our education or environment—the problem seems to be with us. That's when everybody looked at me kind of funny."

"And that's when Roger informed us that we do and say things because we have a sinful nature," Michelle added. "Then Cecelia wanted to know how the sinful nature could be changed."

"Yeah, that's exactly the way I remember it too," Kevin said. "I knew that we didn't have time to fully discuss Cecelia's question, so I decided to invite everyone over to Roger's house since we already wanted to get together. I'm sorry, Roger. I should have asked you first."

"No problem," Roger replied. "The most important thing right now is that we answer Cecelia's question about changing our sin nature. My guess is that all of you did not come today just to enjoy my good cooking. I know better than that. You not only wanted to talk about Cecelia's question, but you probably have some questions of your own that have been bothering you.

Before we can even attempt to answer her question, however, we have to understand some other important truths."

Roger began to explain that everything begins with our concept of God. For the next few minutes he asked each of his friends to describe their idea of God. Although each of them had an opinion of what God is like, they didn't really know how they had come to that conclusion. Roger told them to hold on to that thought because he wanted to discuss it more fully a little later.

Then he explained the options that faced each of them as they considered their personal concept of God. First, there was the choice between supernatural and natural. God was either "a part of" this world or "apart from" this world. He pointed out that each of their descriptions of God indicated a belief in the supernatural.

He went on to explain that if you believe that God is supernatural, then you have another choice to make. God is either some kind of cosmic force or He is personal, intimate with His creation. Many people do believe that there is some kind of cosmic entity that they call god, and that he has some type of relationship to the world and to us. However, no one really knows what this entity is like. Evidently, this god doesn't want us to know anything about himself.

"I believe in a personal God," Roger said. "I believe that God not only created us, but that He has an interest in each of us. This God has made Himself known to us because He wants to have a personal relationship with us."

Roger then went on to explain that the God He worships is not just some unknowable force in the universe. The God he serves is characterized by the following

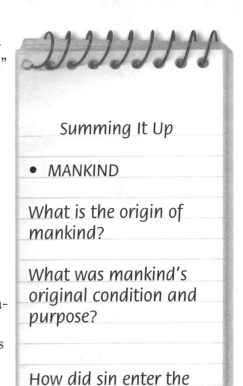

Summing It Up

• MANKIND

What is the origin of mankind?

What was mankind's original condition and purpose?

How did sin enter the world?

What are the results of sin?

How can a person be restored to a right relationship with God?

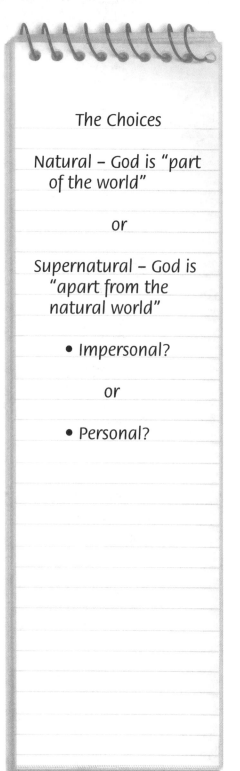

The Choices

Natural – God is "part of the world"

or

Supernatural – God is "apart from the natural world"

• Impersonal?

or

• Personal?

attributes: Spirit, immutable, eternal, infinite, omnipotent, omnipresent, omniscient, loving, righteous, just and holy.

"How can you know so much about God when it seems like everyone else is unsure of what He is like?" Michelle asked.

"A few minutes ago I asked each of you to explain your concept of God," Roger responded. "After each of you told me what you thought God was like, I asked you to tell me how you had come to that conclusion. None of you seemed to know why you believe the way you do. Do you remember that?"

His friends all nodded in agreement.

"That's because you have not yet identified the ultimate authority that guides your beliefs and your life. In other words, upon what basis have you drawn your conclusions about God? Is your concept of God based on your feelings? Is it based on what others have said about God? Is it the result of how the media has portrayed Him? What is your ultimate authority for determining what God is like?"

All four sat in silence. They had never been asked such a pointed question in such a personal way. Although each had a concept of God, they were unable to explain where their idea of God had come from. Finally, they each concluded that their concept of God had come from a variety of sources.

Roger continued, "Isn't it logical that a personal God would want to communicate with His creation? And isn't it logical that His communication would be completely accurate and authoritative?"

Once again, each of his friends nodded in agreement. "My guess is," Kevin interrupted, "that you're talking about the Bible. Why are you so sure that the Bible is God's Word."

"Yes, I do believe that the Bible is God's totally accurate, authoritative communication to mankind," Roger replied. "I believe that the Bible is inspired, or put another way, God-breathed. If you will seriously evaluate every known writing or book that purports to be the communication from a supreme being, you will find that the Bible is the only one that meets a number of objective criteria.

"For example, there is the Bible's accuracy when recording dates, events or locations. The Bible records hundreds of prophecies that have been fulfilled. The Bible maintains extraordinary unity for a book that was written by more than 40 people over a period of 1600 years. It is in the Bible that I learn what God is like. It is also in the Bible that I learn why man is like he is."

As the group continued to listen to Roger, the pieces began to fall into place. Mankind was created in the image of God. Until Adam sinned, the relationship between God and Adam was pure. But when he sinned, that relationship was broken. And, since we are all part of the human race, the results of Adam's sin affected all of us. Roger then read Romans 5:12, ". . . through one man sin entered the world, and death through sin, and thus death spread to all men, because all sinned."

Then Roger tried to explain how every person is thoroughly and totally depraved—hopeless and helpless without God. That doesn't mean that mankind is as bad as he possibly can be, or that he has no sense of

On what basis?

• Feelings?

• Human thinking?

• Others who seem to have greater spiritual acuity?

• God's revelation in the Bible?

Conclusions

- *Mankind was created in God's image.*

- *Mankind sinned and the relationship to God was broken.*

- *Mankind is hopeless and helpless to cure his sin nature.*

- *The only way the sin nature can be changed is through the power of God.*

morality left in him. But it does mean that the principle of evil has infected every part of his nature. Mankind's inclination is not to conform to God's laws, but to resist and rebel against them.

"Let me explain it this way," Roger said. "Sin does not begin with our overt acts, nor is it limited by them. Our sinful acts occur because of our sinful heart and mind. In other words, we are not sinners because we sin; we sin because we are sinners. An apple tree is not an apple tree because it bears apples; it bears apples because it has the nature of an apple tree. Sins are the acts; sin is our corrupt nature."

Cecelia was the first to respond. "So, people who commit such terrible acts against others do so because of their sin nature. Those acts are just the result of who they are apart from God."

"That's right," Roger said. "The acts they commit don't make them sinners. They commit evil acts because they are already sinners."

Cecelia once again raised the question that she asked two weeks ago, "How can the sinful nature be changed?"

Roger was well prepared for that question. "The root problem is sin. Mankind is alienated from God, and therefore is self-centered. The tensions between racial groups, economic classes and nations are nothing more than the self-centeredness of the individual on a worldwide scale. Of course, the things we heard at the conference are just other examples of this sin problem. The only way to solve the sin problem is to change the nature of mankind. The only way to change the nature of mankind is through the power of God as presented in the Gospel."

After reading Romans 5:18–19 to his friends, Roger explained the Plan of Salvation. He then read Romans 5:21 to them. "So that as sin reigned in death, even so grace might reign through righteousness to eternal life through Jesus Christ our Lord."

"The Gospel is the only answer to the sin problem," Roger concluded. "Neither education nor government programs can change the nature of man. Whether or not to receive Jesus Christ as our Savior is an individual decision that all of us—at one time or another—will have to make."

Each journalist looked at the others, knowing that Roger's words made sense. Roger had done all he could do. The rest was up to them as the Holy Spirit confirmed the Gospel to their heart and drew them to Christ.

Therefore, as through one man's offense judgment came to all men, resulting in condemnation, even so through one Man's righteous act the free gift came to all men, resulting in justification of life. For as by one man's disobedience many were made sinners, so also by one Man's obedience many will be made righteous.

Romans 5:18–19

QuestNote 9.1
Roger's Logic

God Is . . .

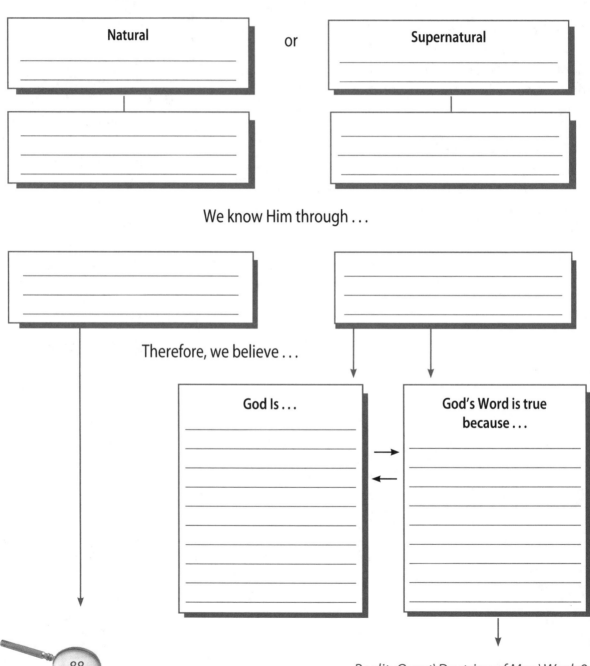

| Natural | or | Supernatural |

We know Him through . . .

Therefore, we believe . . .

God Is . . .

God's Word is true because . . .

QuestNote 9.1
Roger's Logic

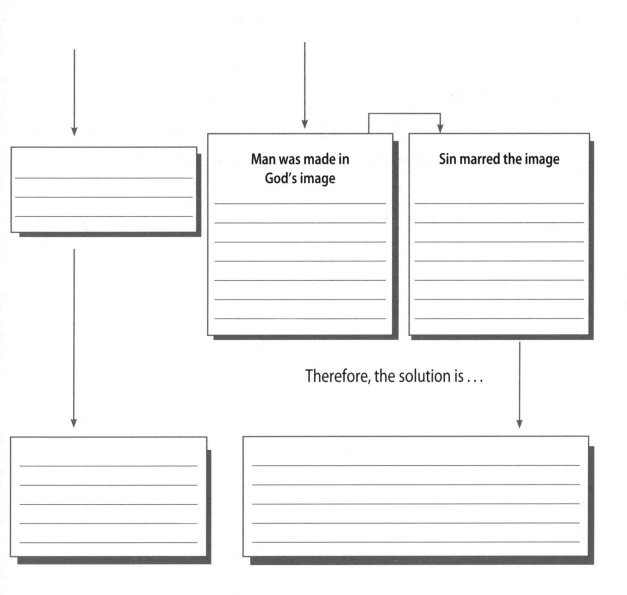

Man was made in God's image

Sin marred the image

Therefore, the solution is . . .

QuestNote 9.2
The Nature of Mankind and Sin

Summarize your study of the nature of mankind and sin.

Topics to Consider

Mankind's Origin	**The Inherited Sin Nature**
Mankind's Original Nature	**The Only Solution to the Problem of Sin**
Mankind's Original Responsibilities	**The Old Vs. the New Nature within a Christian**
The Origin of Sin	
The Consequences of Sin	

QuestNote 9.3
Summing It Up

 God

How do we know God exists?

What is God's nature?

 Bible

What is the origin of Scripture?

How do we know the Bible is true?

What is the purpose of Scripture?

QuestNote 9.3
Summing It Up

➤ *Mankind*

What is the origin of mankind?

What was mankind's original condition and purpose?

How did sin enter the world?

What are the results of sin?

How can a person be restored to a right relationship with God?

Mankind's Need
of Salvation

"This one had a happy ending," Doug thought as he watched the report of the dramatic rescue on television at the motel. Earlier that day the parents of two young boys had reported them missing. After questioning the parents, Joliet officer Mike Kljaich had a hunch where the boys might have been playing.

Immediately the officer headed to an area where dangerous rapids created whirlpools along a craggy bank. As the officer approached the area, he heard a cry for help. Then he saw one of the boys hanging onto a tree limb over a culvert of fast-moving water, surging toward a waterfall that plunged into the Vulcan Quarry off Highway 53.

Kljaich raced to the tree. With one hand, he reached out and grabbed the frightened child. Because the boy was so wet, he almost slipped out of the officer's hand. Finally rescued, the boy wanted to know what had happened to his brother. Fortunately, he grabbed onto some rocks and was able to climb out of the culvert.

As the emergency vehicles arrived, the officer tried to calm the two boys. Interviewed later by the local television station, Kljaich was asked how the boys felt when they were finally rescued. "They were plenty scared," the officer answered. "They believed that their situation was completely hopeless and that no one would arrive in time to save them."

As he was getting ready for bed at the motel, Doug thought about the officer's words, "they believed that their situation was completely hopeless." How many times had people found themselves in similar situations, only to be rescued in the nick of time? He had asked himself that question many times over the past few years. And each time he asked the question, he moved one step closer to a life-changing decision.

Are we basically good but sometimes do bad things? Or are we completely corrupt, even though at times we do good things?

The 6:00 A.M. wake-up call seemed to come unusually early that next morning. As Doug struggled to get out of bed, he remembered the news story he had watched just before turning off the light. The words of officer Kljaich, "they believed that their situation was completely hopeless," kept echoing in his ears. He couldn't get the pictures of that dramatic rescue out of his mind.

Doug was looking forward to getting home again. Although he had only been on this particular assignment for a couple of days, it seemed like he had been gone forever. As an insurance investigator, Doug would sometimes be away from home for as long as two weeks at a time. Many of his friends viewed his job as glamorous and exciting. But Doug knew that most of the time it was just routine investigation. Anyway, it would be good to get home to his wife and two young daughters.

After checking out of the motel, he began the four-hour drive home. As usual, the drive gave him plenty of time to think. But all he could think about was the news story of the rescued boys. The words "situation" and "hopeless" from the officer's interview replayed in his mind. Could it be that this particular dramatic rescue would be the turning point in Doug's life?

By the time he got home, Doug knew that the time had come for him to pursue his dream. Although it had been on his mind for over two years, he had never felt that the time was right to start this special project. For the first time, he was convinced that the right time to start was NOW! He couldn't wait to tell his wife.

Doug's wife was clearly enthusiastic about his decision. "I'm so glad you've finally decided to work on your manuscript," she said. "I've told you all along that I thought it was a great idea to develop a book based on dramatic rescues. I'm sure that each person's experience has its own unique story that readers would love to know. When are you going to get started?"

"I'm ready now. I've just been looking for a special angle that would distinguish my book from all the rest," Doug replied. "The words of Officer Kljaich, after he rescued those two boys, gave me the idea I needed. They believed that their situation was hopeless and that no one would arrive in time to save them. That's the perspective I'm going to use when I write the book. I want to research stories in which the individuals rescued had given up all hope for survival. What do you think?"

"That's a great idea!" she replied.

Doug had always appreciated his wife's enthusiasm when he embarked on a new project. For just a moment, his mind flashed back to his junior year in high school when they first met. Although her name was Melissa, her friends all called her Missy. He remembered her as having lots of energy and spontaneity. That was a big attraction. After eight years of marriage and two children, Missy was still as enthusiastic as ever. He knew that she would support him throughout the entire book project.

"I'm surprised that it was the news report that gave you the idea you needed for your book," Missy observed.

"What do you mean?" Doug asked.

"Think about it. What has been the topic of Pastor Williamson's sermon series for the past three weeks?"

Christ died for sin.

Believers die to sin.

Unbelievers die in sin.

— D. L. Moody

Doug stopped to think for a moment. "Well, I know that it has to do with the nature of man, but I don't understand the connection."

Missy had immediately noticed the relationship between the pastor's messages and Doug's angle for his book. "Don't you remember how many times the pastor has reminded us of mankind's 'hopeless situation' and of mankind's need 'to be rescued'? You might want to consider an additional perspective for your book. Although many people have found themselves in hopeless situations and needing a dramatic rescue, everyone is in a spiritual state of hopelessness, also desperate for rescue."

Doug was amazed at his wife's insight. Of course, following up on her idea would mean additional work. He would have to research not only the stories for his book, but also the doctrine of salvation. Doug certainly wasn't a Bible scholar, but he knew his pastor would be willing to help.

"Honey, I think your idea has real possibilities," Doug finally replied. "I'm going to make an appointment to see if the pastor would be willing to help me with my Bible research." Without waiting for a reply, Doug headed for the telephone to call the church.

The next day, after Doug finished work at the office, he met Pastor Williamson at a restaurant that was conveniently located about halfway between his office and the church. The men ordered their coffee and selected a vacant booth in a far corner. Doug didn't waste any time sharing his book idea and the new angle proposed by Missy.

"I think you really have something there," was Pastor Williamson's response. "I'd be happy to help in any way that I can. When do you want to get started?"

"Would today be too soon for you, Pastor?" Doug asked.

"Not at all. Let's do it," the pastor replied. "Let me share a few thoughts with you about man's spiritual hopelessness. That will give you something to think about. I'll also suggest some reading material. Then let's get together again to talk about other aspects of the doctrine of salvation. The more you know, the better prepared you'll be to write your book."

The pastor began by explaining that the most dramatic rescue story would pale in comparison to mankind's hopeless condition before God. As a result of the Fall, Pastor Williamson explained, the entire human race is infected by sin—sin which is an offense to a holy God. If God were to execute divine judgment upon mankind, it would mean condemnation and hell for every person on the face of the earth. By our own efforts, we are completely hopeless and helpless to save ourselves.

Doug was taken aback by the pastor's powerful description of mankind's condition. As an insurance investigator, he knew that people were capable of extreme evil. But he had never really considered the fact that our sin is an abomination to God.

Sensing Doug's hesitancy, the pastor decided to briefly characterize what mankind is really like. "Mankind lives to please himself," the pastor began.

Grace to you and peace from God the Father and our Lord Jesus Christ, who gave Himself for our sins, that He might deliver us from this present evil age, according to the will of our God and Father.

Galatians 1:3–4

"While people may give lip-service to God, their real motive is to look out for Number 1—themselves. In order to get his way, mankind will try to manipulate people and events in any way possible—including those considered supernatural. And then, if things don't happen as desired, people will blame and curse God, or even deny His existence. Whether we like to admit it or not, we deserve God's condemnation."

"I'm beginning to see your point," Doug said after a brief silence. "Mankind has turned his back on God in so many different ways. Unless God comes to our rescue, there is no hope of salvation."

"You're exactly right!" the pastor responded. "That's what Paul was saying in Romans 1:20–25. Let me read to you what Paul said." Pastor Williamson reached for his Bible and turned quickly to the passage.

For since the creation of the world His invisible attributes are clearly seen, being understood by the things that are made, even His eternal power and Godhead, so that they are without excuse, because, although they knew God, they did not glorify Him as God, nor were thankful, but became futile in their thoughts, and their foolish hearts were darkened. Professing to be wise, they became fools, and changed the glory of the incorruptible God into an image made like corruptible man—and birds and four-footed animals and creeping things. Therefore God also gave them up to uncleanness, in the lusts of their hearts, to dishonor their bodies among themselves, who exchanged the truth of God for the lie, and worshiped and served the creature rather than the Creator, who is blessed forever. Amen.

The pastor pointed out several important facts from the passage. First, mankind is conscious of God's existence, power and divine nature through general revelation. According to Paul, the person who truly seeks God will find Him. Second, mankind chose to worship the creation rather than the Creator. According to Leviticus 10:3 and Romans 15:5–6, our chief purpose is to glorify God. To glorify God is to honor and obey Him. Instead of worshiping God, however, people chose to make images of God's creation and worship them.

"As a result," the pastor continued, "God 'gave them up.' In the Greek language this is a judicial term used for handing over a prisoner for his sentence. When people constantly turn their backs on God, they distance themselves from His grace. Of course, this is not what God wants. His desire is for people to be saved. But if they refuse the truth, they will remain in their hopeless, lost condition."

After some further discussion, Doug thanked the pastor for taking time to meet with him. "You've certainly given me a lot to think about," he said. "Understanding man's spiritual hopelessness has to be the first step in my research. The story of someone's dramatic rescue at sea is futile if that same person has not been rescued from being eternally lost."

As Doug left the restaurant, he felt an even greater passion to write his book. What began as a collection of dramatic rescue stories might now become a tool that God could use to rescue unbelievers into a right relationship with Him.

Relating to the world of people:

1. Be in the world but not a part of it. (John 17:15-16, 18)

2. Be salt and light to the world. (Matthew 5:13–14)

3. Take the Gospel to the world. (Matthew 28:19–20)

4. Pray for those in the world. (1 Timothy 2:1–2)

5. Live honestly, responsibly and peacefully. (Romans 12:17-21; 1 Thessalonians 4:11–12)

6. Avoid the influence of the world. (1 John 2:16)

7. Do not conform to the world. (Romans 12:2)

QuestNote 10.1
Mankind's Need

Write notes based on the class presentation.

The Meaning of Salvation

"How was your meeting with the pastor?" Missy asked as her husband came through the door from the garage. She then added, "Dinner's almost ready; I hope you didn't have a hamburger or fries at the restaurant."

"Don't worry, all we had was coffee," Doug replied, "although I was tempted to order the fries. Anyway, we had a great meeting. Pastor Williamson loved the idea for my book, especially the spiritual angle. He agreed to help me any way that he could. In fact, he gave me some ideas on how to begin my study of the doctrine of salvation."

After dinner, Doug went to the local Christian bookstore to purchase some of the books suggested by the pastor. He had visited the bookstore many times, usually to just browse. Doug was an avid reader but seldom read Christian types of books. And when he did, it was usually fiction. But this trip to the bookstore was different. For the first time, it seemed, he had a specific purpose for coming.

After finding the theology book the pastor had suggested, Doug began looking at the books addressing the subject of salvation. He was surprised at the number of books on the topic. When he left the store over an hour later, he had purchased one theology text and seven various books all related to salvation. Although that seemed like a lot of books on one subject, he wanted to buy more. But these would get him started. Besides, he could always come back. He knew for a fact—bookstores love to sell books!

This is a faithful saying and worthy of all acceptance, that Christ Jesus came into the world to save sinners, of whom I am chief. Now to the King eternal, immortal, invisible, to God who alone is wise, be honor and glory forever and ever. Amen.

1 Timothy 1:15 & 17

By the time Doug got home, the girls were already in bed but weren't asleep yet. He took the stairs two at a time as he went to say good-night. Of course, they had all sorts of questions, mostly to avoid the inevitable "lights out." Why did he go to the bookstore? What books did he buy? He explained as much as their young minds could handle. Finally, he kissed them good night, darkened the room and headed back downstairs.

"Well, the girls had a few questions, but they seem to be satisfied with the answers I gave them," Doug said as he turned the corner to enter the living room. "What was your day like?"

Typically, after the girls were in bed, Missy and Doug spent some time just talking about the events of the day. They both enjoyed some quiet, relaxing conversation each evening. But Missy knew that tonight Doug would want to start reviewing the books he had just purchased.

"It was a good day, Doug," Missy replied, "but we can talk more about it later. I'm sure you'd like to take a closer look at some of those books you bought today. It's all right to spend the rest of the evening on your research. I've got plenty to do."

Doug was pleasantly surprised by Missy's response. "Well, I really would like to start reading tonight if you're okay with it."

Doug settled into an easy chair in his make-shift office. After setting his new books on the corner of his desk, he reached up to turn on the lamp. A quick flash told him the light bulb had just burned out. A little annoyed, Doug went to get a replacement bulb. Of course, at the time he didn't realize how that burned-out bulb would become a significant link in his understanding of the doctrine of salvation.

Over the next couple of hours, Doug reviewed the chapter titles in each of his new books. He prioritized and flagged the chapters that he wanted to read first. He also highlighted words that he didn't completely understand. As an investigator, he had learned years ago that you couldn't just skip over a word because it was unfamiliar. A single word could change the entire meaning of a paragraph.

Several hours passed before he realized he was really tired. As Doug leaned back in his chair, he thought about the many aspects of salvation discussed in the books. It seemed strange, for he had always thought of salvation as a pretty simple event. But it was obvious, from just the chapter titles, that the topic of salvation is actually complex.

At that same moment, Doug noticed the burned-out light bulb still sitting on his desk and the replacement bulb burning brightly in the lamp. Staring more intently at the two bulbs, he realized that the light he was enjoying in his office was far more complex than simply turning on a switch. Before that light bulb could emit light, it required extensive substructure, including transmission towers, power substations, huge dams, generators, wires strung and all types of electrical equipment installed. Tremendous complexity exists behind the simple act of turning on a light switch.

That's when he saw the relationship between the light bulb and the doctrine of salvation. Although salvation seems so simple, it is far more complex than it appears on the surface. Immediately, questions started popping into Doug's mind.

Salvation Facts

1: People must be saved, or face eternal death (separation from God and punishment) as a just consequence of their sin.

2: People cannot be transformed by their own efforts. It is the supernatural work of God by the work of Christ and through the Holy Spirit.

3: The process of conversion differs from person to person. What is important is genuine repentance and faith.

4: Saving faith is more than belief. It is the abandonment of the old life and a commitment to following God.

5: Regeneration produces a new spiritual sensitivity. There is an increasing desire, and ability, to obey God and to conform to Christ's character.

Definitions

Salvation –
A work of God through which the believer is freed from the penalty of sin, the power of sin and the presence of sin

Conversion –
turning/changing from one direction to another with deep commitment and passion; involves repentance and faith; the new birth

Repentance –
Sorrowing over sin, confessing and turning from sin to God; the process brings forgiveness and the fruit of righteousness; an "about-face" from the wrong direction

• How does salvation relate to the whole plan of God?

• Why is Jesus' incarnation significant to salvation?

• Why did Jesus have to die on the cross?

• Could someone be saved if Jesus' resurrection had not occurred?

• What role does the Holy Spirit play in salvation?

• What really happens when you "call on the name of the Lord"?

As a little boy, Doug remembered his parents telling him that all he needed to do was "ask Jesus into his heart" and he would be saved. While it was true that salvation was a simple act of faith, Doug now began to realize that it is a far more multifaceted. And he was determined to understand as much about it as he could. He returned to the stack of books sitting on his desk. This time he was going to focus on the important events and terms related to salvation.

The first thing Doug learned was that salvation is one of the basic themes of Scripture, and it is not just found in the New Testament. Actually, the concept of salvation was formally introduced as early as the sacrifices of Abraham. Interestingly, neither the Old nor the New Testament defines the word "salvation." However, in passages such as Exodus 14:30, Exodus 15:2 and Psalm 33:16–18, salvation means deliverance.

Although most of the Old Testament passages refer to a physical deliverance, the New Testament refers to salvation as a spiritual deliverance. Mankind is saved from his sins (Matthew 1:21); from condemnation (John 3:17); from death (Luke 6:9); and from the wrath of God (Romans 5:9). Salvation is the process of deliverance from the condemnation of God to entrance into favor with God.

The more Doug read, the more he realized that there are four terms that relate specifically to the concept of salvation. He knew that he had to understand these terms to fully appreciate the scope of God's provision of salvation. He began making copious notes.

The first term is "conversion." This is the first step of the Christian life. It is the act of turning in repentance and faith from one's sin to Christ. The second term is "repentance." Some authors describe it as the negative side of conversion because it has to do with turning our back on sin. Repentance also involves a godly sorrow for our sin. The next term is "faith." Faith is the positive side of conversion. It is the heart of the Gospel because it is the means by which we receive the grace of God.

Doug noted that repentance and faith always go together, then continued his writing.

Finally, there is "regeneration." The terms "conversion" and "regeneration" are thought to be synonymous, but are actually two concepts. Conversion is man's response to God's offer of salvation. Regeneration is completely God's work. It is the other side of conversion because it is God's transformation of the individual believer in giving new life.

Faith –
Trusting Christ alone for salvation; a belief so determined that it leads to action; knowing God exists, that His Word is true, and accepting His Son as Savior

Regeneration –
New life given to believers by God through the indwelling Holy Spirit

Conversion =
Repentance + Faith
→ Regeneration

Faith is living, daring confidence in God's grace, so sure and certain that the believer would stake his life on it a thousand times.

—Martin Luther

Faith is a firm persuasion/belief in the mind about the facts related to Christ,

PLUS

a personal surrender of the will to those facts,

RESULTING IN

a lifestyle consistent with the belief.

Although Doug had accepted the Lord over ten years earlier, this was the first time that he had carefully thought about what had actually taken place in his life. He looked again at the burned-out light bulb on his desk. Yes, salvation, just like the emission of light, is far more complex than he had ever realized. There was so much more he wanted to learn about salvation. This wasn't just research for his book now—it was personal. He wanted to fully understand the miraculous work that God had accomplished in his own life.

It was getting late and Doug knew that Missy was ready for bed. As he began to straighten the books on his desk, Doug once again thought about the two boys who had been rescued by Officer Kljaich. They had been "saved" in the physical sense. But what about their eternal salvation? Just like every other human being on the face of the earth, they were guilty before God. Had they been saved from condemnation and restored to fellowship with God? He would probably never know.

What he did know, however, was that he had a responsibility to share God's wonderful message of salvation with all who would listen. His book might be the means to accomplish that objective for his readers.

QuestNote 11.1
Salvation Involves

Write a summary of the concepts presented related to Christ's work and the process of salvation. Include the terms whenever possible.

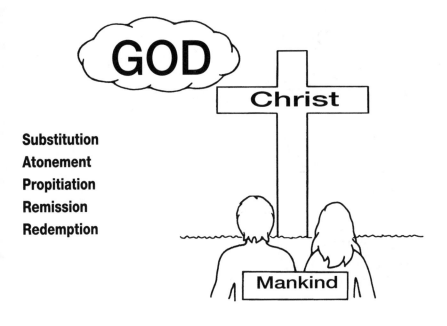

Substitution
Atonement
Propitiation
Remission
Redemption

Amazing Forgiveness

1 On the second ring, Pastor Williamson answered his phone. "Hello?" The pastor recognized Doug's voice immediately. "How are you, Doug? How's the research for your book going?" He listened patiently to Doug's response and then was surprised by the last-minute invitation to lunch. "Yes, I know where the restaurant is. I'll meet you there in an hour."

2 When the pastor arrived, he saw that Doug's car was already in the parking lot. Pastor Williamson had hardly stepped through the door when he saw Doug coming to greet him. The big grin on Doug's face assured him that there wasn't a problem.

3 "Thank you, Pastor, for meeting with me on such short notice," Doug said as he extended his hand in greeting. "I've learned so much in the last few days that I think I'm starting to drive Missy nuts telling her about everything I've read."

4 "So she told you to call me and drive me nuts for awhile. Is that what I'm supposed to think?" the pastor asked with a grin on his face.

5 "Oh, no! That's not it at all. It was my idea to call you. I wanted to discuss with you what I've learned to make sure that I understand everything correctly. Now that I've collected enough rescue stories and have completed the study, I'm going to start the first chapter this evening."

6 "That's great!" the pastor responded as the server approached their table. "Let's go ahead and order lunch, and then you can tell me what you've learned since we met last week."

7 Soon Doug was launching into a detailed explanation of what he had studied. First he reviewed some of the controversy surrounding the doctrine of salvation that had been debated throughout church history. He then made sure that he had a correct understanding of the key terms related to the doctrine. But most importantly, Doug wanted to be sure that he understood the process of salvation—conversion, repentance, faith and regeneration. When lunch arrived at the table, Doug was still involved with his report, so Pastor Williamson ate his meal while Doug talked.

8 "I'm surprised at how much you have learned in such a short time," the pastor said finally. "However, there are three important Biblical concepts related to salvation that you haven't mentioned. Although they may not relate directly to the focus of your book, they are essential to the doctrine of salvation."

9 "You mean there's more?" Doug replied, thinking he had studied every possible aspect. "What are you referring to?"

10 As Doug began eating, the pastor finished his lunch and sat back in his chair. "Let me tell you a little story to illustrate the first concept," he said. "Of course, this is a fictional story, but I'm sure that you'll get the point."

A man dreamed that he died and was met at the gates of Heaven by one of God's angels. As the man approached the gate he asked, "What do I have to do to get in?"

The angel replied, "It takes 10,000 spiritual points to get in." Noting the confusion on the man's face, the angel explained that a person earns points for his actions in life. "What have you done during your time on earth?" the angel asked.

"Well, let's see," the man began. "I attended church every week and went to the mid-week service at least twice a month. I was very careful to give my tithe to the Lord. I financially supported three missionaries. And then, of course, I gave to the building fund and helped the youth group purchase their new van."

"Was there anything else?" the angel inquired, checking his clipboard.

The man quickly replied, "I served on the deacon board most of my adult life. I also taught Sunday School and served as an usher. One weekend each month I helped clean and maintain the grounds. I was very involved with our church."

"Was there anything else?" the angel asked once again.

Beginning to get a little irritated, the man continued to list his good works. "Every Thanksgiving I went to the rescue mission and helped serve food to the homeless. At Christmas I delivered gifts to needy families. I even went to the senior citizens' home every other weekend to visit the shut-ins."

"Was there anything else?" the angel asked once again.

The man stood before the angel in disbelief. "No, I can't think of anything else," he replied. "Isn't that enough?"

"Although you did many good deeds in your life," the angel responded, "it only adds up to zero. It isn't enough."

Some steps of salvation defined:

Repentance – a change of mind; new mind about God.

Conversion – a change of life; new life for God.

Regeneration – a change of nature; new heart for God.

Adoption – a change of family; a new relationship toward God.

Sanctification – a change of service; separation unto God.

Glorification – a change of place; new condition with God.

–Found on the flyleaf of a Bible belonging to D. L. Moody

Mercy - pity, sympathy, caring, compassion that causes a person to want to help; the motivation for loving action to meet a need.

Grace - the favor—love and kindness—of God (undeserved and unearned by our own works, extended for our benefit on the basis of Christ's work of redemption.

Forgiveness - cleansing from the guilt and eternal consequences of sin

The man was shocked. "You mean to tell me that everything I've done, the money I've given and all the time I've spent, is only worth ZERO POINTS? I've got zero points and it takes 10,000 points to get into Heaven?"

The angel nodded and began to turn away from the man. All of a sudden, the man cried out in a loud voice, "OH, LORD, HAVE MERCY ON ME!" The angel noted his clipboard and made a checkmark.

The man continued, "I REMEMBER THE DAY I REPENTED OF MY SINS." The angel made another mark.

"I TRUSTED GOD ALONE FOR MY SALVATION!"

Upon hearing the man's cry, the angel turned and replied. "That's it! The sum now is 10,000 points. You may enter into Heaven."

11 "Okay, Pastor, I get the point. God has provided for our salvation. It's His mercy that is important," Doug admitted.

12 "Not just mercy, Doug, but grace as well. It is important that you understand both words." With that, the pastor began to explain that mercy is God's tenderhearted, loving compassion for His people. Mercy sees man as miserable and needy. Pastor Williamson then read Psalm 103:13. "'As a father pities his children, so the Lord pities those who fear Him.' Mercy provides the motivation for God to act on our behalf."

13 He continued, "Grace, on the other hand, reflects God's goodness and generosity in actually saving us. Both mercy and grace are attributes of God. Because

we are sinners, God has compassion (mercy) upon us. And though we deserve punishment for our sins, God grants us salvation on the basis of His goodness and generosity (grace), and not because of anything we have done."

14 The pastor turned once again in his Bible and read Ephesians 2:8–9. "For by grace you have been saved through faith, and that not of yourselves; it is the gift of God, not of works, lest anyone should boast."

15 "You know, Pastor, it's amazing that anyone is saved at all," Doug commented upon hearing the explanation of mercy and grace. "If God gave to people what we deserve, none would be saved. Everyone would be lost and condemned to an eternal hell."

16 Pastor Williamson saw that Doug was serious about what he had just said. "You're exactly right, Doug. It is only because of God's mercy and grace that we can receive His gift of salvation. But there is still one more important term related to the doctrine of salvation that you must know. It is not only one of the most wonderful words in our language, but it's also one of the most amazing concepts in the Bible. It is called forgiveness."

17 The pastor explained that forgiveness is the act of excusing, or pardoning, someone in spite of what that person may have done. For the next few minutes, both men talked about the many times that they had needed the forgiveness of their wife, their children or one of their friends. They couldn't even imagine life had they not been forgiven for the offenses they had caused others.

18 "You're right, Pastor," Doug agreed. "Forgiveness is one of the most wonderful words in our language."

Justification - declared not guilty, but righteous, by a holy God; "just as if I'd" never sinned; given right standing before God

Sanctification - made holy; set apart for service; the continuing process of the work of the Holy Spirit to conform us to the image of Christ; becoming more like Him

Glorification - the future perfect transformation into the presence of God forever

Have mercy upon me, O God, according to Your loving-kindness; according to the multitude of Your tender mercies, blot out my transgressions. Wash me thoroughly from my iniquity, and cleanse me from my sin. Hide Your face from my sins, and blot out all my iniquities.

Psalm 51:1–2, 9

19 "But more than that, it is one of the most amazing concepts in the Bible," the pastor replied. "Forgiveness in the Bible refers to the God of the universe pardoning our sins. Did you know that there is no religious book—except the Bible—which teaches that God completely forgives sin?"

20 "Is that really true?" Doug asked.

21 "Yes. Biblical researchers have studied every known religion in an attempt to understand beliefs about various gods and their view of man's sin and salvation. They have determined that the Bible is the only book that teaches that God completely forgives sin. Doug, take a look at Psalm 51:1–2 and 9. You'll find God's mercy, grace and forgiveness."

22 "You know, Pastor, those verses really do put everything in perspective," Doug concluded. "There is one real difference between the physical rescue stories I'm including in my book and what I've learned about my own spiritual rescue. All of the stories I've collected describe how humans accomplished the rescue. But spiritual rescue—salvation—is accomplished completely and totally by God."

23 "Your book is going to be a bestseller, Doug. I'm sure of it," the pastor said as they left the restaurant. "You have selected some exciting, breathtaking stories to tell your readers. And I hope they realize, after finishing the book, that the greatest rescue story in all of history is a spiritual one. It is the story of how God provided salvation through the work of Christ on the cross."

QuestNote 12.1
Salvation Involves

Use the graphics and words to help you summarize the truths about salvation you have studied this week.

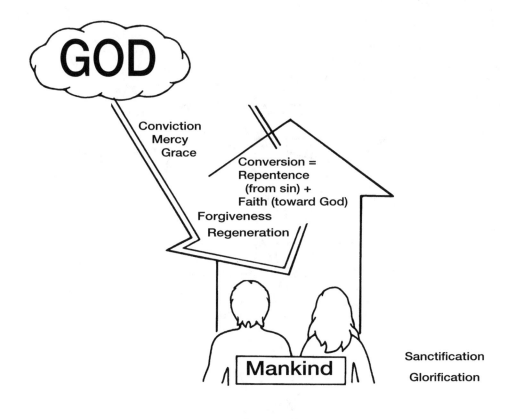

_____

_____

_____

_____

_____

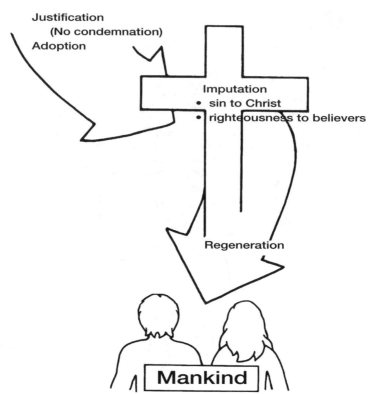

QuestNote 12.2
Truths of Salvation

Write your own doctrinal statement regarding salvation. The questions are meant to guide your thinking. Be sure to use the vocabulary and references you have studied.

1. What circumstances led to mankind's need to be saved?

2. How do we know that God's Plan was for the salvation of mankind?

3. How were the deaths of animals symbolic of Christ's death on the cross?

4. How did Christ's death redeem mankind from the penalty of sin?

5. What must a person do in order to be converted?

6. What is a believer's relationship to the Holy Spirit after salvation?

7. What is a believer's relationship to God after salvation?

8. What does it mean to be saved from the power of sin, and eventually the presence of sin?

QuestNote 12.2
Truths of Salvation

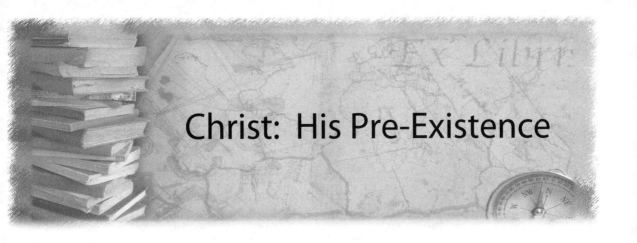

Christ: His Pre-Existence

"You've Got Mail!" the digitized voice cheerfully reported, and Darren immediately took note. It had been over a week since he had e-mailed his sister. Could this be her response? He sure hoped so.

Darren quickly moved the cursor to open his mail. He scrolled down through the 14 new items. As usual, most of it was junk. He soon realized that his sister had not replied. What he had written must have upset her more than he imagined. For the first time, he doubted whether he should have been so transparent about the struggle going on in his life.

"How's the research going, Darren?" Tom asked as he entered the room. Tom, Carlos and Darren had been good friends since high school. Although they had attended different colleges, they landed jobs in the same city after graduation. Since three can live cheaper than one, they decided to share an apartment. As a result, they lived in one of the most beautiful—and expensive—apartment complexes in the city.

"I was just checking my mail," Darren responded. Pointing to the weather outside, he continued, "I'll bet you had a pretty tough day. I heard that the airport was shut down for almost an hour because of thunderstorms. Are things back on schedule now?"

Although Tom had now been working as an air traffic controller for almost a year, bad weather still shook him up just as much as it did his first day on the job. "No, the planes are still running 30 minutes behind schedule. But at least we had no incidents." It was the "incidents" that Tom feared. Managing hundreds of aircraft during the day was stressful enough. But when bad weather hit, the chances of an incident increased dramatically.

A Skeptic's Challenge

To explain apart from a supernatural God . . .

- the existence and function of the universe

- the nature and purpose of humans

- why humans can even conceive of God

- why humans have a sense of right and wrong

- why there exists a book such as the Bible

- why Biblical prophecies have come true

"I'm glad to hear it," Darren responded as he returned his attention to his computer screen. Tom proceeded to the kitchen for a snack to hold him over until Carlos got home from the hospital. The three young men, and their girlfriends, were planning to go to dinner together to celebrate Darren's promotion.

Carlos' job as a lab technician made it difficult for him to predict the exact time he would get off work. So Darren knew that he had ample time to check the newest Web site he had created, "The Skeptics Corner." As the site came into view, he was greeted by his own words of introduction:

If you consider yourself a skeptic of any type, you are warmly welcomed to The Skeptics Corner. My name is Darren and I am the Webmaster. I am also a skeptic. As you read my story, I encourage you to tell your story as well.

The Web site was the result of Darren's promotion at *Newswatch*, one of the most widely respected weekly magazines in the country. As the new assistant editor for culture and religion, one of his major responsibilities was to develop human-interest stories that would entice undecided readers to purchase the magazine.

After all, increased circulation was the name of the game. Sometimes the news itself wasn't too interesting. Unless you had a consistently large number of people buying your magazine, advertisers might choose to spend their marketing dollars somewhere else. Without the steady stream of advertising revenue, the *Newswatch* organization would be unable to maintain its worldwide news bureaus.

Not long after Darren was hired at *Newswatch*, his creative talents were obvious to the editorial staff. After giving him a number of short assignments, his bosses recognized that he was a talented writer. So, when the assistant editor's position became available, they agreed that Darren was the best candidate for the position.

His first major assignment was a perfect fit for him. Realizing that religion was an important part of people's lives, the magazine's editorial board wanted to look at the "other side" of religion—skepticism. As a skeptic from a family of skeptics, Darren couldn't have been more pleased with the assignment. The first thing he did was create "The Skeptics Corner" Web site. By inviting other skeptics to share their stories, he would have a wealth of material for his article.

"Any new stories?" Tom asked as he walked back through the room holding a ham sandwich. "It amazes me how people will share their personal stories with strangers on a Web site."

Darren didn't have time to answer before Tom bounded up the stairs to his own office. Actually, he was glad that Tom had not stuck around for a response. Darren really didn't want Tom or Carlos to know that many of the stories showing up on his Web site were not from skeptics, but from converted skeptics!

At first he had ignored the stories, but now he found himself intrigued by what these people had to say. Jennifer's story, the one he had e-mailed with his letter to his sister, had particularly caught his attention. Although he had read it many times, Darren decided to go through it once more.

- why Jesus Christ has had more profound influence in the world than any other person

- why millions of believers have experienced dramatic conversions and changed lives

- why humans have a sense of destiny and eternity

> In the beginning was the Word, and the Word was with God, and the Word was God. And the Word became flesh and dwelt among us, and we beheld His glory, the glory as of the only begotten of the Father, full of grace and truth.
>
> John 1:1 and 14

She had caught his attention, and that of other readers, with her title, "Jennifer's Story—A Witch Finds Christ." As if visiting with an old friend, Darren began reading.

I am the oldest daughter of an alcoholic, socialist family. I have a sister, a brother and a foster brother, all much younger— also two nephews, a constantly varying herd of guinea pigs which we rehabilitate, and most importantly, the best husband in the world, Dennis.

I grew up without any real religious training. In fact, my father was adamantly anti-religious, and he forbade us to participate in church-type activities. But at college my horizons broadened in a big way. That's where I was introduced to witchcraft. One thing led to another, and I eventually dropped out of college. I found that I could make pretty good money as a practicing witch and fortuneteller. All I needed was a gullible audience.

For the next twelve years I continued to be heavily involved in the occult and New Age practices. During those years of "doing my own thing," both my parents died. I had no idea how much that would affect me. Although I professed to believe in reincarnation, I knew (somewhere deep inside me) that I would never see either of them again. I continued to believe that I had to work out my own salvation and enlightenment—that "oneness with the Divine" which comes as the result of a lifetime of effort. And yet, no matter how hard I tried, the goal seemed further away with each passing day.

I worked so hard at "resolving my own karma" that I eventually became emotionally depressed and physically ill. I found myself constantly bedridden with stress-related illnesses. Every day, I was medicated into insensibility so that I wouldn't become sicker or try to commit suicide.

Dennis was beside himself with worry. He didn't know how to help me. Nobody did. Because I was unable to work, and Dennis had to spend lots of extra time caring for me, we soon found ourselves deeply in debt. Our financial situation added to the stress and depression. I'm sure Dennis felt like giving up on me.

We were both searching for help—any kind of help—when it happened. Although it may not sound like much of a miracle to you, we are convinced that God prepared Eric just for us. He showed up at our door one evening with two bags of food. We knew that he was from the church a couple of blocks from our house, because they had tried to give us food before. This time we were so desperate, we gladly invited him in.

That was the beginning of a friendship that changed both of us. Over the next few weeks, Eric visited us frequently. Of course, we expected that he would ultimately want to talk with us about Christianity. But now, for the first time, we really didn't mind. Dennis and I received Christ as our Savior after realizing that NOBODY can fix his own life. Anyone who claims he can create his own reality is lying. No one is capable of saving himself . . . or herself.

> I commend my soul into the hands of God, my Creator, hoping and assuredly believing, through the merits of Jesus Christ my Savior to be made partaker of Life everlasting.
>
> –William Shakespeare
> Written at the close
> of his Last Will
> and Testament

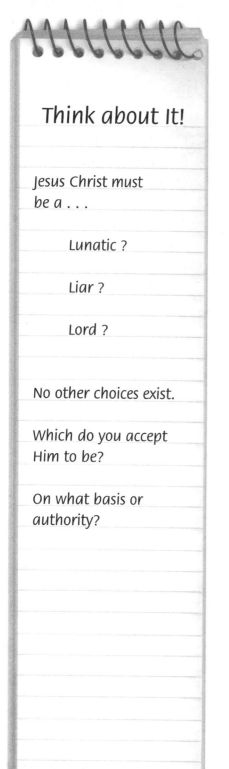

Think about It!

Jesus Christ must be a . . .

    Lunatic ?

    Liar ?

    Lord ?

No other choices exist.

Which do you accept Him to be?

On what basis or authority?

As I look back on those visits Eric made to our house, I still remember him explaining what C. S. Lewis said about Jesus Christ: He is either LIAR, LUNATIC or LORD. I now know that Jesus is neither a liar nor a lunatic. He is the Lord of the universe just as He claims to be."

Darren looked up from his computer screen, once again thinking about the C. S. Lewis quote. Although he had been a skeptic all of his life, he couldn't get Jennifer's story out of his mind. There was something about her struggles that affected him. He wasn't sure why her story "connected" with him, but it did! That's why he had e-mailed his sister a few days earlier. Darren wanted to know what she thought of Jennifer's experience.

Of course, Darren thought he knew a lot about Jesus Christ. After all, he hadn't grown up in some pagan country. But he just couldn't understand how this Christ could make such a dramatic difference for someone who had practiced witchcraft most of her life.

Just then, Carlos came through the door and interrupted Darren's thoughts. "Sorry I'm late," he said. "Just give me a few minutes to clean up and change clothes."

Momentarily startled by the interruption, Darren blurted out the question that had been bothering him for days. "Who do you think Jesus Christ is?"

"What?" Carlos replied, almost tripping over the chair in front of him. "Did you say what I think you said?"

Realizing that Carlos had just come in the door, Tom came back downstairs from his office. The look on Carlos' face surprised him. "What's the matter, Carlos?

Before Carlos could respond, Darren repeated his question. The two friends were at a loss for words. "What's come over you?" Tom asked. "Are you getting religion or something?"

"I'm serious. Who do you think Jesus Christ is?" he asked. Darren then told them Jennifer's story, concluding with the quote from C. S. Lewis. "Lewis says we only have three options when it comes to determining who Jesus is. At one time I would have believed that Jesus was either a liar or a lunatic, but now I'm not so sure."

By now Tom and Carlos knew that Darren wasn't kidding around. "Why don't we talk about this at dinner tonight?" Tom offered. "I think that we would all enjoy the topic. Besides, Cathy has been trying to get me to go to church with her for months now. Let's get going—I'm hungry."

Darren knew that Tom and Carlos did not understand the predicament he was in. He knew that it was his neutrality—even skepticism—that had landed him the promotion to Assistant Editor for Culture and Religion. Now he was starting to have second thoughts about Christianity and Jesus Christ. Could he perform his job objectively? In fact, could he have been wrong about Jesus Christ? If so, that was even more important than his job.

The young men left the apartment and headed for their cars. In a few minutes they would meet at the restaurant for what was sure to be an interesting exchange of ideas.

For thirty-five years of my life I was, in the proper acceptation of the word a nihilist—not a revolutionary socialist, but a man who believed in nothing. Five years ago my faith came to me. I believed in the doctrine of Jesus, and my whole life underwent a sudden transformation . . . . Life and death ceased to be evil; instead of despair, I tasted joy and happiness that death could not take away.

–Leo Tolstoy
Russian author

QuestNote 13.1
Pre-Existence of Christ

Write summary information presented by your classmates.

1. **The Question: What do we know about the pre-existence of Christ prior to the creation of the world?**

A. Testimony of Scripture:

B. Christ's activities prior to the creation of the world:

2. **The Question: Was Christ merely a man, or is He God?**

A. Testimony of Scripture:

B. Attributes—the same as God's:

   1.
   2.
   3.
   4.

C. Sinlessness:

   1.
   2.
   3.

QuestNote 13.1
Pre-Existence of Christ

3. **The Question: What was/ is Christ's work in relation to Creation?**

A. Testimony of Scripture:

   1. _____

   2. _____

B. What is the intent of the plural name for God *(Elohim)* and plural pronouns?

   _____

   _____

4. **The Question: What was God's plan regarding salvation through Christ?**

A. When was the plan formulated?

   _____

B. What does the plan entail?

   1. _____

   2. _____

   3. _____

   4. _____

   5. _____

   6. _____

C. How were people in the Old Testament saved?

   _____

QuestNote 13.2
Christ in the Old Testament

Summarize two truths about the pre-incarnate Christ in the Old Testament.

1. **Theophanies:**
   - meaning of the word

   - appearances to . . .

2. **Prophecies:** List at least ten prophecies fulfilled by Christ.

QuestNote 13.3
Essential Summaries

Write a paragraph that summarizes each of the major truths you have studied this week. Titles for the paragraphs have been supplied as a help in getting started.

Truth 1: *Pre-Existence of Christ—His Eternality and His Work*

Truth 2: *Salvation in Christ—God's Plan*

QuestNote 13.3
Essential Summaries

Truth 3: *Christ Was Active in Creation*

Truth 4: *Christ Appeared in the Old Testament*

Truth 5: *Christ Was Prophesied in the Old Testament*

Christ: His Incarnation

"Well, that was quite an evening," Carlos commented as he walked through the living room door. Darren and Tom had already arrived home after dropping off their dates. "I'm not sure that I can handle so much excitement in one night," he continued sarcastically.

Darren knew he was right. He had put a bit of a "damper" on the evening when he asked, "Who do you think Jesus Christ is?" As expected, Cathy was super interested in the topic and had a lot to say. But Darren knew that wasn't what everyone else wanted to talk about. Besides, it was supposed to be a celebration dinner for his new position, but the tone of conversation had been more serious than celebratory.

"I know what you mean, Carlos," Darren replied. "I'm sorry if I spoiled the evening for everyone. I didn't mean to. I've just had a lot of questions ever since I read Jennifer's story."

In an effort to make peace Tom responded, "Hey, don't worry about it, Darren. We're just giving you a hard time. We all had a great time tonight—just a little more somber than we expected. But, you know, we talked about some pretty important stuff. I know a lot of facts about Jesus Christ but have never really considered Him as someone who could solve my problems and fears. I probably should take a closer look for myself." Unfortunately, Tom's efforts didn't make Darren feel much better.

Tom and Carlos called it a night and headed to their rooms. Darren decided to check his e-mail once more just in case his sister had written. As the online connection was made, the familiar words "You've got mail" were heard. Darren quickly scrolled through the messages, hoping to see his sister's name.

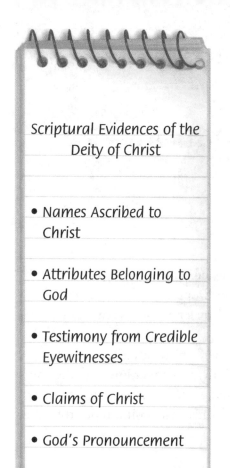

Scriptural Evidences of the Deity of Christ

- Names Ascribed to Christ

- Attributes Belonging to God

- Testimony from Credible Eyewitnesses

- Claims of Christ

- God's Pronouncement

Her letter was the second message from the bottom of the list. Without hesitating, he clicked the open icon. Although her message was very short, Darren was encouraged by what she said. "I've been thinking seriously about your e-mail. Please call me on Monday. I need to talk to you."

Darren knew his sister well enough to know that Jennifer's letter had gotten through to her also. He wondered what she thought of the quote from C. S. Lewis. Unfortunately, he would have to wait three days to learn the answer. Evidently, his sister wasn't going to be home over the weekend. Otherwise, she would have wanted him to call earlier. On the other hand, maybe she just wanted more time to think about what he had written. Either way, he would just have to be patient.

Saturday passed uneventfully. That was usually the time the guys did their laundry and took care of other housekeeping chores. Typically, they saw very little of each other. Sunday was pretty much the same as other Sundays. The guys all slept late and then went out to have a late breakfast together. Tom and Carlos planned to play golf that afternoon. Darren made a lame excuse then headed home to work on his article for *Newswatch*.

As expected, it began as a very quiet Sunday afternoon. But that changed when the telephone rang. Darren picked it up, and at the other end of the line was his editor, Dr. Hastings. As initial pleasantries were shared, Darren tried to figure out why Dr. Hastings was calling him on a Sunday afternoon. Before he could even develop a good hypothesis, Dr. Hastings stated his reason.

"Yesterday," Dr. Hastings began, " I was reading the first draft of your article for the upcoming issue. As usual, I was pleased with your unique topic selection. I believe our readers would be very interested in how various religions portray their gods. But I do have a question for you."

Darren was waiting for the shoe to drop. He knew that Dr. Hastings wasn't calling just to compliment him on his article. Dr. Hastings would not have taken the time on a Sunday afternoon to call unless something was wrong. Darren then realized he had to respond to his boss's comment. "What is your question, sir? You know that I'll do all that I can to help."

"Why did you devote so much of your article to the incarnation of Jesus Christ?" Dr. Hastings asked.

Darren was both surprised and embarrassed by the question. He now realized that Jennifer's story had gotten to him more than he thought. Evidently, his own struggles and uncertainties had been reflected in his article. As a reporter, he knew that he was supposed to be objective and unbiased. Obviously he had failed—and on his first assignment as Assistant Editor.

"I'm sorry, Dr. Hastings," Darren replied. "I didn't intend to be so one-sided in my article. I really tried to represent the various religions fairly." Darren waited anxiously for a response.

"You didn't answer my question, Darren," he replied. "I didn't ask you about representing all of the religions equally. Please meet me in my office at 9:00 tomorrow morning. I have several questions I want to ask about your article. Good-bye."

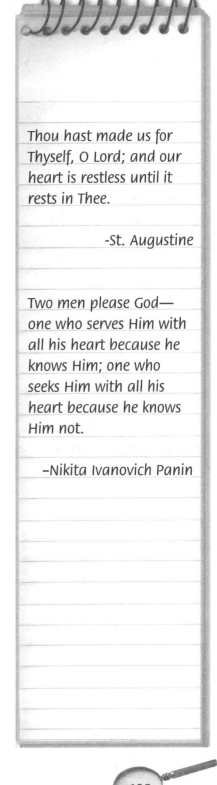

Thou hast made us for Thyself, O Lord; and our heart is restless until it rests in Thee.

-St. Augustine

Two men please God— one who serves Him with all his heart because he knows Him; one who seeks Him with all his heart because he knows Him not.

–Nikita Ivanovich Panin

Let this mind be in you which was also in Christ Jesus, who, being in the form of God, did not consider it robbery to be equal with God, but made Himself of no reputation, taking the form of a bondservant, and coming in the likeness of men. And being found in the appearance as a man, He humbled Himself and became obedient to the point of death, even the death of the cross.

Philippians 2:5-8

With that, the line went dead. Darren found himself standing there, holding the telephone and wondering what kind of questions Dr. Hastings wanted to ask him.

Looking forward to Monday was bittersweet. On one hand, Darren wanted to talk with his sister. He was curious to know what she thought about Jennifer's story and the C. S. Lewis quote. On the other hand, he had to meet with Dr. Hastings about his article. He had a bad feeling about that meeting. It would be an understatement to say that Darren had difficulty sleeping Sunday night.

Monday morning, Darren arrived at his office earlier than usual. He didn't want to take any chances of getting stuck in traffic then being late for the meeting. Just before appointment time, Darren entered the elevator and pushed the button for the tenth floor. He felt as if he were going to his own execution.

"Come on in," Dr. Hastings said as he welcomed Darren to his office. "Thank you for coming to see me on such short notice. I'm sure that you're wondering what this meeting is all about."

Darren thought to himself, "Sure enough! He is being nice to me considering he's probably going to fire me before my first article even goes to press."

"Did you know that I am traveling to Palestine and Egypt next week?" Dr. Hastings asked, breaking Darren's train of thought.

"No, sir, I didn't," Darren replied, rather startled at the nature of the question as well as Dr. Hastings' gentle manner.

"I have to be there next Tuesday. I have several interviews and some research I need to do. I will probably be gone for almost a month." Dr. Hastings looked out the window at the beautiful skyline below before continuing. "As I read your article I couldn't help but realize that I was going to many of the places where Jesus was supposed to have lived and taught."

He paused again and looked out the window. Darren could tell that his boss didn't quite know how to proceed. He wasn't sure whether Dr. Hastings was unhappy with the article or concerned that he was traveling to a dangerous part of the world for such a long period of time. Finally, Dr. Hastings spoke.

"You asked some very critical questions about Jesus in your article—questions that I need to try to answer while I'm on this trip. Although I'm not a religious man, that doesn't mean that I haven't thought about the subject. For some reason, in the last few months, I've thought a lot about Jesus Christ. I don't know if it is because I'm planning to travel to Palestine or if there is some other reason. But when I read your article, the questions you asked were many of the same questions that have been on my mind. I just wanted to talk with you before I left."

Darren was stunned by what he had just heard. "When I came into this office," he thought, "I expected to be either demoted or fired. Now my boss wants to talk about Jesus!" He thought of the many testimonies on his Web site about the unusual ways that people had encountered Jesus. Of course, it was Jennifer's story that had really caught his attention. Could he now be living through a "Jennifer story" of his own? And what about his boss?

Jesus Christ

More God than man, or more man than God?

The Son of Man — The Son of God

The God-Man

Incarnation

God's Son clothed in human flesh

All God and all man

In the Incarnation . . .

- the infinite became finite.

- the eternal was conformed to time.

- the invisible became visible.

- the supernatural Creator of the universe reduced Himself to be a part of the natural creation.

However, at no time did Jesus cease from being fully God.

Dr. Hastings motioned for Darren to sit at the conference table. "Let's review the questions that you asked in your article," Dr. Hastings began. "As you can see, I've put each question on a card and arranged them on the table."

As Darren sat down, he saw the neatly arranged index cards on the table. He scanned the questions.

- *Who is Jesus Christ in relationship to God?*

- *Why did God become a man?*

- *How could Christ be completely human and completely God at the same time?*

- *Did Christ really perform miracles?*

- *How did other religious leaders view Christ?*

- *What were the circumstances surrounding Christ's death?*

- *Is there any proof for the resurrection?*

- *If Jesus did rise from the dead, where is He now?*

- *If it's all true, what does it mean?*

"I've thought of even more questions than these," Dr. Hastings noted when Darren had finished scanning the questions on the table. "But this is a good place to start. You seem to have a good understanding of Christianity. I want you tell me the answers to these questions."

For the second time since coming to Dr. Hastings' office, Darren was at a loss for words. He was no authority on Christianity. In fact, he still considered himself an atheist. Sure, he had some of the same questions about Jesus Christ. But he had very few, if any, answers. Darren struggled with how to respond to his boss.

"Well, sir," Darren began slowly, "all I know about Christianity is what I've read in books. Unfortunately, I haven't spent much time personally thinking about the questions. That is, until recently."

Darren paused and looked at his boss. He was surprised by what he saw. For the first time, there was disappointment in Dr. Hastings' face. His boss had hoped for answers, but Darren didn't have any. There was an awkward silence that seemed to go on for a very long time. And then Darren knew what to say next.

"Dr. Hastings, I would like to tell you Jennifer's story . . . ."

> In the one person, Jesus Christ, there are two natures, a human nature and a divine nature, each in its completeness and integrity, and these two natures are organically and indissolubly united, yet so that no third nature is formed thereby.
>
> –A. H. Strong
> Systematic Theology

QuestNote 14.1
Scriptural Evidences of the Deity of Christ

Summarize the central Bible truths for each evidence.

Names Ascribed to Christ — — — — — — — —

_____

_____

_____

Attributes Belonging to God — — — — — — —

_____

_____

_____

Testimony from Credible Eyewitnesses — — — —

_____

_____

_____

Claims of Christ — — — — — — — — — —

_____

_____

_____

God's Pronouncement — — — — — — — —

_____

_____

_____

QuestNote 14.2
Scriptural Evidences of the Humanity of Christ

1. List at least six events or characteristics that show Christ's humanity.

2. What response would you make to a person who claims that Christ never lived at all?

3. Explain incarnation.

   > Definition:

   > Importance:

4. Explain the phrase "Christ—the God-Man."

QuestNote 14.3
This We Believe . . .

Summarize the traditional doctrines regarding Jesus Christ.

His Birth:

_____

_____

His Humanity:

_____

_____

His Deity:

_____

_____

His Incarnation:

_____

_____

Christ: His Miracles and Teachings

Although Darren was sitting in his car on the drive home, he felt like he was floating on a cloud. What had started as possibly one of the worst days of his life had turned out to be one of the most unforgettable days of his life. As he rehearsed each event in his mind, he savored the joy of every moment.

He first remembered his near panic when entering Dr. Hastings' office. He felt sure that he was going to be demoted, or maybe even fired, for the article he had written. But then Dr. Hastings wanted to know even more about Jesus Christ. His editor had been thinking about Christianity for some time. Darren would never forget the look of disappointment on Dr. Hastings' face when he admitted how little he knew about Jesus Christ.

And then he felt compelled to tell Dr. Hastings "Jennifer's story." He actually began by describing the "Skeptics Corner" Web site. After hearing "Jennifer's story," Dr. Hastings immediately wanted to go to the Web site to read the other unusual conversion experiences. For the next two hours, the two of them read and discussed the stories on Darren's Web site. It became increasingly obvious to both of them that something about Jesus Christ had a profound effect on these people.

Next came lunch. Together they took the elevator to the top floor where the executive dining suite was located. Since this dining room was only open to the senior executives, Darren had never been there. In fact, until that moment, he never thought he would ever have the opportunity to eat there.

> How shall we escape if we neglect so great a salvation, which at the first began to be spoken by the Lord, and was confirmed to us by those who heard Him. God also bearing witness both with signs and wonders, with various miracles, and gifts of the Holy Spirit, according to His own will?
>
> Hebrews 2:3–4

But it wasn't the incredible food, the opulent environment or the fact that he was having lunch with the president of the company that made the time memorable. It was when Dr. Hastings leaned toward him and asked if Darren would be willing to join him on his trip to Palestine and Egypt. Dr. Hastings wanted him to work on finding answers to the questions they both had about Jesus Christ.

What a day it had been!

But now there was so much to do to get ready for the trip. Darren was so engrossed with plans that he almost didn't notice the light flashing on his answering machine as he entered the apartment. Immediately he knew that it was a message from his sister. Without hesitation, he pressed the play button.

"Hi, Darren." Wow! How good it was to hear his sister's voice. "I'm sorry I've been so difficult to reach. But there's a lot going on in my life. Anyway, when you e-mailed me Jennifer's story, I knew my prayer had been answered. That's right, I was praying! Listen, I don't want to tell you everything on an answering machine. I know that you will be home soon, so I'm going to stay here until you call. I want to tell you how Jennifer's story has become my story. Talk to you later. Bye."

Darren couldn't believe what he had just heard. Could it be true? Had his sister become a Christian? As the questions raced through his mind, he picked up the phone and dialed her number. It only rang once before he heard her "Hello" at the other end of the line. "Cindy, this is Darren. What's going on?"

Almost an hour later, Darren said "Goodbye" and hung up. There was no question about it. His sister had become a Christian. He rehearsed her story in his mind, especially the part about the visiting professor who spoke in her philosophy class. Although his topic wasn't all that interesting, something about him intrigued her. Her curiosity motivated her to attend an evening event sponsored by Campus Crusade where he was speaking. Even the title of his presentation, "Christianity for Skeptics," fascinated her.

Just as Jennifer's story had been a turning point in Darren's life, the presentation at the campus meeting had changed the course of his sister's life. As a result of her call, he now understood that Jennifer's story and the C. S. Lewis quote had been—to use her own words—an "answer to prayer." After reading his e-mail, Cindy knew that God was drawing her to Himself. Two days after reading his letter, she had received Jesus Christ as her Savior.

Darren suddenly realized that he was still standing by the telephone. In one sense, he was relieved to hear that his sister was all right and didn't think he had lost his mind. In another sense, he didn't know what to think about her conversion. Was it for real? Could it just be an emotional reaction to something going on in her life? Darren didn't know whether to be happy or concerned. Then it occurred to him—he had just heard another "Jennifer's story." Only this time it could be titled "Cindy's story."

For the time being, he had to quit thinking about what had happened to his sister and focus on preparing for his trip with Dr. Hastings. After all, it was a tremendous honor to be asked to accompany his boss on such an important trip. Dr. Hastings made it quite clear that this

Miracle Worker

Nicodemus said, "No one can do these signs that You do unless God is with him."

Jesus said, "The works that I do in My Father's name, they bear witness of Me."

Luke said, "God anointed Jesus of Nazareth with the Holy Spirit and with power, who went about doing good and healing all who were oppressed by the devil, for God was with Him."

Teacher

God said, "This is My beloved Son . . . Hear Him!"

Jesus said, "Therefore, whatever I speak just as the Father has told me, so I speak."

His enemies said, "No man ever spoke like this man."

His friends said, "We know that you are a teacher sent from God."

would not be a vacation. The days would be long and the work intense. Darren knew that he had to prepare thoroughly, even though he had very little time to do so.

It wasn't just his packing for the trip. Dr. Hastings had directed him to conduct further research about Jesus Christ. He wanted Darren to pay special attention to Jesus' claim to be God, the evidence surrounding Jesus' resurrection, and the role Jesus played in God's overall plan. It was obvious to Darren, from this assignment, that Dr. Hastings had already spent considerable time reading about Jesus Christ.

Knowing that he had to complete this research prior to their departure, Darren had picked up several books at the library on his way home. He wanted to get started right away. He knew that this would be a good evening for reading because Tom and Carlos would not be home until much later. After a quick meal of take-out tacos, he settled into his most comfortable chair with the books and a notepad.

After less than an hour of concentrated study, Darren felt compelled to begin putting his thoughts on paper. Although he was still a novice writer compared to many of his colleagues, the words flowed easily.

Emerging from the Judean desert nearly 2000 years ago, Jesus was an unknown itinerant preacher, proclaiming to His listeners that the Kingdom of God was at hand. Many said that He was a healer and a gifted teacher. Others noted that He challenged conventional wisdom and spoke with authority. In the villages and hillsides of Galilee, curious crowds gathered to witness His miracles and hear His teachings.

Some hearers became followers, believing He was God's anointed one—the Christ. Others dismissed Him as a faker and a troublemaker. Less than three years after He began His ministry, He was arrested in Jerusalem and executed on a Roman cross. Surely no one believed at the time that His death, His resurrection and the witness of His followers would change the course of history.

It is still true today that Jesus of Nazareth remains one of history's most intriguing and enigmatic figures. Christianity, the religion founded on His teachings, counts nearly a third of the world's population as members. However, His words and deeds and the meaning of His life, death and resurrection continue to be the subjects of intense debate. In spite of all that is known about Him, the question is still asked, "Who is this Jesus?"

While an entire lifetime could be devoted to a study of the teachings of Jesus, it is His miracles that are even more astounding. The four gospels report 37 of them directly and allude to hundreds more. These miracles range from healing the sick, performing exorcisms to walking on water and raising the dead. Is He the divine Son of God, as taught by the early disciples, or was He just a uniquely gifted teacher who was also a magician and deceiver of people?

Our science-dominated educational system has found little place for miracles. Science depends upon observation and replication. While the scientific method is useful for studying nature, it has little relevance for the supernatural. Just as entertainers are speaking outside their field of expertise when they appear on television to tell you what medicines to take, so scientists are speaking outside their field when they address theological issues like miracles, the resurrection or the ascension.

Buddha is not essential to the teaching of Buddhism, or Muhammad to Islam, but everything about Christianity is determined by the person and work of Jesus Christ. Christianity owes its life, substance, and character in every detail to Christ. He was:

- the author of its teachings,
- the object of its doctrine,
- the origin of its salvation,
- the fulfillment of its hopes,
- the source of its power,
- the founder of its church, and
- the one who gave the Holy Spirit as a legacy to those who believe.

–Paul E. Little
Know What You Believe

In Christ, we have. . .

A love that can never be fathomed;

A life that can never die;

A righteousness that can never be tarnished;

A peace that can never be understood;

A rest that can never be disturbed;

A joy that can never be diminished;

A hope that can never be disappointed;

A glory that can never be clouded;

But the testimony of history, especially during the time that Jesus walked upon this earth, reveals that miracles do happen. All evidence indicates that Jesus did cast out demons, exercise power over nature, feed thousands, and even raise the dead! Could He be who He said He is? Is Jesus the Messiah, the Son of God? If His miracles were the only proof that He was God, there is no doubt that this testimony would stand up in any court in our nation.

Darren sat back and reviewed what he had just written. He believed that his words clearly conveyed the first obstacle that he and Dr. Hastings would have to overcome in order for them to give credence to Jesus' teachings. After all, if the miracles were fakes, why should they believe anything that He said?

With that in mind, Darren continued writing his thoughts.

Miracles have played a strange role in the history of faith. Sometimes they have provided a strong reason for belief, while at other times a strong reason for disbelief.

The Bible is a book of miracles. Beginning with the Creation in the opening chapters of Genesis to the events described in the book of the Revelation, one miracle after another unfolds. Moses at the burning bush, Daniel in the lions' den, the fire that Elijah called down from Heaven, the virgin birth and the resurrection—all are evidence of God stepping into human history.

For the Christian, the miracles provide a clear confirmation of God's message. But to the doubter, miracles are a stumbling block. In the world of the skeptic, there is no God who intervenes in the laws of nature. Bushes do not burn and remain unconsumed. Lions do eat people—especially when they are hungry. Fire does not come down from the sky. Pregnancy only happens as a result of insemination. When someone dies, that person stays dead! In the mind of the skeptic, the miracles of the Bible are no more believable than the fairy tales enjoyed before bedtime during childhood.

When studying the teachings of Jesus, the significance of miracles cannot be discounted. After all, Jesus pointed to His miracles as one of the proofs of His deity. The truth of Christianity depends entirely on the reality of Jesus Christ. If the miracles were nothing more than elaborate scams, then Jesus is either a liar or a lunatic. But if the miracles occurred exactly as recorded in the Bible, then there can be no question that Jesus is Lord.

Darren knew that the last two sentences reflected the quote from C. S. Lewis. But now, more than ever, he understood the significance of what Lewis had said. He knew that this trip to Palestine and Egypt was more than just a research trip. It was a personal quest to learn the truth.

The evening was late and Darren knew he had to get some rest. There were so many details to take care of before leaving. But a good night's sleep would enable him to better organize his thoughts.

As he walked to his bedroom, he thought again about Jennifer's story, his meeting with Dr. Hastings and his conversation with his sister. It was obvious that the events in his life were taking him down a dramatically new path. The problem was, he didn't know where this path would end. But he was sure of one thing—his invitation to assist Dr. Hastings with his research was no accident. It was just the next chapter in what was now becoming "Darren's story."

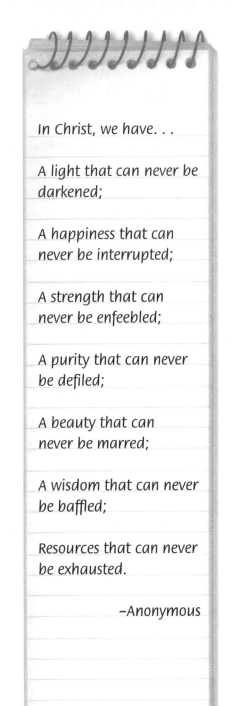

In Christ, we have. . .

A light that can never be darkened;

A happiness that can never be interrupted;

A strength that can never be enfeebled;

A purity that can never be defiled;

A beauty that can never be marred;

A wisdom that can never be baffled;

Resources that can never be exhausted.

–Anonymous

QuestNote 15.1
Christ's Teachings

Summarize each topic as a means of review.

1. Select at least four major themes in Christ's teachings, and summarize them.

   1. _____

   2. _____

   3. _____

   4. _____

2. What are parables, and what purpose did they serve?

   _____

   _____

   _____

3. List at least three parables Christ taught, and state two principles illustrated in each.

   1. _____

      a. _____

      b. _____

   2. _____

      a. _____

      b. _____

3. _____

    a. _____

    b. _____

4. Why should we accept Jesus' teachings as being from God?

    1. God's testimony: _____

    2. Christ's testimony: _____

    3. The scribes' testimony: _____

    4. Their impact on the world: _____

5. What must be proved if Jesus' teachings were not from God?

_____

_____

_____

_____

_____

_____

QuestNote 15.2
Christ's Miracles

As a means of review, summarize each topic.

1. Explain what is meant by "miracle."

_____

_____

2. Name at least two miracles Christ performed related to His power over . . .

• nature _____

• disease and disability _____

• demons _____

• death _____

3. What are two reasons for Christ to perform miracles?

_____

_____

4. List three issues that must be addressed if a person doesn't believe that Christ performed miracles.

_____

_____

_____

5. Why are miracles a powerful proof that Jesus is the Christ?

_____

_____

_____

QuestNote 15.3
Summarizing the Facts

Write a summary paragraph for each of the topics.

1. **Christ's Teachings Show His Deity**

_____

_____

_____

_____

_____

2. **Christ's Miracles Show His Deity**

_____

_____

_____

_____

_____

3. **Christ, the Only Name By Which We Must Be Saved**

_____

_____

_____

_____

QuestNote 15.4
Your Story

The worktext refers to "Jennifer's story," Cindy's story" and "Darren's story." Do you have a story or are you on a path to your story? Summarize it here or in your personal journal.

_____

_____

_____

_____

_____

_____

_____

_____

_____

_____

_____

_____

Christ: His Death and Resurrection

Darren couldn't believe how difficult it was to go through customs at the Tel Aviv airport. He had heard that there was tight security in Israel, but he had not expected the interrogation. Dr. Hastings, an experienced world traveler, seemed to take it all in stride.

As both men boarded the hotel van, they looked forward to a hot shower, something to eat other than airline cuisine, and a good night's rest. It had been a long, 15-hour overnight journey from the United States to Israel. The change of planes in Frankfort, Germany, just made the trip seem that much longer. Darren's body clock was really out of sync. The setting sun told him it was evening. But it was actually eight hours earlier back home. Regardless, he was tired and ready for a bed instead of an airplane seat.

As the driver made his way through the city, Darren and Dr. Hastings sat quietly in the van. Although they had talked for hours during the flights, the combination of lack of sleep and finally reaching their destination caused both men to relax and reflect upon the tasks ahead of them.

For some strange reason, Darren found himself thinking about the conversation that he and Dr. Hastings had somewhere over Iceland at 35,000 feet. As they discussed the purpose of their trip, he remembered what Dr. Hastings said at the end of their conversation. "There is a twofold question I want to answer on this trip. Was Jesus of Nazareth a real person who actually walked the dusty roads of Palestine in the first century? Or, were His life, death and resurrection, as recorded in the four gospels, events that belong entirely to the realm of faith, or even fantasy?"

As a matter of fact, however, it may be stated categorically that no archaeological discovery has ever controverted a Biblical reference. Scores of archaeological findings have been made which confirm in clear outline or in exact detail historical statements in the Bible. And, by the same token, proper evaluation of Biblical descriptions has often led to amazing discoveries. They form tesserae in the vast mosaic of the Bible's almost incredibly correct historical memory.

—Nelson Glueck
Rivers in the Desert

Recalling his questions further convinced Darren that this trip was more than a research assignment for *Newswatch* magazine. Dr. Hastings was on a personal quest for the truth—a quest that Darren had now embraced as his own. Surely their trip to Palestine would answer these questions once and for all.

Moments later the van pulled up to the hotel. Tomorrow the two men would begin looking at the artifacts, traveling to archaeological sites and talking with some of the best historians in the country. But for now, it was time to call it a day and get some sleep. Dr. Hastings had outlined a demanding schedule that would begin early the next morning.

Darren didn't need a wake-up call. As a result of the time change, he was awake over an hour before the telephone rang. It didn't take him long to get ready and head to the restaurant to meet Dr. Hastings for breakfast.

Although he arrived early, Darren was surprised to find Dr. Hastings already sitting at a table having coffee. It seemed that even the most experienced travelers couldn't avoid the effects of jet lag. Darren was also surprised to see an elderly gentleman sitting at the table talking with Dr. Hastings.

"Good morning, Darren," Dr. Hastings said as he motioned Darren toward a chair. "I want you to meet Dr. Kumir. Steve and I have known each other for over 30 years. We not only attended the same graduate school, but we also worked on several research projects in our younger years. He's in town for a conference and just happens to be staying at this hotel."

"It's a pleasure to meet you," Darren replied as he took his place at the table. "I guess it is a small world, after all."

Over the next hour, the three men discussed the research project that had brought Dr. Hastings and Darren to Israel. Since much of Dr. Kumir's work took place in the Middle East, his advice was invaluable.

As if in a classroom setting, Dr. Kumir instructed his friends. "Recent archaeological finds in the Holy Land have provided a wealth of insights into the culture from which the belief in Jesus Christ has emerged. The most controversial of these discoveries were the 800 or so Hebrew and Aramaic texts unearthed during the 1940s from caves at Qumran near the Dead Sea. Biblicists have long hoped to locate more of them. Recently, Israeli archaeologists began excavating newly-discovered caves in the same area."

At this point, Darren felt compelled to interrupt. "I'm familiar with the Dead Sea Scrolls. But what do they contribute to our understanding of life during the time of Jesus?"

"Scholars originally thought that the Dead Sea Scrolls, with their references to the imminent coming of a Messiah, represented the teachings of a radical group of Jewish ascetics known as Essenes," Dr. Kumir responded. "But most experts now believe that the texts, which even include fragments of early legal codes, actually represent beliefs which were widely held by Judaism during the first century.

"The scrolls show that the Holy Land during the time of Jesus was filled with apocalyptic fervor. Ordinary Jews were anticipating the arrival of a Savior who would lead

I know of no one fact in the history of mankind which proved by better and fuller evidence of every sort, to the understanding of a fair inquirer, than the great sign which God has given us that Christ died and rose again from the dead.

—Thomas Arnold
1859

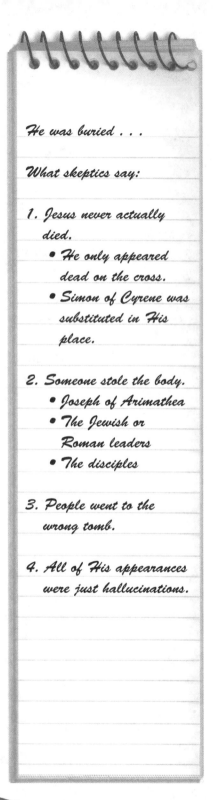

He was buried . . .

What skeptics say:

1. Jesus never actually died.
- *He only appeared dead on the cross.*
- *Simon of Cyrene was substituted in His place.*

2. Someone stole the body.
- *Joseph of Arimathea*
- *The Jewish or Roman leaders*
- *The disciples*

3. People went to the wrong tomb.

4. All of His appearances were just hallucinations.

them in a holy war against Rome. When Jesus claimed to be the Messiah for the spiritual Kingdom of God, many Jews were disillusioned, and some were angry. Because they desired immediate relief from Roman authority, Jesus was not what they had hoped for."

"So Jesus did not meet the Jews' criteria for the Messiah?" Dr. Hastings asked. "Yet He was an actual historical person. Since Darren and I are on a fact-finding trip, we'd like to know what evidences there are that the record of Jesus' life is correctly portrayed in the gospels."

Dr. Kumir smiled apologetically, "Actually, there are far more evidences than I have time to share with you this morning. Let me tell you about just a few of the more recent significant ones.

"In 1990 archaeologists in the Jewish Quarter of Jerusalem's Old City uncovered an ossuary (repository for bones) with the inscription JOSEPH, SON OF CAIAPHAS. According to the gospels, the high priest Caiaphas presided at the Sanhedrin's trial of Jesus. This finding was the first archaeological evidence that Caiaphas was a real person.

"You may already know that in 1961 archaeologists found a fragment of a plaque indicating that a building had been dedicated by PONTIUS PILATUS, PREFECT OF JUDEA. The undisputed evidence of the existence of these two men certainly lends support to the record of Jesus' trials as presented in the gospels.

"We also know that Capernaum, on the Sea of Galilee, played a major role in Jesus' life. It was there, according to the gospels, that He began His public ministry. Archaeologists have uncovered a first-century house in Capernaum that, according to tradition, was the home of Peter. The building contains a meeting room that was likely used for worship. Some experts speculate that this was the synagogue where Jesus preached, as recorded in John 6:59. This site has been extensively excavated and is a "must see" as you tour some northern sites.

"Repeatedly, archaeologists have validated Scriptural references. Discoveries of an astonishing variety of first-century coins, for example, helped explain the need for moneychangers. If you will remember, Jesus drove moneychangers from the Temple on two separate occasions. So, as you can see, there are many evidences that the gospel accounts of His life and ministry are true."

Both Darren and Dr. Hastings remained unusually quiet as Dr. Kumir brought his "lesson" to a close. They both had many more questions, but they knew that Dr. Kumir had an appointment. Finally, Dr. Hastings spoke. "May I ask you just one more question?"

"Certainly. What is it?" Dr. Kumir responded as he counted out some money to pay for his part of the check.

"Did the resurrection of Jesus actually happen?"

Although Dr. Kumir had already started to get up, he sat back down and looked carefully into his friend's face. "Are you asking me if I believe that Jesus Christ is the Messiah, the Son of God?"

"Actually," Dr. Hastings responded, "I'm more interested in whether or not the stories about His resurrection are true."

. . . and rose again . . .

What the Bible says:

1. He was seen alive by many witnesses.

2. The witness of Scripture

3. The grave clothes

4. The dramatic change in the disciples

5. The development of Christian churches

6. The change of the day of worship from Saturday to Sunday

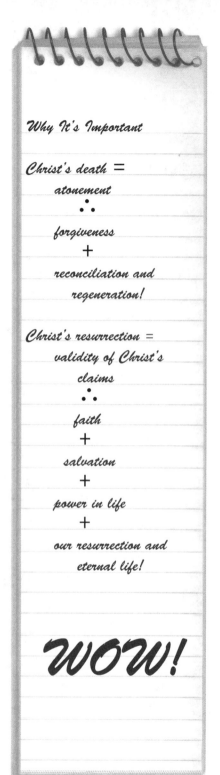

Why It's Important

Christ's death =
atonement
∴
forgiveness
+
reconciliation and
regeneration!

Christ's resurrection =
validity of Christ's
claims
∴
faith
+
salvation
+
power in life
+
our resurrection and
eternal life!

WOW!

"This may come as a surprise to you, but I became a Christian six years ago. I do believe that Jesus Christ rose from the dead. Only God could do what Jesus did."

"We're here to determine whether or not Jesus Christ is who He said He is," Darren interjected. "Can you give us some direction in our research?"

Once again, Dr. Kumir engaged his lecture mode. "I'm sure you know that there are a number of alternate explanations for the resurrection of Jesus Christ. However, none of these so-called explanations adequately accounts for the facts.

"For instance, there are those who believe that Joseph of Arimathea took the body. But you have to ask, why would Joseph want to take Jesus' body? Then there are those who believe that the Roman or Jewish authorities took the body. Yet that explanation makes no sense either.

"According to Matthew 28:11–15, the Roman soldiers and the Jewish authorities accused the disciples of stealing the body of Jesus.

"That explanation has a number of problems. First, on the night of His arrest they did not even understand that He was going to die, let alone be raised from the dead. You need to read John 13:36. We also know from John 20:19 that the disciples were afraid of the Jews. Does it make sense that these men would try to steal His body from a heavily guarded tomb? Finally, if this hypothesis is true, then the disciples later died for something they knew to be a lie. That just doesn't make any sense at all.

"I believe that Jesus not only died, but that He rose from the dead in the same physical body in which He died. There is proof that Jesus rose from the dead. Over

500 people saw Him on twelve different occasions. There is certainly more proof for the resurrection of Jesus Christ than there is for many 'facts' contained in history books.

"I have to leave now, or I will be late for my appointment. However, before you begin your research, I encourage you to read 1 Corinthians 15:3–6. Remember, Paul was a highly educated man who spent the early years of his life persecuting Christians. In these verses, the Apostle Paul explains the reality of the resurrection."

Dr. Kumir picked up his coat, said "goodbye" and walked out of the restaurant. For a few moments, Dr. Hastings and Darren sat quietly at the table. Then Dr. Hastings reached into his briefcase and pulled out a Bible. The fact that Dr. Hastings was carrying a Bible startled Darren. Yet he tried not to show the surprise on his face.

"Before we begin," Dr. Hastings said as he turned the pages of his Bible, "let's see exactly what Paul says in 1 Corinthians 15. I want to know what my friend was referring to." After finding the passage, Dr. Hastings began to read.

Afterward Dr. Hastings closed his Bible and looked up. "Darren, if the resurrection of Jesus is true, then the claims of Christianity must be true. There is no record of any other religious leader who has come back from the grave. We can't delay any longer. We must examine the evidence."

Their first full day in Israel had begun with a coincidental meeting with Dr. Kumir. But Darren wasn't convinced that the meeting had happened by chance. That "God-incident" idea kept gnawing at the back of his mind.

For I delivered to you first of all that which I also received: that Christ died for our sins according to the Scriptures, and that He was buried, and that He rose again the third day according to the Scriptures, and that He was seen by Cephas, then by the twelve. After that He was seen by over five hundred brethren at once, of whom the greater part remain to the present, but some have fallen asleep.

1 Corinthians 15:3–6

QuestNote 16.1
The Day Christ Died

Summarize class discussions regarding Christ's death on the cross.

1. Was Christ's death a surprise . . .

   - To His followers? _____

   - To Jesus Himself? _____

2. Had Jesus anticipated what would happen to Him? _____

3. Did Jesus resist having to die on the cross? _____

4. Was there some other way that God could have solved the problem of sin? _____

5. So Christ died for sin; what else was accomplished by His death?

   - _____

   - _____

   - _____

   - _____

   - _____

What it all means to me:

_____

_____

_____

QuestNote 16.2
Christ Died According to the Scriptures

Summarize what you have learned about the Atonement.

1. When was the plan for Christ's death formulated?

2. How was His death predicted in the Old Testament?

3. For what purpose did Christ say that He came to earth?

4. How did the disciples respond to Christ's teachings regarding His death?

5. What did Christ's death accomplish in relation to God?

6. What did Christ's death accomplish in relation to mankind?

7. What did Christ's death accomplish in relation to believers?

QuestNote 16.3
He Rose Again According to the Scriptures

Summarize the class discussion related to the Resurrection into succinct notes.

1. What are some responses to skeptics' explanations regarding Christ's resurrection?

   - Jesus never actually died. _____

   - Someone stole the body. _____

   - People went to the wrong tomb. _____

   - All His appearances were just hallucinations. _____

2. Explain some facts of the resurrection of Christ.

   1) He was seen alive. _____

   2) The witness of Scripture _____

   3) The grave clothes _____

   4) The dramatic change in the disciples _____

   5) The development of Christian churches _____

   6) The change of the day of worship from Saturday to Sunday _____

3. Explain the significance of the Resurrection. _____

QuestNote 16.4
Summing It Up

State the truths related to the death and resurrection of Christ.

The Death of Christ and Its Importance

QuestNote 16.4
Summing It Up

The Resurrection of Christ and Its Importance

Christ: His Present and Future Ministry

Although the sun had not yet come up, Darren and Dr. Hastings were already climbing into their Jeep. Day 21 in Israel was under way.

"I can't believe we have been here three weeks," Darren commented as they drove onto the highway. "It seems like we just arrived yesterday."

"I know what you mean," agreed Dr. Hastings. "We have gathered so much information, and yet there is still so much more that needs to be done. By the way, how are you coming on the assignment I gave you a couple of days ago? Have you figured out how Jesus Christ fits into God's overall plan as revealed in the Bible? Since it's going to be a while before we get to the museum, why don't you tell me what you've learned so far."

Darren was more than happy to have Dr. Hastings' undivided attention for the next hour. It seemed that during most of their three weeks in Israel, the two men were so focused on their individual tasks that they had little time to compare notes. This was a welcome opportunity for Darren to demonstrate his research abilities, and share all that he had learned.

"Let me get my notes," Darren began. "I have some quotations that I am sure will be of interest to you. Let's begin with this one." Darren settled back in his seat and starting reading.

"Taken as a whole, the Bible differs in its subject and purpose from any other book in the world. It stands supreme as reflecting the place of man and his opportunity of salvation, the supreme character and work of Jesus Christ as the only Savior, and gives in detail the infinite glories that belong to God Himself.

Truths Leading to Salvation

1. I had to know the truth about Jesus Christ. (See Jeremiah 29:13; John 8:32.)

2. Because we are sinners, and God is holy, the relationship between us has been broken. (See Romans 3:10-12; Isaiah 59:2.)

3. Knowing that there was no way mankind could restore that relationship on his own, God provided a way through His Son, Jesus Christ. (See Romans 5:8; John 3:16.)

It is the one book that reveals the Creator to the creature and discloses the plan by which man in all his imperfections can be reconciled and in eternal fellowship with the eternal God." (Major Bible Themes, *Lewis Sperry Chafer, Zondervan Publishing House, Grand Rapids, Michigan, 1974, p. 29*)

"I wanted to begin with that quote," Darren explained, "because it is in the Bible that God presents Jesus Christ, His Son, as well as His plan for mankind. If we do not accept the accuracy of the Bible, then we cannot believe anything that it says about Jesus Christ."

Darren looked up from his notes to see if there was any response from Dr. Hastings. When nothing was said, Darren began reading from another section in his notes.

"If Jesus were not fully God, He could not be our Saviour. But if He were God and yet did nothing on our behalf—that is, did not do something to bring us to God—He would not be our Saviour. Being God qualified Jesus Christ to be Saviour, but His atoning death for us made Him our Saviour. Jesus not only could save men, He did." (Know What You Believe, *Paul E. Little, Victor Books, Wheaton, 1997, p. 43*)

Dr. Hastings thought for a moment before commenting. "It's obvious, then, that the death of Jesus Christ is useless if He is not God. No matter how perfect a man Jesus may have been, He cannot be our Savior if He is not God. What other quotations do you have?"

"Do you remember when we were talking about sin the other day?" Darren asked. "This following quotation helped me to understand the relationship of sin to the plan of God."

"The first exciting experience of a sin makes the second easier. The second encourages the third, and so on until we find that we do not want to think of life without the fleeting pleasures of sinning. But we reach a point where we cannot give it up. By that time it should be obvious that we cannot have the pleasure of sin without paying a price. Sin, then, is a form of slow death.

The Christian view of sin is realistic because it explains both the dignity of man as a creature of God and the ruin of man in his self-chosen rebellion. Man has joined the ranks of the resistance. He is wandering through life far from his spiritual home, the only source of his true identity. Above every other concern, then, he needs to find his way back to his Father's house." (Christian Theology in Plain Language, Bruce L. Shelley, Word Books, Waco, Texas, 1985, pp. 58–60)

All of a sudden it became very quiet in the Jeep. The only sounds heard were the rocks hitting the underside of the vehicle as it made its way down the unpaved road. Both men sat quietly, reflecting on what Darren had just read. Dr. Hastings was the first to speak.

"I don't know about you, but it's almost as if those words were written with me in mind. I know I've done wrong—committed sin, that is. And every time I've committed sin, I've found it easier to commit sin the next time. Sin is a slow form of death. There are so many times that I wish I could turn my back on sin, but I can't.

4. All that remains is for us to accept what Jesus Christ has done on our behalf. (See Romans 10:9-10; John 1:12.)

Jesus Now

- Seated with God (Ephesians 1:20; Colossians 3:1; Hebrews 1:3–4)

- Exalted by God (Acts 5:31; Ephesians 1:21; Hebrews 7:26; Philippians 2:9–11; 1 Peter 3:22)

- Preparing a home for believers (John 14:2; 2 Corinthians 5:5)

- Serving as priest and advocate (Hebrews 5:5–6 and 9:24; 1 John 2:1; Revelation 12:9–10)

- Interceding for believers (Hebrews 4:14–16 and 7:24–27; John 14:13–14)

"You know, Darren, I had an ulterior motive for making this trip to the Holy Land. While it is true that we are here to conduct further research for future *Newswatch* articles, I wanted to make this trip for a very personal reason. For almost two years, I have been on a spiritual journey. I have been trying, as the author of your last quote said, to find my way back to my Father's house. No matter how many religions I studied, I have always come back to Christianity. That's why I had to make this trip. I had to know the truth about Jesus Christ."

"So, when you saw my article, you knew that I was searching too," Darren responded.

"Yes. I could tell by what you wrote that you were also trying to find the truth. I knew immediately that I wanted you to join me on this trip. Now I know that this may sound hard to believe—and maybe even a little 'spiritualeze'—but I was sure that God had brought you my way. Then, when you told me about Jennifer's story, I knew I was right. God meant for us to make this trip together."

Darren sat quietly, not knowing quite how to respond. For the first time, all the events of the previous weeks were starting to make sense. From the moment he had received the promotion at *Newswatch*, everything that happened seemed to lead him closer to God. It all began with "Jennifer's story." Now he was in a Jeep, thousands of miles from home, listening to the president of his company confessing that he had been trying to find God for two years. "Where is this all going?" Darren asked himself.

Finally, he responded. "I have one final quotation I would like to read if that's all right with you." Dr. Hastings nodded his approval.

170

"The real barrier to our forgiveness, therefore, is not our sin, but the very fact that we are asking God to do the forgiving, because in the end, sin is ultimately against God's character itself. Since to maintain His justice as God, He must judge all sin, on what basis can God forgive any sin without compromising His own justice and integrity?

"The story is told about a judge whose daughter was brought into the courtroom for breaking the law. Because the judge was just but also loved his daughter, he faced a dilemma: If he simply forgave his daughter, he would compromise his justice. But if he passed judgment on his daughter, he would compromise his love for her.

"What did he do? First, he declared that his daughter was guilty and ordered that a fine be paid. Then he took off his robe, stepped down from the bench, and paid the fine himself.

"In the Scriptures we see the glory of God as judge on the disrobed face of Christ (2 Corinthians 4:4, 6). As the judge of the world, Christ first came as its Savior in order to make it possible by His own death for God to save sinners without sacrificing His own righteous character." (This We Believe, *Akers, Armstrong, Woodbridge, editors, Zondervan Publishing House, Grand Rapids, Michigan, 2000, p. 87)*

"So," Dr. Hastings began, "God's plan is all about restoring our relationship with Him. Because we are sinners, and God is holy, the relationship between us has been broken. Knowing that there was no way mankind could restore that relationship on his own, God provided a way through His Son, Jesus Christ."

- *Enabling believers (John 14:12; Hebrews 13:20–21; Ephesians 4:8, 11–12)*

- *Waiting for the fulfillment of God's Plan (John 17:4; Acts 3:20–21; Ephesians 4:10; Hebrews 10:12–13)*

- *Sending the Holy Spirit (John 7:39, 14:23 and 16:7; Acts 1:5 and 2:33)*

- *Calling people to be saved (John 3:13–15 and 10:16; Acts 5:31, Romans 10:1–4; 2 Peter 3:9*

- *Building His church (Matthew 16:18 and 28:19–20; John 10:16; Acts 2:42; Ephesians 3:8–10)*

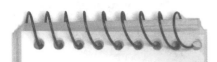

Therefore God also has highly exalted Him and given Him the name which is above every name, that at the name of Jesus every knee should bow, of those in heaven, and of those on earth, and of those under the earth, and that every tongue should confess that Jesus Christ is Lord, to the glory of God the Father.

Philippians 2:9–11

"At first it sounds so complicated," Darren interrupted. "But actually, it makes a lot of sense."

"Yes, it does," Darren's boss continued. "Through the death of Jesus Christ, God's payment for sin has been fully satisfied. All that remains is for us to accept what Jesus Christ has done on our behalf. Now I understand what Paul was saying."

Dr. Hastings pulled alongside the road. By now the sun had come up sufficiently that no additional light was needed for Darren to read from his notes. But it wasn't Darren's notes that Dr. Hastings wanted to read. He reached into his backpack and pulled out his Bible. Turning quickly to Romans 5:6–10, he began to read.

For when we were still without strength, in due time Christ died for the ungodly. For scarcely for a righteous man will one die; yet perhaps for a good man someone would even dare to die. But God demonstrates His own love toward us, in that while we were still sinners, Christ died for us. Much more then, having now been justified by His blood, we shall be saved from wrath through Him. For if when we were enemies we were reconciled to God through the death of His son, much more, having been reconciled, we shall be saved by His life.

"I don't think we have to drive any farther," Dr. Hastings said as he closed his Bible. "I now understand the role Jesus Christ played in God's plan. Because He died for me, my relationship with God can be restored."

After Dr. Hastings spoke, Darren took the Bible from his hands. "When I first began earnestly reading the Bible," Darren said as he turned to the gospel of John, "I read two verses that I haven't been able to get out of my mind. Now I realize that these verses are a summary of God's plan. Let me read what John says in 3:16 and 17."

For God so loved the world that He gave His only begotten Son, that whoever believes in Him should not perish but have everlasting life. For God did not send His Son into the world to condemn the world, but that the world through Him might be saved.

"The mission of Jesus is the result of God's supreme love for an evil, sinful world of humanity. It is no more complex than that."

Dr. Hastings quickly agreed, adding, "And our response to what Jesus has done should be simple faith. The Bible tells us to confess our sins and trust Him as our Savior. Darren, I believe that it is time for both of us to take that step of faith. My search is over."

"So is mine," Darren replied quietly.

As the sun climbed higher into the sky, the two men bowed their heads.

> When I say "Jesus," I mean that He is the Son of God, the second member of the trinity who existed before the creation of the world, who participated with the Father and the Holy Spirit in creation, and who became human. This Jesus of Nazareth, being born of a virgin, came to earth to do the will of God the Father. He died for our sins, came to life again, was bodily resurrected, ascended into heaven, and will come again some day to judge sin and establish permanent righteousness on earth.
>
> —Dr. D. James Kennedy
> Coral Ridge Ministries

QuestNote 17.1
Christ's Present and Future Ministry

Summarize the answers based on class discussion.

1. What were the events related to Christ's ascension? (Mark 16:19–20; Luke 24:49–53; Acts 1:1–11)

2. Where is Christ now? (Ephesians 1:20; Colossians 3:1; Hebrews 1:3–4)

3. What is Christ's position now? (Acts 5:31; Ephesians 1:21; Hebrews 7:26; Philippians 2:9–11; 1 Peter 3:22)

4. What is Christ doing now in Heaven?

   1) (John 14:2; 2 Corinthians 5:5)

   2) (Hebrews 5:5–6 and 9:24; 1 John 2:1; Revelation 12:9–10)

   3) (Hebrews 4:14–16 and 7:24–27; John 14:13–14)

   4) (John 14:12; Hebrews 13:20–21; Ephesians 4:8, 11–12)

   5) (John 17:4; Acts 3:20–21; Ephesians 4:10; Hebrews 10:12–13)

QuestNote 17.1
Christ's Present and Future Ministry

5. What is Christ's present ministry on earth?

   1) (John 7:39, 14:23 and 16:7; Acts 1:5 and 2:33)

   2) (John 3:13–15 and 10:16; Acts 5:31; Romans 10:1–4; 2 Peter 3:9)

   3) (Matthew 16:18 and 28:19–20; John 10:16; Acts 2:42; Ephesians 3:8–10)

6. What will Christ's future ministry be?

   1) (John 14:3; 1 Thessalonians 4:16–17; Revelation 1:7)

   2) (John 5:22–23, 30; Acts 17:31)

   3) (Matthew 24:29–30; 1 Timothy 6:15–16; Revelation 20:1–4)

   4) (Hebrews 12:22–24; 2 Peter 1:10–11 and 3:10–13; Revelation 21:3–7)

7. Summarize the present and future ministry of Christ.

QuestNote 17.2
Doctrine of Christ

Write your own personal statement of the doctrine of Christ. The outline is provided as a help in organizing your thoughts. You can write over it.

Who Jesus Christ Is:

Pre-existence and Plan of God:

Old Testament Presence, Prophecies and Foreshadows:

Incarnation and Miraculous Birth:

Teachings and Miracles:

Death on the Cross and Its Necessity for Salvation:

Resurrection and Ascension:

Present Ministry:

Future Return:

Review of Truths

The Doctrine of God

1.1   Why does mankind instinctively sense that God exists?

1.2   How does nature witness to the existence of God?

1.3   How does the innate knowledge of right and wrong (morality) affirm the existence of God?

1.4   Why is the knowledge of God gained through nature and conscience insufficient?

1.5   How has mankind explained the existence of God from a natural point of view?

1.6   How has mankind explained the existence of God from a supernatural point of view, apart from the Bible?

1.7   What means of special revelation does God provide so that mankind can know Him?

1.8   What does it mean to say that God is a Spirit?

1.9   What does God mean when He says, "I AM THAT I AM"?

1.10 What does the eternality of God mean?

1.11 What does the omnipotence of God mean?

1.12 What does the omnipresence of God mean?

1.13 What does the omniscience of God mean?

1.14 What does the sovereignty of God mean?

1.15 What does the holiness of God mean?

1.16 How can we believe that "God is one" and still believe in the Trinity?

1.17 What does the immutability of God mean?

1.18 How do we know that God is merciful, kind and bountiful?

1.19 How do we know that God is love?

1.20 What is the tension between the love of God and the justice of God?

1.21 What is the meaning of God's grace?

The Doctrine of the Bible

2.1   Why would God provide a book such as the Bible?
2.2   How do we know the Bible is God's inspired Word?
2.3   What major story does the Bible tell from beginning to end?
2.4   What part of the story is told in Genesis 1 and 2?
2.5   What part of the story is told in Genesis 3 through 11?
2.6   What part of the story is told in Genesis 12 through Malachi?
2.7   What part of the story is told in Matthew, Mark, Luke and John?
2.8   What part of the story is told in Acts?
2.9   What part of the story is told in Romans through Jude?
2.10 What part of the story is told in Revelation?
2.11 How does the Bible's unity (being written over 1600 years by 40+ authors) support its inspiration?
2.12 How does the Bible's inerrancy support its inspiration?
2.13 How does fulfilled prophecy support the Bible's inspiration?
2.14 What does the Bible itself say about how it was written?
2.15 What is meant by "plenary verbal inspiration" of the Bible?
2.16 In contrast to dictation, how do Bible authors express their own backgrounds and personalities?
2.17 How does archaeology support the fact that the Scriptures have been preserved as originally written?
2.18 Why should we accept that the canon of Scripture is complete, rather than accepting new writings?
2.19 What is the difference in revelation and illumination regarding Scriptures?
2.20 Of what benefit are the Scriptures?

The Doctrine of Sin

3.1   What were the circumstances leading to the first sin committed by mankind?
3.2   How is Satan related to the origin of sin?
3.3   What were the spiritual results of the first sin?
3.4   What were the earthly results of the first sin?
3.5   How do we know that God was aware that mankind would sin?
3.6   How was the sin nature passed to all mankind?
3.7   In what ways did mankind's sin become worse and worse?
3.8   How can sin be defined?
3.9   What is meant by "total depravity"?
3.10 What is the difference in temptation and sin?

3.11　In what three ways do temptations come?

3.12　What is the sequence leading from a thought (temptation) to actual sin?

3.13　How can a person resist temptation?

3.14　How does a person receive forgiveness from sin?

3.15　What does it mean to say that believers are saved from the penalty, power and presence of sin?

3.16　What are the eternal consequences for failing to repent of sin and trust Christ as Savior?

The Doctrine of Man

4.1　What is the origin of humans?

4.2　How are theories of evolution in opposition to Scripture?

4.3　In what ways was mankind created in the image of God?

4.4　How is a person a tripartite being—body, soul and spirit?

4.5　At death, what happens to the body of a person?

4.6　At death, what happens to the soul and spirit of a person?

4.7　How do humans differ from animals?

4.8　What is mankind's purpose in relation to God?

4.9　What original commands were given to mankind?

4.10　What happened to spoil the original innocence of mankind?

4.11　What is the effect of the sin nature within a person?

4.12　How can a person receive a new nature?

4.13　What is the relationship between the old and new nature after a person has been saved?

4.14　What is the earthly outcome of receiving a new nature?

4.15　What is the eternal outcome of receiving a new nature?

The Doctrine of Salvation

5.1　When was God's Plan of Redemption formulated?

5.2　How does the general, five-point outline of the Bible reflect this Plan?

5.3　What promise was made to Adam and Eve regarding her "Seed"?

5.4　What promise was made to Abraham (and other patriarchs) regarding their "Seed"?

5.5　What promise was made to David regarding his family line?

5.6　How was the death of the first animals a picture of atonement?

5.7　How was the Passover, in Egypt at the time of Moses, a picture of the Atonement?

5.8　How were the sacrifices and other aspects of Israel's worship a picture of the Atonement?

5.9   How were people in the Old Testament made right with God?

5.10   How can people now become right with God?

5.11   What is the meaning and importance of conviction related to salvation?

5.12   What is the meaning and importance of repentance related to salvation?

5.13   What is the meaning and importance of faith related to salvation?

5.14   What is the meaning and importance of receiving Christ related to salvation?

5.15   What is the meaning and importance of conversion related to salvation?

5.16   What is the meaning and importance of forgiveness related to salvation?

5.17   What is the meaning and importance of redemption related to salvation?

5.18   What is the meaning and importance of being born again related to salvation?

5.19   What is the meaning and importance of regeneration related to salvation?

5.20   What is the meaning and importance of imputation of sin related to salvation?

5.21   What is the meaning and importance of substitutionary death related to salvation?

5.22   What is the meaning and importance of atonement related to salvation?

5.23   What is the meaning and importance of justification related to salvation?

5.24   What is the meaning and importance of declared righteousness related
       to salvation?

5.25   What is the meaning and importance of no condemnation related to salvation?

5.26   What is the meaning and importance of reconciliation related to salvation?

5.27   What is the meaning and importance of Christ as mediator related to salvation?

5.28   What is the meaning and importance of adoption related to salvation?

5.29   What is the meaning and importance of security related to salvation?

5.30   What is the meaning and importance of sanctification related to salvation?

5.31   What is the meaning and importance of glorification related to salvation?

5.32   Why is it impossible for a person to earn salvation?

5.33   What must a person do to be saved?

5.34   What are the consequences of salvation?

5.35   What are the consequences of not receiving Christ as Savior?

The Doctrine of Christ

6.1   What does the pre-existence of Christ mean?

6.2   What does the pre-incarnation of Christ mean?

6.3   What is Christ's relationship to God the Father?

6.4   What attributes does Christ share with the Father?

6.5   What was Christ doing prior to the creation of the world, and time as we know it?

6.6   How do we know that Christ was present and active in Creation?

6.7   What does the "proto-evangel" verse (Genesis 3:15) mean in relation to Christ?

6.8   Why do we believe that "Christ was slain before the foundation of the world"?

6.9   How does the shedding of blood in the Old Testament relate to Christ?

6.10 What significance are the Old Testament appearances (theophanies) of Christ?

6.11 What are some Old Testament prophecies that are fulfilled in Christ?

6.12 What is meant by the Incarnation of Christ?

6.13 What is meant by the virgin birth of Christ?

6.14 As the "Logos of God," for what purpose did Christ come to earth?

6.15 In what ways was Christ fully divine?

6.16 In what ways was Christ fully human?

6.17 What is meant by the impeccability of Christ?

6.18 Why was Jesus baptized?

6.19 Why was Jesus tempted?

6.20 Why did Christ have to be the God-Man in order to fulfill the purposes of salvation?

6.21 How did Christ's miracles confirm that He was God's Son?

6.22 Over what various elements did Christ demonstrate His power while
       performing miracles?

6.23 How did Christ's teachings confirm that He was God's Son?

6.24 What were some major themes of Jesus' teachings?

6.25 Why did Christ's teachings and actions bring Him into conflict with established
       religious leaders?

6.26 How did Christ's own statements regarding Himself confirm that He was God's Son?

6.27 How did God verbally confirm that Christ was His Son?

6.28 How did His followers verbally confirm that Christ was God's Son?

6.29 How do we know that Christ actually lived, and is not some myth?

6.30 What does it mean to say that a person must accept that Christ was a liar, lunatic
       or Lord?

6.31 Why was the death of Christ imperative?

6.32 How do we know that Christ actually died, rather than His death being explained by vari-
       ous theories?

6.33 How do we know that Christ actually was raised from the dead?

6.34 Why is the Resurrection so fundamental to Christianity?

6.35 What was the significance of the post-resurrection appearances of Christ?

6.36 What was the significance of Christ's ascension?

6.37 How did God glorify and exalt Christ?

6.38 What is Christ's present ministry in Heaven?

6.39 What is Christ's ministry as our High Priest in Heaven?

6.40 What is Christ's present ministry on earth?

6.41 What will Christ do in the future?

QuestNote 18.1
Review of Doctrines

Succinctly state the essential truths related to the doctrines studied this semester.

1. **The Doctrine of God**

2. **The Doctrine of the Bible**

QuestNote 18.1
Review of Doctrines

3. The Doctrine of Man

4. The Doctrine of Sin

5. **The Doctrine of Salvation**

6. **The Doctrine of Christ**

QuestNote 18.2
Review of RealityQuest

On the basis of the doctrines studied, describe the three top commitments you need to make in your life.

1. _____

_____

_____

_____

2. _____

_____

_____

_____

3. _____

_____

_____

_____

Describe how you feel this course has helped you thus far.

_____

_____

_____

_____

Personal QuestNotes

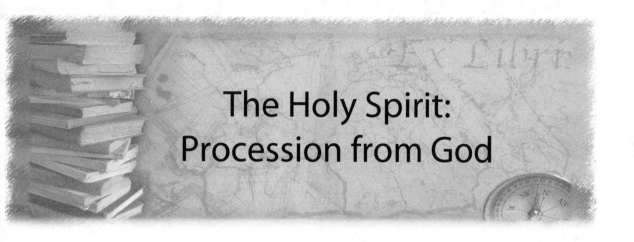

The Holy Spirit: Procession from God

As Debbie settled into her chair, she silently asked herself, "How many years has it been?" Everyone in the class was so much younger than she was. Although they all seemed friendly enough, she quickly realized she had very little in common with any of her classmates. The majority of them were only a few years older than her son and daughter—both high school students.

As the class came to order, Professor Taylor introduced himself and then explained that for the next few minutes, he wanted to get to know the members of the class better. As part of each person's introduction, the students were to tell something interesting about themselves. That's when Debbie realized that although much had happened since she began her graduate program over 20 years earlier, some things would never change. Even though two decades had passed, teachers still had not discovered more creative ways to have students introduce themselves.

Debbie's introduction of herself was brief and to the point. She didn't want to draw any more attention to herself than necessary. But it soon became apparent that the professor wasn't going to let her off so easily.

"Mrs. Howe, I think the students would be interested to know why you have enrolled in this class. Why don't you give them a little more background about yourself and why you are here."

Now she remembered why she hated these "introduction" sessions. She never liked being the center of attention, especially when she was so different from the rest of the class. But there was nothing she could do about it now. Everyone in the class seemed to be staring at her.

Holy Spirit

• True Person

  • mind
  • will
  • emotions
  • actions
  • acted against
  • responded to

• True God

  • eternal
  • omnipresent
  • omniscient
  • omnipotent
  • creative
  • gives life
  • sovereign
  • loving

"You have probably all noticed," she began, "that I'm considerably older than all of you. I hope you don't think that I've spent the last 20 years trying to complete my master's degree!"

Everyone in the class laughed. The tenseness that Debbie felt was soon gone. She found it much easier to tell her story.

"Before I got married, I had started my graduate program in psychology. I only had a few classes left to take, then writing my thesis, in order to receive my degree. Only a year after my husband and I married, our son Jonathan was born. A little over a year later, our Cheryl was born. Well, it was important for me to stay home with my children, so I never completed my program.

"My son will graduate from high school this year and has already been accepted at the university. When he filled out his application, I started thinking about returning and completing my program. My family was excited about my decision . . . and . . . here I am!

"It's been a long time since I've been in school, but I'm ready for the challenge. Matter of fact, I've already given considerable thought to my topic for my master's thesis."

Up until that point, the professor already knew what Debbie was sharing. But he didn't know that she had been thinking about her master's thesis. Since he was her academic advisor, he wanted to talk with her about her topic. After all, the department was pretty strict about what they would allow as a topic for thesis work.

Debbie was the last student "introduction." The professor then began explaining the course syllabus, the papers the students would need to write, and the reading that was assigned for the next class period. Since it was the first class of the term, it was dismissed early. As the students filed out of the room, the professor asked Debbie to remain after class.

"Am I in trouble already?" Debbie asked half jokingly.

"Of course not," Professor Taylor responded. "However, you did mention that you have been thinking about the topic for your master's thesis. We need to discuss it before you start your research. Could you meet with me about 30 minutes before our next class?"

"No problem," Debbie replied with a sense of relief.

On the way home, Debbie started thinking about how she would explain the choice of her thesis topic to Professor Taylor. After all, she couldn't just walk into his office and announce that she wanted to do her research on the Holy Spirit. This was a graduate psychology program —not a seminary. Her thesis committee probably would never allow her to write on such a topic without a clear connection to human behavior.

The drive home was a fairly long one—more than 40 miles from the university to her home. Debbie decided to turn off the CD player and use the time to think about what she would say to Professor Taylor. She realized that if her advisor did not like her thesis topic, then it wouldn't even have a chance of making it to the committee.

At first she struggled with how to make the presentation. But then the words "changed lives" popped into her mind. She knew immediately that this was the approach to take. After all, it was her interest in the life-changing experiences of people that had first gotten her interested in psychology. And the more she read about the dramatic

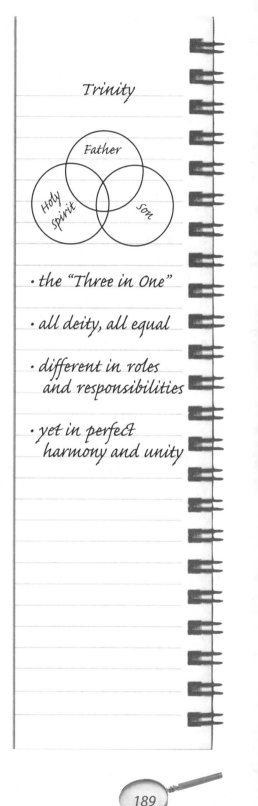

Trinity

- the "Three in One"

- all deity, all equal

- different in roles and responsibilities

- yet in perfect harmony and unity

> *"And when He has come, He will convict the world of sin, and of righteousness, and of judgment: of sin, because they do not believe in Me; of righteousness, because I go to My Father, and you see Me no more; of Judgment, because the ruler of this world is judged."*
>
> *John 16:8-11*

changes that people had experienced, the more she became aware of the work of the Holy Spirit.

For example, there was the story of the change that took place in Kevin's life. This young man had once been in prison but was now a pastor. Throughout his youth, he had been in and out of jail cells. He had seen beatings, drug dealing and horrific crimes. Although it scared him at times, he had accepted these things as part of his life.

After nearly 12 years in various juvenile detentions and prisons, he was released. His mother demanded that he get a job, or he could not return home. Due to his lack of education and his inability to focus on specific tasks, he could not hold a job for more than a few weeks at a time. In a three-year period he had eleven different jobs. But he didn't really care. A job was just a way to keep him out of trouble with the law . . . and with his mother!

But then Kevin encountered Roy. Although the two men worked together, they didn't really know each other. One Monday, during the lunch break, Kevin asked Roy what he was writing. Roy responded that he was working on his Sunday School lesson for the high school class he taught. This led to a 30-minute discussion about the Bible, God, Jesus Christ and salvation. Throughout the rest of the day, Kevin pondered what Roy had said.

The next morning, Kevin awoke to a voice in his own mind telling him, "Jesus Christ is who He says He is. You must become a Christian." It was such a bizarre, overwhelming experience that Kevin immediately went outside to get a breath of fresh air. As he walked along the street, he became more and more aware of his sin and his need of a Savior. Describing the event, Kevin used words very similar to those spoken by John Wesley, "My heart was strangely warmed." At that point he felt compelled to kneel to the ground and ask Jesus to forgive his sins and save him.

The fruit of being "born again" soon became evident to everyone. The craving for nicotine disappeared. He quit taking illegal drugs. Every aspect of his life dramatically changed. His desire was to be with others who knew Jesus Christ as Savior. He constantly felt God's presence within him, guiding his decisions and giving him the strength to overcome sin.

Kevin returned to school and ultimately entered the ministry. Presently, he and his wife Colleen and their two sons serve the Lord in a small church outside of London, England.

Stories like Kevin's had prompted Debbie to conduct a more in-depth study as a part of her master's thesis. She not only wanted to gain a better understanding of the work of the Holy Spirit, but she also wanted to study the specific types of life changes that took place.

Debbie knew that it would be a difficult study because many would be skeptical of the topic. After all, most people would probably put the work of the Holy Spirit in the same category as the Force in *Star Wars* or the power that enabled Harry Potter's magical abilities. Some probably even believed that the Holy Spirit provided guidance to astrologers or could cause a levitation. If she wasn't careful in the presentation of her thesis topic, she could be subjected to considerable ridicule.

For the first time, a sense of panic swept over her. How would she explain to her advisor the topic she wanted to research? Would she now be perceived as some kind of religious fanatic? Was it possible that her desire to pursue this subject would make her the laughing stock of

The Holy Spirit

Sent to me to . . .

- *help me*

- *abide in me*

- *lead me*

- *reveal truth to me*

Sent to the world to convict / convince people of . . .

- *sin*

- *righteousness (in Christ)*

- *judgment (consequences of unbelief)*

The Holy Spirit in the Old Testament

· Creation

· inspiration of Scripture

· enabled leaders

· care of Israel

· restrained Satan's power

the entire psychology department? Maybe going back to school wasn't such a good idea after all.

The last five miles of the trip home seemed to last forever. By the time Debbie walked through her front door, she had almost given up her dream to complete her master's degree. The task just seemed too overwhelming. The expression on her face showed her disappointment.

"What's the matter, Mom?" Jonathan asked. Debbie knew she couldn't hide her feelings. As she sat down in her favorite chair, her daughter and husband joined the conversation. Although none of the family members had any idea what had happened at school, they knew by the look on Debbie's face that something had gone terribly wrong.

Beginning slowly at first, Debbie explained the events as they unfolded in class. Soon she realized that the class had actually gone quite well. She was even encouraged by her professor's willingness to meet with her right away regarding her thesis topic. Her doubts and fears had come during the drive home. No detail was left out as Debbie revealed to her family why she was so discouraged.

Don, Debbie's husband, was the first to speak. "You know, you have been preparing to re-enter the master's program for almost six months. The application process, including tests and interviews, has been challenging. But during each step of the way, you repeatedly told us that you were confident that God was guiding you in this decision. Do you think God would have brought you this far just to have you drop out of the program?"

"Yeah, Mom," Cheryl chimed in. "I know that you can do this, because it's part of God's plan for your life. Remember, we all talked about it the first night you mentioned to us that you wanted to go back to college."

Debbie quickly realized the incredible support that she had from her family. But, more importantly, she was reminded once again that God had led her to re-enter the program, and He certainly wasn't going to abandon her now. The words of Jesus in John 14:16 and 17 were comforting. Jesus said, "And I will pray the Father, and He will give you another Helper, that He may abide with you forever—the Spirit of truth." Later in that same chapter (verse 26), Jesus revealed this Helper to be the Holy Spirit.

"You know," Debbie began, "I want to study how the Holy Spirit changes lives. Yet I haven't sought His help as I've tried to figure out how to present my thesis topic to my advisor. How ironic that I want to study how the Holy Spirit works in others, but I've been unwilling to allow Him to work in my own life."

As the Howe family sat together in the living room, what they needed to do next was obvious. They began to pray for the enabling power that only God's Holy Spirit can provide.

The Holy Spirit in the Life of Christ

· conception

· anointing

· leading

· empowerment

· death and resurrection

QuestNote 19.1
The Holy Spirit

Summarize your knowledge of the Holy spirit in relation to the statements.

1. The Holy Spirit is a person.

2. The Holy Spirit is deity.

3. The Holy Spirit is a member of the Trinity.

QuestNote 19.2
The Holy Spirit

Summarize your knowledge of the Holy Spirit in relation to the Old Testament and the life of Christ.

1. Old Testament Ministry of the Holy Spirit

2. Ministry of the Holy Spirit in the Life of Christ

3. Application of Bible Truth to My Own Life

QuestNote 19.3
The Holy Spirit

Summarize the ministries of the Holy Spirit as taught by Christ.

Revealer of Truth

Helper\Comforter

Convicter of the World

The Holy Spirit:
His Coming and Ministry

Since there was a week between classes, Debbie had plenty of time to think about how she could present her thesis proposal to Professor Taylor. She knew that she would use "changed lives" as the link between the work of the Holy Spirit and her research in psychology. From the informal research she had already done for years, she wanted to show that God had produeced radical, miraculous changes in many people. Colin's story was a perfect example. She opened a computer file named Colin.

Although Colin's parents had divorced, he knew that they both really loved him. In spite of their differences, they did all that they could to encourage and help him. But his grandmother was the only one who taught him about Jesus. Until the time of her death when he was a junior in high school, she would teach him about the Bible every time they were together.

Upon completing high school, Colin joined the Air Force "to see the world." After the Air Force, he went to college to become an engineer. During the last couple of years in college, he secured a high paying job with a successful chemical company. By the time he received his degree, he was earning a six-figure salary. He was making more money than he ever dreamed possible. The money allowed his family to do and buy anything they wanted.

But the money also provided him with the opportunity to do everything he shouldn't. In addition to excessive drinking, Colin started using illegal drugs. His life quickly went into a downward spiral. He was fired from the chemical company, he lost

The Holy Spirit . . .

· *relates a believer to God*
— *Regeneration!*

· *relates a believer to self*
— *Indwelling!*

· *relates a believer to the church* —
    · *spiritual baptism*
    · *filling*
    · *gifts*
    · *empowerment*

his wife and children, he lost their home, and he lost the respect of all his friends. From every outward indication, his life was over.

Six months later, while drowning in his destructive habit, Colin was busted for drugs. Although he thought his life couldn't get any worse, he soon found out that it would. After appearing before several judges and pleading unsuccessfully for leniency, he was sentenced to seven years in the state prison.

His memory of stepping into his cell for the first time was chilling. He felt that there was no hope, that he would die before ever leaving prison. As he threw himself on his bunk, the tears started to flow. Colin didn't sleep that night. He just lay on his bed, scared and alone.

A few days later, some men from the Gideons organization came to the prison to pass out New Testaments. It was something the businessmen voluntarily did on a regular basis. The first thing that Colin thought of when he saw the little Bible was his grandmother. He remembered how she would read to him and try to help him understand what it meant. Although he hadn't been too interested as a child, he was surely interested now. He gratefully accepted a New Testament and took it back to his cell. Before the day was over, he had read it from cover to cover.

For the second time since entering the prison, Colin couldn't sleep. Maybe it was his own fear that was driving him, but he kept thinking about the many times Jesus' disciples were scared and confused. The first instance he remembered was when Jesus walked on the water. Colin once again opened his New Testament and read from Mark 6:47–50.

Now when evening came, the boat was in the middle of the sea; and He was alone on the land. Then He saw them straining at rowing, for the wind was against them. Now about the fourth watch of the night He came to them, walking on the sea, and would have passed them by. And when they saw Him walking on the sea, they supposed it was a ghost, and cried out; for they all saw Him and were troubled. But immediately He talked with them and said to them, "Be of good cheer! It is I; do not be afraid."

Colin then turned to John 20:19. Here was another example of the disciples' confusion and fear as Jesus appeared to them after the resurrection. Yet, once again, Jesus tried to comfort them.

Then, the same day at evening, being the first day of the week, when the doors were shut where the disciples were assembled, for fear of the Jews, Jesus came and stood in the midst, and said to them, "Peace be with you."

As long as Jesus was with His disciples, He was able to comfort and help them. But when the ascension occurred, Jesus was no longer physically present. Once again, Jesus' disciples must have been confused and fearful.

Now Colin understood the promise of a Helper that Jesus made in John 15:26. That

The Spirit gives . . .

- different talk

- different walk

- different thinking

- different feelings

- different actions

- different priorities

- different perspectives

Produces improved judgment — not impaired judgment

> *And suddenly there came a sound from heaven, as of a rushing mighty wind, and it filled the whole house where they were sitting. Then there appeared to them divided tongues, as of fire, and one sat upon each of them. And they were all filled with the Holy Spirit and began to speak with other tongues, as the Spirit gave them utterance.*
>
> *Acts 2:2–4*

promise was fulfilled in Acts with the coming of the Holy Spirit. As he read more verses about the Holy Spirit he understood, for the first time, that it was the Holy Spirit who was convicting him of his sin and drawing him to the Savior.

At the end of the small New Testament there was a copy of the "Sinner's Prayer." It seemed as if it had been written just for him. Right there in his cell, Colin dropped to his knees and began to pray. That simple step changed his life forever.

As Debbie thought about Colin's story, she became even more determined to move forward with her thesis topic. She had overwhelming evidence that the lives of people were being changed as a result of the work of God's Spirit. In a world where people are searching for meaning and answers, Debbie wanted to introduce them to the power of the Holy Spirit as revealed in the Bible.

Debbie reached for her Bible and turned once again to the story of Pentecost in Acts 2. It came seven weeks after Passover, when Jesus had been crucified. Excitement in Jerusalem was at a fever pitch. During the festival about 120 disciples of Jesus were meeting in a home when an unusual event happened. God's Spirit suddenly fell upon those gathered there. Some thought it was a violent wind, while others believed that tongue-like flames of fire were resting on each of them.

Afterward Peter stood before a huge crowd and told them that the miracle they were witnessing was a fulfillment of the prophet Joel's promise about the outpouring of God's Spirit in the "last days." Peter then explained that God had made Jesus of Nazareth, who had just been crucified, Lord and Messiah by raising Him from the dead!

Then Peter said to them, "Repent, and let every one of you be baptized in the name of Jesus Christ for the remission of sins; and you shall receive the gift of the Holy Spirit. For the promise is to you and to your children, and to all who are afar off, as many as the Lord our God will call." (Acts 2:38–39)

The book of Acts made it very clear that the growth and spread of the Gospel throughout the Mediterranean world was the result of the work of the Holy Spirit in Jesus' disciples. But what exactly did the Holy Spirit do? What was His work during the time of the New Testament church? And, more importantly, is He still working in the same way today?

For the next couple of hours, Debbie searched the New Testament to study the work of the Holy Spirit. When she was finished, she organized her research under four headings, all beginning with the letter "C". From the New Testament she learned that the work of the Holy Spirit included conviction, comfort, counsel and confidence.

Conviction – From John 16:8 Debbie read *"And when He has come, He will convict the world of sin, and of righteousness, and of judgment."* Further study revealed that the word convict has two meanings. On one hand, it refers to the judicial act whereby someone is convicted and then sentenced. It is a courtroom term. On the other hand, convict is used to convince us of the need of something. In the case of this verse, the Holy Spirit is showing (convicting, convincing) us of our need of the Savior. Debbie concluded that one of the works of the Holy Spirit was to make people aware of their sin and their need of Jesus Christ.

Some Ministries of The Holy Spirit

Conviction: "And when He has come, He will convict the world of sin, and of righteousness, and of judgment." (John 16:8)

Comfort: "And I will pray the Father and He will give you another Helper, that He may abide with you forever." (John 14:6)

Counsel: "However, when He, the Spirit of truth, has come, He will guide you into all truth; for He will not speak on His own authority, but whatever He hears He will speak; and He will tell you things to come." (John 16:13)

Comfort — The Holy Spirit's work of comfort is best described in John 14:6 where it says, *"And I will pray the Father and He will give you another Helper, that He may abide with you forever."* Debbie learned that the word Helper is the translation of the word paraclete. Helper is a good translation because the word actually means one called alongside to help. However, the word paraclete also includes the idea of providing comfort. After studying many other passages, Debbie realized that a second work of the Holy Spirit is to come alongside to help and comfort believers.

Counsel — As our Counselor, the Holy Spirit leads us to understand the truth. Because we live in a world filled with falsehood and lying, we must be able to discern truth from error. Of course, this was especially true during the time of the early church. Thus, the Holy Spirit abides in us to counsel us in the way of truth. *"However, when He, the Spirit of truth, has come, He will guide you into all truth; for He will not speak on His own authority, but whatever He hears He will speak; and He will tell you things to come"* (John 16:13).

Confidence — As Debbie carefully studied Acts 1:8, she began to understand a very important work of the Holy Spirit that also transcended the time of the early church. She realized that every time she had previously read the verse, she had focused on the word power. *"But you shall receive power when the Holy Spirit has come upon you; and you shall be witnesses to Me in Jerusalem, and in all Judea and Samaria, and to the end of the earth."* While it was true that the Holy Spirit gave the Apostles the ability and strength to share the Gospel, the Holy Spirit also gave them the confidence to carry out their task. The Apostles knew that by preaching the Gospel, they would likely face persecution and death. As a result, the Holy Spirit gave

Confidence: "But you shall receive power when the Holy Spirit has come upon you; and you shall be witnesses to Me in Jerusalem, and in all Judea and Samaria, and to the end of the earth." (Acts 1:8)

them both the power to preach and also the confidence to overcome their fears.

Although she had summarized her research in four simple categories, Debbie realized that the work of the Holy Spirit is far more comprehensive than she had described in her notes. Before ending her studies for the evening, she decided to reread the first two chapters of Acts, one of her favorite passages of the Bible.

As she read Acts 2:42–47, the idea of "changed lives" once again emerged from the text. The converts from Peter's sermon not only experienced a new life through Jesus Christ, but a new lifestyle as well. According to the passage, the new believers celebrated their new life in Christ in five important ways.

- They listened to the Apostles' teaching.
- They shared meals in a spirit of common fellowship.
- They praised God through their worship.
- They shared what they owned with one another.
- They cared for the needs of each other.

It was very clear that the Holy Spirit worked in a mighty way during the time of Pentecost. Lives were changed, churches were established and the Gospel was preached throughout the known world. But the work of the Holy Spirit did not cease at the end of the first century. The Spirit is still at work today.

As Debbie prepared to call it a night, she knew the direction her research would take next. She would have to answer the question "What is the Holy Spirit's ministry today?" The answer to that question was crucial to the presentation of her thesis topic.

For Believers, the Holy Spirit . . .

- *assures believers that we are God's children*

- *teaches and guides in what is true*

- *comforts us*

- *prays, and helps us to pray*

- *strengthens us*

- *prompts us toward purity*

- *frees from the bondage of sin*

- *inspires worship, praise and joy*

- *produces fruit*

QuestNote 20.1
The Holy Spirit Relates Believers to . . .

```
┌─────────────────────────────────────┐
│          The Holy Spirit            │
└─────────────────────────────────────┘
        /                      \
┌──────────────────┐    ┌──────────────────┐
│                  │    │                  │
└──────────────────┘    └──────────────────┘
```

QuestNote 20.2
Because the Holy Spirit . . .

1. Assures believers that we are God's children, I _____

_____

(Romans 8:16; Galatians 4:6; 1 John 4:4)

2. Teaches and guides in what is true, I _____

(John 14:26; John 16:13–14; 1 John 2:20, 27; 1 Corinthians 2:12–13; Romans 8:14)

3. Comforts us, I _____

_____ (John 14:16–18; John 14:26; John 16:7; 2 Corinthians 1:4–5)

4. Prays, and helps us to pray, I _____

_____ (Romans 8:26–27; Ephesians 2:18; Ephesians 6:18; Jude 20)

5. Strengthens us, I _____

_____ (Ephesians 3:16; Colossians 1:10–11)

6. Prompts us toward purity, I _____

_____ (1 Corinthians 3:16; 1 Corinthians 6:17–20)

7. Frees from the bondage of sin, I _____

_____ (Romans 8:2–4; Galatians 5:16–18; 1 John 5:4)

8. Inspires worship, praise and joy, I _____

_____ (Ephesians 5:18–20; John 4:23)

9. Produces fruit in a believer's life, I _____

(Galatians 5:22–25; Romans 14:17; Romans 5:5; John 15:2; Ephesians 4:1–2)

QuestNote 20.3
The Holy Spirit Relates Believers to His Church

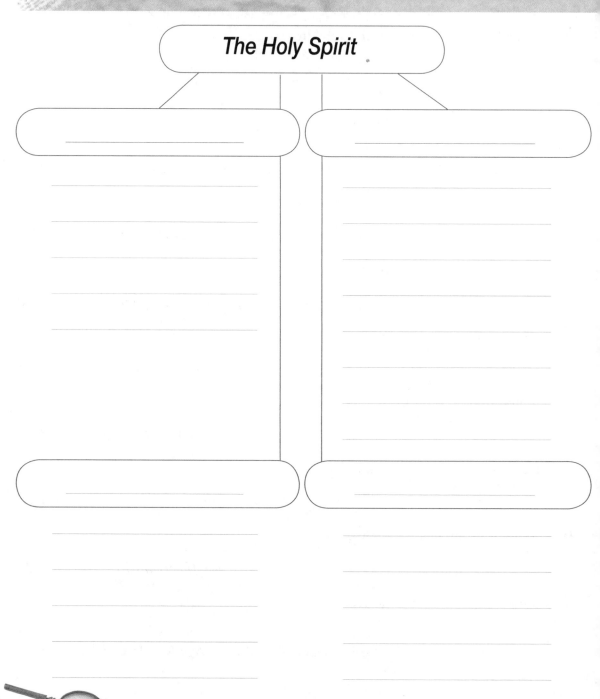

The Holy Spirit

The Holy Spirit: Making God Personal

This was the day Debbie had looked forward to, and yet dreaded. A week had passed since her first class. Later that afternoon she would once again make the drive to the university. However, this time she would be meeting with Professor Taylor before class to explain her thesis topic. While Debbie was excited about sharing her research, she was also concerned that he would dismiss her topic as religious fanaticism.

Before Debbie had time to give any more thought to the meeting with her professor, the front door bell rang.

"Come on in, Ashley," Debbie said as she opened the door. "I'm glad that you could meet for lunch today."

Debbie and Ashley had been friends since high school. Although they lived in the same city, they couldn't see each other as often as they liked. But Debbie had a special reason for wanting to get together. Ashley was a family therapist known for her strong Christian approach in counseling. If there was anyone who would understand what Debbie wanted to accomplish with her master's thesis, it would be Ashley.

"It's so good to see you again, Deb," Ashley said, giving her a hug. "I'm glad you called and arranged for us to get together. After hearing that you had resumed work on your master's degree this term, I wanted to find out how things are going."

"Funny you should ask," Debbie responded as they headed toward comfortable chairs in the living room. "I was hoping that after lunch, you could give me some tips on presenting the topic I would like to use for my thesis."

> But the manifestation of the spirit is given to each one for the profit of all. But one and the same Spirit works all these things, distributing to each one individually as He wills.
>
> 1 Corinthians 12:7 and 11

After catching up on the latest family news, Debbie served lunch. Then the conversation turned to her thesis topic and meeting with Professor Taylor later that afternoon.

After Debbie explained her concerns, Ashley concluded, "I see a strong connection between the idea of changed lives, the work of the Holy Spirit and the field of psychology. You are clearly on the right track in your thinking. I'm sure that Professor Taylor will help you focus the statement of your thesis so that it will be accepted by the entire committee."

"So, you do believe I have a chance with this topic?" Debbie responded with relief in her voice. "I was so sure that I would be viewed as some type of religious fanatic because I wanted to include the work of the Holy Spirit in my research."

"I know Professor Taylor pretty well," Ashley replied. "This topic will intrigue him. Although I don't think he's a Christian, he does have respect for the religious views of others. I think he will be very supportive of what you want to do. However, I do have some advice for you."

Debbie raised her eyebrows and looked intently at her friend. "You know I want to hear what you have to say. That's part of the reason I invited you over today."

"Well," Ashley began slowly, "it's important in the presentation of your thesis topic that you do not compromise who you are. Sometimes a student, especially at the graduate level, is tempted to try to be someone they're not in order to appease others. This approach to life dishonors both the person and God."

"I think I understand what you're saying, but . . . ."

Ashley raised her hand to interrupt her friend's response. "Do you remember Mark from high school?"

"I sure do. That's one guy who changed a lot between his freshman and senior year."

"Well, I know a little more about Mark than you realize," Ashley began. "After Mark became a Christian, he gave me permission to tell what happened in his life.

"During high school, he tried desperately to deconstruct and then reconstruct his personality. For starters, he hated being a Southerner. He wanted to disassociate himself from his upbringing because he saw that many entertainment outlets portray Southerners as ignorant and backward."

"Did he really believe all that?" Debbie asked in amazement.

"Yes, I'm afraid he did," Ashley continued. "Vowel by vowel, he worked on his accent. By the time he went to college, no one would have known that he was from the South. But his attempt to reconstruct himself didn't stop there. He began to make changes in his life that had absolutely nothing to do with his Southern heritage. For example, he even changed his handwriting, forcing himself to form each letter in a different way than he had before."

"This is really hard to believe. But what does it have to do with me and my master's thesis?" Debbie asked with a bit of hesitancy.

The Fruit of the Spirit helps me have . . .

love — be genuinely more interested in what benefits others rather than myself

joy — have a deep sense of well-being — a positive mental attitude

peace — have a deep sense of contentment as I trust the sovereign care of God

longsuffering — be patient with both difficult people and difficult situations as I learn to surrender my rights

kindness — think of others first and treat them as I would want to be treated

goodness — do the right thing as a reflection of the godly character I develop within

faithfulness — be dependable, a person others can count on

gentleness — treat others with respect, showing true care and concern as I try to solve problems, not make them worse

self-control — keep my natural self in check as I yield to the Holy Spirit's desires for me

"Be patient," Ashley responded. "You'll see my point in a moment." Ashley continued her story.

"By and large, the makeover worked. As Mark finished his senior year in college, he felt that he now had a personality that he thought was acceptable. But over the next few years, he realized that there were limits to a self-constructed personality. Although he had changed the way he spoke, the way he dressed, the way he thought about things, and even the way he wrote, he continued to be selfish, joyless, loveless, and lacking compassion.

"To make a long story short, Mark became a Christian about three months after his first appointment with me. You see, Mark needed to understand that an outward change would never bring peace and happiness. He was so focused on presenting himself the way he thought others wanted him to be that he failed to realize his own need to be an 'authentic' individual. He needed to first understand that he was a sinner in need of a Savior. Then he needed to allow the Holy Spirit to reconstruct his life in a way that was pleasing to God."

"I'm really happy to hear what happened in Mark's life," Debbie interrupted. "But I still don't understand what this has to do with my meeting."

"Here's my point," Ashley continued. "It's natural for you to be concerned about what Professor Taylor or your committee thinks about your research topic. But more importantly, you need to be concerned about how your life reflects your faith. Just as the Holy Spirit has brought about these changed lives that you want to include in your research, the Holy Spirit has also changed your life. It may not be as dramatic as the change that took place in Mark's life, but because you are a Christian the Holy Spirit continues to work."

Debbie thought for a moment before responding. "I want to please the Lord in my work, but I also don't want to come across as a nutcase."

"You'll be okay. Think about addressing life changes as a result of inner changes rather than modifying just some externals. Mark realized that while he was trying to reshape his life, what he really needed to do was allow God's Holy Spirit to be fully in control of his life. With the exception of self-control, he lacked all nine of the fruit of the Spirit listed in Galatians 5. He came to realize that his entire project of reconstructing himself had been misguided."

"I think I'm beginning to see your point," Debbie admitted. "God has chosen me and given me the opportunity to be a witness for Him to the members of my committee. My responsibility is to demonstrate how God has changed my life as well as those that I want to study in my research."

Ashley slowly nodded in agreement. "Including yourself makes your research authentic—believable. The work of the Holy Spirit is the culmination of God's work on earth. The Israelites in the Old Testament approached God with fear and trembling through an elaborate series of rituals under the direction of priests. Although Jesus' disciples had a much more personal connection with God, they failed to fully understand His mission on earth until after He had ascended to Heaven. Then the Holy Spirit personalized God's presence to each of them in unique ways that were tailored to their individual needs. Like them, the first step for us is to allow God's Holy Spirit to have full control—to be filled with His presence."

An Authentic Christian:

Not being changed on the outside through personal effort, but being changed on the inside through the work of the Holy Spirit

The friends talked for a while longer before saying goodbye. After Ashley left, Debbie began to more fully understand the significance of what her friend had said. Pleasing the committee had consumed her thinking. It had been obvious to everyone but her. She also needed to focus on what would please the Lord.

For a few moments Debbie once again thought about the irony of the situation. While she wanted to research how the Holy Spirit changed others, it was actually her life that needed to have some additional changes. She needed to allow the Holy Spirit to personalize God's presence in her life to meet the unique challenges she currently faced.

Debbie opened her Bible to Galatians 5:22 to remind herself of what the Apostle Paul said about the fruit of the Spirit. These were the godly attitudes that characterize the life of a person who belongs to God. She asked herself if these nine characteristics were a reality in her life.

As always, her study of one passage of Scripture led her to other passages. She was surprised at how much the New Testament says about the attitudes that should characterize believers. In 1 Corinthians 13:3–8 Paul discusses love. In Philippians 4:8 he describes the types of things we should think about. And in Colossians 3:12–16 he lists those things we should "put on." Later Peter provides a list of attitudes to be added to our faith. These characteristics must grow within the inner person through the work of the Holy Spirit (2 Peter 1:5–8). Only then can they be expressed outwardly as evidence of a changed life.

Debbie then realized that all five of these passages answered a similar question, "What characterizes the life of a true believer?" And once again, she asked herself if the characteristics found in these passages were a reality in her life.

In a very real way she sensed God working in her. The fears and doubts about her meeting with Professor Taylor, her master's thesis and meeting with the committee were no longer consuming her thoughts. Now her main desire was to allow the Holy Spirit to personalize God's presence in her life.

QuestNote 21.1
The Spirit's Work in My Life

Take a personal inventory of how effective the Holy Spirit's ministry is in your own life. Circle the numeral that best applies to each statement.

	Not so good	Could be better	About right	Par excellence

1. I am a believer and know that the Holy Spirit lives in me.

    1   2   3   4   5   6   7   8   9   10

2. I am submissive to (controlled/ filled by) the Holy Spirit.

    1   2   3   4   5   6   7   8   9   10

3. I experience the Holy Spirit's prompting and guidance to do the right thing.

    1   2   3   4   5   6   7   8   9   10

4. I experience conviction from the Holy Spirit when I sin.

    1   2   3   4   5   6   7   8   9   10

5. I am able to break sin habits in my life by depending on the Holy Spirit.

    1   2   3   4   5   6   7   8   9   10

6. The Holy Spirit gives me a deep sense of joy and contentment.

    1   2   3   4   5   6   7   8   9   10

7. The Holy Spirit comforts me and gives me peace when things go wrong.

    1   2   3   4   5   6   7   8   9   10

8. The Holy Spirit enables me to have courage when standing against sin.

    1   2   3   4   5   6   7   8   9   10

9. The Holy Spirit enables me to have courage when witnessing for God.

    1   2   3   4   5   6   7   8   9   10

10. The Holy Spirit is producing fruit (good character) in my life.

    1   2   3   4   5   6   7   8   9   10

11. The Holy Spirit has given me ability that I use in serving others.

    1   2   3   4   5   6   7   8   9   10

12. I think it is obvious to others that I am a Spirit-filled person.

    1   2   3   4   5   6   7   8   9   10

QuestNote 21.2

> ### *The Holy Spirit*

_____ | _____

Explain in your own words how to not mistreat the Holy Spirit.

_____

_____

_____

_____

The most important personal lesson I have learned in this unit:

_____

_____

QuestNote 21.3
Doctrine of the Holy Spirit

Write a concise essay regarding what Christians believe about the Holy Spirit. Include who He is, His ministry in the Old Testament, in the life of Christ, in believers' lives and in the church.

QuestNote 21.3

The Christian Life:
New Resources

As the sun made its way up over the surrounding hills, a new week was beginning on campus. The bright rays betrayed the cold that was still in the air. Although signs of spring were beginning to appear, it was still winter in the Connecticut countryside.

The cadets made their way quickly across the campus, determined to be in their seats when the bell rang for class. Being on time and being prepared were just two examples of the disciplined lifestyle expected daily of the cadets. In addition, they were required to maintain a strict dress code, daily physical training and a carefully monitored study time every night. This was certainly not the typical college experience. But the typical college experience is not what most cadets want.

Contrary to public opinion, the majority of young men and women who attend military academies do not plan to enter the armed services upon graduation. They attend military academies because of the regimented and disciplined lifestyle. The typical cadet actually enjoys the highly structured environment, both in and out of class.

As the bell rang and classes began all over campus, nearly 2000 cadets were in their seats ready to begin the week. But for three cadets, the week would be a turning point. At roughly the same time, in every class on campus, every cadet heard the same announcement.

"Classes have been cancelled for this afternoon," Captain Peterson announced to his morning government class. "We have the distinct honor of having Colonel Hensley visit our campus today. He will address the entire faculty and student body at 1400 hours. I encourage you to arrive early because there will be lots of media coverage for his presentation."

Sanctification may be defined as that gracious and continuous operation of the Holy Spirit by which He . . .

- purifies the sinner from the pollution of sin,

- renews his whole nature in the image of God,

- and enables him to perform good works.

– Louis Berkhoff
Manual of Christian
Doctrine
1933

As Captain Peterson began the day's lesson, David leaned toward Maria. "Who is Colonel Hensley?"

"I'll tell you after class," Maria whispered.

As usual, the cadets had a lengthy reading assignment for the evening. They quickly filed out of class, some on their way to other classes, while others headed to different responsibilities. Once outside the door, Maria explained to David who the special speaker was.

"Colonel Hensley was held hostage in Lebanon for almost two years by an Islamic Jihad terrorist group. I've read several articles about him. I can't believe that he's actually here to speak to us this afternoon."

"I knew something was up," David replied, "when they cancelled our afternoon classes. They don't even do that when we have three feet of snow! I'll be seeing Brent in my next class. How about the three of us getting together for lunch, and then we can go straight to the field house?"

"Sounds good to me," Maria said as she turned toward the library. "I want to make sure that we get the best seats possible."

The morning passed quickly and the cadets were soon seated comfortably only seven rows from the podium. Captain Peterson was right. The media had arrived in full force. There were television cameras and reporters everywhere.

Almost on cue, General Shelley, the president of the academy, and members of his administration made their way to the stage. After they took their positions, Colonel Hensley entered the room. The applause was deafening.

And as close as they were to the stage, the bright lights from the cameras were almost blinding. The Colonel acknowledged the students and took his seat next to General Shelley.

After a long standing ovation by the students and visitors, General Shelley stepped to the podium. "I will not take time to give a lengthy introduction of our speaker this afternoon. Obviously everyone here knows who he is and what he has experienced. I would rather have him tell you his story in his own words.

"But I had a second reason for asking Colonel Hensley to speak to us today. When I was in Washington, D.C., a few months ago, I heard him lecture on survival techniques. What he said that day is important for you to hear today. These techniques are just as applicable right now as they would be if you were in a prison cell in Lebanon."

General Shelley ended his remarks and welcomed the distinguished guest to the school. Once again, the applause was deafening as Colonel Hensley took his place in front of the microphone.

"Thank you, General Shelley, for your kind invitation to address these cadets. It is a privilege to be with you.

"Why do I believe so strongly that I am qualified to speak to you today about survival techniques? The answer is simple. I was a hostage of Islamic Jihad terrorists in Lebanon for nearly two years. Chained to the floor, blindfolded, beaten, tormented, deprived of food—and finally I was isolated in an underground prison cell. I had only two options available to me—either learn to survive or just give up and die. I was determined to live! Over the months, I learned some techniques that enabled me to survive. These

Let the word of Christ dwell in you richly in all wisdom, teaching and admonishing one another in psalms and hymns and spiritual songs, singing with grace in your hearts to the Lord. And whatever you do in word or deed, do all in the name of the Lord Jesus, giving thanks to God the Father through Him.

Colossians 3:16-17

techniques worked for me as a hostage and now serve me as a citizen of a complicated, confusing world."

Maria, Brent and David glanced quickly at each other. The expressions on their faces revealed their awe and respect for the soldier standing less than 20 feet from them. They couldn't wait to hear what he would say next.

"I'm not going to describe the details of my capture and imprisonment to you today. Instead, I want to talk about what I learned during those two years, as well as what I've learned from other hostages. The survival techniques that I outline today are lessons that you need to make a part of your life.

"Remember, life is not always fair. How are you going to respond when you are confronted with a major problem in your life? I'm talking about serious issues like illness, physical disability, death of a loved one, divorce or addictions. Most people don't know how to respond positively to tragic events. Unfortunately, problems take control of the individual rather than the individual taking charge of the problems.

"Although I was caged like an animal, the experience taught me how to survive adversity and still maintain my sanity, values and faith. This audience is primarily comprised of students. So, students, I want you to get out a piece of paper and write down the survival techniques I am about to give you."

Two thousand students responded immediately to his request. Throughout the building, notebooks were opened and pens stood ready to write. In just moments the field house was transformed into a giant classroom.

No spiritual discipline is more important than the intake of God's Word. Nothing can substitute for it. There simply is no healthy Christian life apart from a diet of the milk and meat of Scripture. . . . We find in Scripture how to live in a way that is pleasing to God as well as best and most fulfilling for ourselves. None of this eternally essential information can be found anywhere else except the Bible. Therefore if we would know God and be godly, we must know the Word of God intimately.

– Donald S. Whitney
Spiritual Disciplines for the Christian Life
1991

Colonel Hensley continued. "Number one, you must possess a true faith in God. You may be sitting here today not knowing if there is a God. Let me ask you a question. Don't you think it's about time to settle this issue once and for all? I am constantly amazed at how many times people put off the most important decisions in life. What makes you think that you are going to have a 'tomorrow' in which to make that decision? You can no more know the future than I could have known that I would end up as a hostage on the morning I casually entered Beirut.

"And then there are those who profess to believe in God but have never experienced a true relationship with God. These people are like the Pharisees and Sadducees that Jesus challenged in the New Testament. Is your belief, like theirs, only academic, or have you personally experienced His true work of grace?

"My ability to survive began with my faith in God. It was a faith that began many years ago, not when I found myself in a prison cell. It gave me, and many others like me, the strength to survive."

Although Maria, David and Brent were Christians, they were surprised that Colonel Hensley's first survival technique was "a true faith in God." Even more, they were astounded when he shared his second technique.

"Next, you have to realize the power of prayer. I not only believe in God, but I also believe that He cares for me and wants to communicate with me. Sure, He communicates to me through the Bible. However, He has also established a personal line of communication through prayer. For two years, I had no access to a Bible. But I still had access to God. The power of prayer is always available to you, even in the darkest hours of adversity."

God's Word

Read and hear it.
(Deuteronomy 31:11–13; 2 Timothy 4:13; Revelation 1:3)

Meditate on it.
(Psalm 1:2; 63:6–8; Proverbs 22:17–19)

Study it.
(Acts 17:11; Ezra 7:10)

Memorize it.
(Psalm 119:11, 16)

Apply it.
(Matthew 4:4; James 1:25; Luke 11:28)

Grow in it.
(1 Peter 2:2; 2 Peter 1:4–6)

Obey it.
(1 Timothy 4:16; Matthew
7:26; Psalm 119:111–112)

Defend it.
(Jude 3; Philippians 1:27;
Revelation 6:9)

Teach and explain it.
(Acts 5:42; 1 Timothy 4:6–
7, 11; 2 Timothy 2:15; 4:2)

Share it.
(Romans 15:13–14;
1 Corinthians 14:24–25;
Matthew 28:19–20)

David continued to take notes as Colonel Hensley explained several other survival techniques such as "thoughts of loved ones," "exercise" and "focusing attention on specific tasks." But his note-taking became mechanical. His mind blurred on these subsequent techniques as he focused only on the first two. The Colonel's words about God and prayer brought a sense of deep conviction.

When the Colonel ended his address, thunderous applause broke out all over the building. The students had never heard anything like it. Everyone stood to show their respect to this man who had endured so much.

"I need to talk to you two," David said as the cadets made their way to the door. "Let's meet for a soda in thirty minutes."

A half-hour later the three cadets entered their favorite restaurant just a block off campus. "What's up?" Maria asked as David sat down at their table. "You looked pretty serious at the end of Colonel Hensley's speech. Is anything wrong?"

David quickly replied, "Yes, there is something wrong, Maria. There is something wrong with me."

Brent interrupted, "Are you hurting somewhere? Is there something we can do?"

"I'm not physically hurt," David reassured them. "But I know that things are not right between God and me. As Colonel Hensley discussed his first two survival techniques, it was like God was using him to talk directly to me. I know that I'm saved and going to Heaven when I die. But beyond that, I really haven't wanted too much involvement with God in my life. And I certainly don't spend any time praying."

For a few moments, all three of them sat in silence, not even bothering to sip their sodas. They had each indicated, at one time or another, that they were Christians. They had even gone to church together a couple of times. But David's comments were certainly out of character for him.

David continued, "I want to know God in a different way. I want to have the same kind of faith and courage that Colonel Hensley has. I don't know how long it's going to take, but I am determined to know God in a personal and real way. I'm going to begin by finding out everything I possibly can about prayer."

"I hear what you're saying," Brent responded. "If you don't mind, I'd like to know what you learn." Maria nodded in agreement. Brent quickly spoke again, "Then it's agreed. David will do the research, and we'll all get together to discuss what he discovers."

Smiles spread around the table as the three friends shook hands. What had begun as an afternoon out of classes was now a personal, spiritual project. But this project would continue for a lifetime.

QuestNote 22.1
Spiritual Growth Project

Design a project that would move you from an academic relationship with God to a truly personal relationship with God.

Where would you begin?

_____

_____

_____

_____

What steps would you take?

_____

_____

_____

_____

_____

What goals would you expect to achieve?

_____

_____

_____

_____

Is this do-able for you? _____ When will you begin? _____

QuestNote 22.2
Developing a More Personal Relationship with God

Summarize the meaning, importance and the steps to achievement in the areas you have studied this week.

Sanctification

Commitment

QuestNote 22.2
Developing a More Personal Relationship with God

Bible Study

Prayer

The Christian Life:
New Responsibilities

Almost a week had passed since David, Maria and Brent attended the special assembly with Colonel Hensley. Although they saw each other frequently during that week, very little was said about David's progress on his research. It wasn't that Maria and Brent weren't interested; they just weren't quite sure if he would follow through as he had indicated.

The weekend finally arrived. The cadets always looked forward to some down time and the opportunity to enjoy a slightly more laid-back schedule. Normally, the three friends would get together with their roommates for a mid-morning brunch at The Hangar—a local restaurant that had catered to cadets for nearly six decades. But last-minute schedule changes forced the group to forego their usual plans.

In order to not waste the whole morning, Maria suggested that they grab a quick bite to eat and then see an early movie. David agreed, but Brent wasn't in the mood to go to a movie.

"Why don't you guys go ahead, and I'll meet you in the library later this afternoon," Brent said. "I really need to locate information for my English paper, and this would probably be a good time to do it."

"That's all right with us," Maria responded before David could say anything. "We'll meet you at the library at 3:30. Come on, David, let's get something to eat. I'm starved."

Since it was still relatively early, the two friends decided to walk to the restaurant. "How are things with you and Matt?" David asked Maria.

> God's plan for you is nothing short of a new heart. If you were a car, God would want control of your engine. If you were a computer, God would claim the software and the hard drive. If you were an airplane, He'd take His seat in the cockpit. But you are a person, so God wants to change your heart.
>
> — Max Lucado

Maria and Matt had dated since their junior year in high school. Although they attended different schools, their relationship had continued to grow. Matter of fact, Matt was coming to see Maria the following weekend.

"Things are going great," Maria replied with a smile. "He's a great guy, and I really enjoy being with him. How about you and Denise?"

David had started dating Denise the prior summer. The two met while working at Greenleaf, a golf resort set high in the mountains. Denise worked at the registration desk, and David spent most of his time maintaining the golf course. For both of them, it was great summer employment. Neither had anticipated the added benefit of meeting each other.

"Actually, we've been writing quite a bit lately," David answered. "But a lot of things have been running through my mind these last few days. I'm not so sure I should continue our relationship."

There was silence for the next few minutes as Maria contemplated what to say next. The two turned the corner and their destination came into view. Maria decided that it would be best to continue this conversation at the restaurant.

Since the breakfast rush had passed, they almost had the entire restaurant to themselves. They selected a booth, but neither bothered to look at a menu. They were regulars at this place and they both knew what they wanted. As soon as their order was placed, Maria wasted no time pursuing the comment that David had made only minutes earlier.

"Tell me why you are questioning your relationship with Denise. Did she do something to upset you?"

"Oh no," David quickly replied. "She hasn't said or done anything at all. It all started with Colonel Hensley."

"What does Colonial Hensley have to do with you dating Denise?" Maria questioned.

"Do you remember when we all got together after the Colonel's speech and I said that I wanted to get to know God better? Well, that's exactly what I've been trying to do. I've learned a lot about prayer, and I've really tried to be more consistent in my prayer life. But I've been doing a lot of reading too. I'm beginning to realize that, as a Christian, I have certain responsibilities in my relationships with others."

Maria was obviously becoming impatient. "Is there a point to all of this? What does this have to do with whether or not you date Denise?"

"Chill, Maria," David replied rather defensively. "Like I said, I've been doing a lot of reading and thinking this week. I've written down some verses that have really made me rethink some of my relationships. Here, let me show you one of them."

David reached into his pocket and pulled out some neatly folded pieces of paper. Quickly looking through them, he chose the one he wanted Maria to read and handed it to her. Unfolding the paper, she discovered the words from 2 Corinthians 6:14–15. "Do not be unequally yoked together with unbelievers. For what fellowship has righteousness with lawlessness? And what communion

For this reason we also, since the day we heard it, do not cease to pray for you, and to ask that you may be filled with the knowledge of His will in all wisdom and spiritual understanding; that you may walk worthy of the Lord, fully pleasing Him, being fruitful in every good work and increasing in the knowledge of God.

Colossians 1:9–10

God has one destined end for humans—holiness. He is not an eternal "blessing machine" for people. He did not come to save people out of pity; He came to save people because He had created them to be holy.

— Oswald Chambers

has light with darkness? And what accord has Christ with Belial [a heathen god]? Or what part has a believer with an unbeliever?"

As soon as Maria finished reading the passage, David explained the connection. "You see, Denise is not a Christian. We've haven't talked about it a lot, but I do know that she really doesn't have any interest in Christianity. I'm beginning to realize that if I'm going to have a closer relationship with God, then I cannot ignore what these verses say.

"I like Denise and we've had a lot of fun together. I don't know if we would ever get married, but I am sure of one thing—I want to honor God in my home. While I was doing my research, I also found this quote."

Once again, David pulled out slips of paper and found the quotation he was looking for. "Listen to this," he said in a very serious tone.

"Christian homes are created by Biblical people. We can discern a clear pattern—Biblical people become Biblical partners, who can then become Biblical parents. Only believing people can enter Christian marriage, otherwise the marriage is not Christian." (*Building a Christian Family*, Kenneth and Elizabeth Gangel, Chicago, Moody Press, 1987, p. 16)

David looked across the table at Maria. She was silent. It was obvious that she was seriously thinking about the verses from 2 Corinthians and the quotation.

Finally, Maria spoke. "You're serious, aren't you? You know, I've read those verses before. And I guess I do agree with them. But I'm not sure I would have the courage to break up with someone I really like if the only problem was that he was not a Christian. If we dated, maybe I could convince him to become a Christian."

"Do you realize what you just said?" David quickly replied. "You said, 'if the only problem was that he was not a Christian.' So many Christians treat the principles of God's Word as if they were suggestions that we can choose whether or not to obey. I'm becoming more and more convinced that if I am going to have a closer relationship with God, then I have to be serious about what He says in His Word."

"Slow down, David," Maria interrupted. "I agree with you. Honest! I've just never heard anyone say it quite that way before."

At that moment the server arrived with their food. Both cadets sat back in their chairs, waiting to resume their conversation. David had given a lot of thought to a Christian's responsibility in relationships. During his prayer times, he made some important promises to God. Since he had already shared his misgivings about dating Denise, he might as well tell Maria about some other things God was teaching him.

After the server walked away, Maria and David's eyes met once again. It was obvious that David had more to say. For that reason, Maria didn't even bother to pick up her fork. She just waited for David to say what was on his mind.

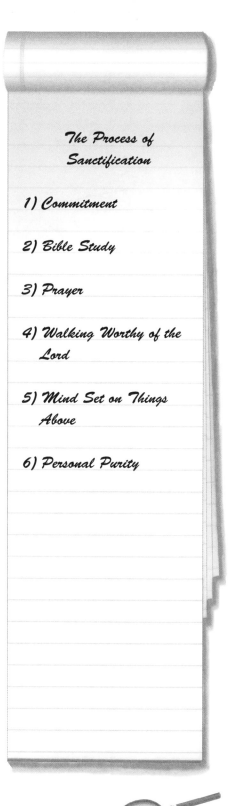

The Process of Sanctification

1) *Commitment*

2) *Bible Study*

3) *Prayer*

4) *Walking Worthy of the Lord*

5) *Mind Set on Things Above*

6) *Personal Purity*

Take Control of Your Mind!

GIGO

- *As a person thinks, so is he.*

- *From the heart proceed the issues of life.*

- *Out of the abundance of the heart a person speaks and acts.*

"Maria," David began, "I've become very convicted about a number of other things in my life, especially one part of my life. This is going to be very hard for me to say, but I hope you'll understand if I'm totally honest with you."

David paused for a minute, wondering if he had the courage to say what he knew had to be said. He looked at Denise for some sort of indication that she understood the struggle he was facing. The compassion in her eyes gave him the assurance he needed. Although he had already sought God's forgiveness, it was time for David to openly admit to something in his life that he had kept hidden for many years.

"You know," David began slowly, "God has a lot to say about our relationships. For one thing, He wants us to have compassion for one another. I've been doing a lot of thinking about how self-centered I am. And God also tells us to build others up rather than tear them down. I've dishonored the Lord many times by the way I've been so critical and cutting. But my relationship with the opposite sex is where God is dealing with me the most right now. You see, I have a real problem with . . . with . . . how I think about girls. The Bible word is . . . lust."

Now he had said it. How would Maria respond? Would she be disgusted, hurt, amused, or have no reaction at all? Would she even understand how serious this was to him?

Finally, Maria asked a question that David had not expected. "Do you mean you're into pornography?" Maria was almost afraid of what his response would be.

At first, David wanted to deny with an emphatic "NO!" But then he realized that he couldn't sugar-coat what had been taking place in his life. He not only needed to be honest with God, but with himself and his friends.

"Well, yes, but probably not in the way you are thinking," David started to explain. I don't buy pornographic books or attend X-rated movies. But still I'm hooked. Here, listen to this verse."

Once again, David reached into his pocket and pulled out a piece of paper. "Come to think of it, you have probably read this verse many times before, just like I have. Listen to what Jesus said in Matthew 5:28. *But I say to you that whoever looks at a woman to lust for her has already committed adultery with her in his heart.*'"

"Maria," David said looking up from the piece of paper, "I want you to know that I am really serious about having a closer walk with God. I've realized that means more than just reading my Bible, praying and attending church. It means cleaning out the secret corners of my life so that God can have complete control. I can't pick and choose the parts of the Bible I want to obey. I don't want to be a Christian who tries to walk the middle of the road between Heaven and the world. It has to be all or nothing."

Maria slowly nodded her head as David continued to explain how God had been working in his life. Finally, the two cadets picked up their forks and began eating. It was obvious that neither of them had any desire to go to the movie. This conversation was far from over. The movie could wait for another day.

Those who walk with Christ in the clean garments of real, practical holiness here, and keep themselves unspotted from the world, shall walk with Christ in the white robes of honor and glory in the life to come. This is a suitable reward. The purity of grace shall be rewarded with the perfect purity of glory.

– Matthew Henry

QuestNote 23.1
Walk Worthy

Describe the walk of a believer in relation to the four characteristics described by Paul.

1. **Knowledge and wisdom**

2. **Consistency**

3. **Positive attitude**

4. **Consideration for others**

QuestNote 23.2
Set Your Mind

List six principles related to developing and controlling the mind in the process of spiritual maturity.

1.	4.
2.	5.
3.	6.

What scripture most impressed you during this study?

QuestNote 23.3
Personal Purity

Summarize some Biblical principles you have learned.

1. What does God expect from believers related to personal purity?

2. On what basis does God expect pure lifestyles among believers?

3. Explain how sexual impurity is a sin against:

   1) Christ and His Spirit

   2) One's own body

   3) Others

4. How will sins involving sexual impurity be judged?

5. What should a believer do who wants to commit to personal purity?

The Christian Life: New Relationships

Weekends always ended too quickly. Before they knew it, the cadets were back in class. But for Maria, this was a special week. On Friday, Matt would arrive shortly after dinner. And to make it even better, it was a three-day weekend! David and Brent knew, just by the look on Maria's face, that she could hardly wait.

As expected, the week did pass by quickly. David turned in his assigned papers, Brent completed his part in a group presentation, and Maria successfully passed a major test in sociology. In every way, it was a typical week for a college student.

But this was a special week for another reason. The third Wednesday evening of each month, under the direction of the chaplain's office, every student was invited to attend a program called "Take Five." It was always a lot of fun because you never knew what was going to happen. Plus, there was always plenty of free food!

Over the years, "Take Five" had become a tradition on campus. Cadets still talked about the year the circus came to town. Somehow the chaplain had arranged for the circus to give a command performance during "Take Five." The event made the papers all over the country.

Never knowing what was going to happen, cadets seldom missed "Take Five." David, Brent and Maria were no exception, and they made sure to be caught up on all their assignments. By Wednesday, all types of rumors were spreading around campus regarding the evening program. Sometimes the rumors were almost as much fun as the program itself.

And whatever you do in word or deed, do all in the name of the Lord Jesus, giving thanks to God the Father through Him. And whatever you do, do it heartily, as to the Lord and not to men, knowing that from the Lord you will receive the reward of the inheritance; for you serve the Lord Christ.

Colossians 3:17, 23–24

"Take Five" always began at 9:00 P.M. As usual, the cadets left early to make sure they got good seats. Upon entering the field house, they immediately got a sense of what was coming. Everywhere they looked, they saw different types of equipment. It seemed as if they were in one gigantic weight training room. This was going to be good!

Promptly at 9:00 P.M., the lights throughout the field house dimmed. On a small stage at the far end of the building, a very physically fit young man held a microphone in his hand. What became immediately obvious was how he was dressed. The red, white and blue uniform proudly displayed the "U.S. Olympic Team" insignia. Members of the U.S. Olympic weightlifting and gymnastic teams had come to display their skills for the cadets. The young man began to speak.

"There is no question that our nation is caught up in a fitness craze. Right now, physical fitness is a billion-dollar business in the United States, and there's no end in sight to its growth potential. Young adults are more health conscious today than at any other time. In many respects, I feel like I'm 'preaching to the choir' at this academy. I know that every cadet is required to occasionally complete some PT."

All at once the entire audience broke into laughter. There was nothing occasional about physical training (known as PT). Every month each cadet had to successfully complete a difficult PT routine. That meant the cadets had to discipline themselves to run and exercise daily. If they didn't, they could not pass their monthly PT test.

As the laughter subsided, the young man once again addressed the audience. "Turn on your TV and you will find an "infomercial" describing the latest fitness product on the market. Have you ever noticed the creative names they give these products? Here are some of my favorites:

'The Thigh-Master'
'The Body-Builder'
'The Ab-Tightener'

"I'm thinking about starting my own business with a product called 'The Gut-Be-Gone'!"

Once again, the audience broke into laughter. He had made his point. Almost everyone was concerned about weight and physical fitness. However, it was ironic that Americans, so concerned about their health and fitness, were seldom willing to follow even the basic routines to achieve good health and fitness.

The young athlete continued his talk. "Have you also noticed that these products come with their own training videos? I actually sent away for *The Ab-Tightener* so I could receive the video called *Abs of Steel*. It would be fun to combine some of my interests into one great video. I even have a name picked out for the promo video—*Line Dancing Aerobics with the Man of Steel*."

Again laughter filled the field house. Now the cadets were really getting into the monologue. From every corner of the room you could hear shouts giving suggestions for workout video titles. This was getting good.

> *This conformity of nature between God and man is not only the distinguishing prerogative of humanity, so far as earthly creatures are concerned, but it is also the necessary condition of our capacity to know God, and therefore the foundation of our religious nature.*
>
> *– Charles Hodge*
> *Systematic Theology*

The young man had the audience right where he wanted them. In addition to being an Olympic athlete, he was also a pretty good comedian. He then introduced the other men and women who had come to perform for the evening. For the next 45 minutes, the cadets were treated to a remarkable display of athletic abilities. By the time the exhibition ended, there was no doubt in anyone's mind that they had seen some of the finest athletes in the world.

The lead speaker once again appeared on the small stage at the far end of the field house. "Physical fitness is the result of a regular routine of diet and exercise, not some gimmick sold on TV. There is no shortcut to good physical health. The requirements are simple: You need to eat a balanced diet, exercise regularly and get adequate sleep.

"I want you to also know that there is no shortcut to good spiritual health and fitness. Please listen to the words of the Apostle Paul in 1 Timothy 4:7–8." The cadets watched as the young man opened his Bible. *"But reject profane and old wives' fables, and exercise yourself toward godliness. For bodily exercise profits a little, but godliness is profitable for all things, having promise of the life that now is and of that which is to come.'"*

Closing his Bible, he began to explain the point of the passage. "Don't think for a moment that Paul sees exercise as a waste of time. Actually, he is placing physical exercise in its proper perspective. Bodily exercise is important but limited. It affects the physical body during this earthly life. Its benefits last for 70 years or so.

"Paul wants us to understand that it is far more important that we 'exercise . . . toward godliness.' Exercise is an athletic term that describes the rigorous, sacrificial training an athlete undergoes. Likewise, it is the same purposeful, spiritual self-discipline that becomes our path to godliness.

"There is an interesting parallel between physical exercise and spiritual exercise. For example some people talk about exercising, and others actually do it. Some talk about wanting a close walk with the Lord, and others take the necessary steps to have that godly walk."

The young man made several good suggestions, but David, Brent and Maria continued to think about the connection he had described between physical and spiritual exercise. They had never thought about it quite that way.

All too soon the program ended, and the three friends made their way back to their barracks. Brent was the first to verbalize what they were all thinking.

"You know, this is the second time that we've gone to an assembly at the field house where we've been challenged to think about our spiritual commitments. I think God used Colonel Hensley's testimony to get my attention. For the first couple of days, I thought a lot about what he had to say. Then I just pushed his words out of my mind. I really didn't want to think about that kind of responsibility to God. Now I think God's giving me another opportunity to get serious about my relationship with Him."

"Me too," Maria added. "I did the same thing. I know I'm a Christian and I try to avoid gross wrongs, but still I don't have a close relationship with God. Although I'm willing to maintain rigorous physical training, I just haven't been willing to do the same thing in my spiritual life."

- *The change is to occur from the inside out.*

- *True believers will display character and actions reflective of the commands of God.*

- *To achieve spiritual maturity, believers must discipline themselves toward godliness.*

- *Therefore, they must be fully committed to both learn and do what God commands.*

IF NOT YOU,

WHO?

IF NOT NOW,

WHEN?

Finally it was David's turn to speak. "I understand exactly what you're saying. God has not let go of me since Colonel Hensley spoke to us. The more I read, the more I realize how important it is for every part of my life to be under the control of Jesus Christ. And that can only happen if I fully yield to the guidance of God's Holy Spirit in my life."

"Brent," Maria began, "last weekend David and I talked about our responsibility as believers in our relationships with others. I haven't been able to get that conversation off my mind. I realized that David was ready to make a very difficult decision because that was the only way he could honor God. That really made an impression on me. I have some relationship issues that I need to deal with in my own life as well. Now I'm beginning to realize that I cannot draw closer in my relationship with God unless I am willing to actually exercise . . . toward godliness."

Just a few feet away was the sidewalk leading to Maria's barracks. As they started to say good-night, the three cadets stopped and looked intently at each other. It was almost as if each could read the others' mind. God's Spirit was working and they didn't want to push Him aside this time. No longer did they want to keep God at a distance. They wanted a real, intimate relationship with Him. It was time to stop playing religious games. This was serious—eternally serious.

Although no words were spoken, the desires of their hearts had been clearly communicated. God had met with each of them in a personal way. Their lives would never be the same again.

QuestNotes 24.1
New Relationships

1. Summarize the essential truths you have learned regarding a Christian's speech and actions toward others.

2. Summarize the essential truths you have learned regarding a Christian's responsibility to people in authority.

3. Summarize the essential truth you have learned regarding a Christian's responsibility to persevere in exercising toward godliness.

QuestNote 24.2
Doctrinal Summary—The Christian Life

Study the outline provided then summarize the truths presented in Scripture.

A Christian's Life Is Characterized by . . .

(1) **Sanctification through the Holy Spirit** _____

_____

_____

(2) **Commitment to cooperate with the process** _____

_____

_____

(3) **Conscientious Bible study** _____

_____

_____

(4) **Consistent prayer** _____

_____

_____

(5) **Walking worthy of the Lord** _____

_____

QuestNote 24.2
Doctrinal Summary—The Christian Life

(6) **Mind (and heart) set on things above** _____

_____

_____

_____

(7) **Personal purity** _____

_____

_____

_____

(8) **Right treatment of others** _____

_____

_____

_____

(9) **Submission to authority** _____

_____

_____

_____

(10) **Exercising toward godliness** _____

_____

_____

_____

Personal QuestNotes

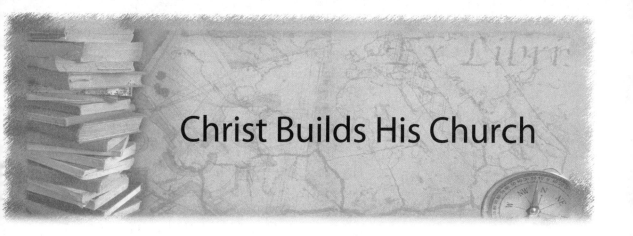

Christ Builds His Church

"I really don't want to have anything to do with the church," the elderly man replied after listening to the pastor's invitation to attend next Sunday. "The church is filled with a bunch of hypocrites who attend only because they want to look good to their friends. I don't need the church—and the church certainly doesn't need me!" Without allowing the young pastor to respond, the elderly man closed the door in his face.

Ted Stevens, known as Pastor Ted to his small congregation, had faithfully invited people to the church ever since he arrived in town. At least twice each week, for the past three months, he had gone door to door to talk to whoever would listen. Although some responded favorably to his invitation, only twice had the people actually showed up for services.

Everyone who knew Pastor Ted liked him. And, for a young man just out of seminary, he was a good speaker. The church's leadership was truly thankful that God had sent Pastor Ted and his wife Traci. For years the little congregation had struggled to survive. Now with Pastor Ted leading them, expectations for the future were high.

Although Pastor Ted was an optimist by nature, even he was beginning to have difficulty facing the repeated rejection by those he invited to church. "Why are people so resistant to church?" he asked himself as he walked down the street to the next house. "It's not like we're going to brainwash them the minute they walk through the door."

Throughout that afternoon Pastor Ted continued to talk to people about their relationship with Christ and to invite them to church. Even though a few people were willing to talk with him, no one had eagerly committed to attending church the following Sunday. After almost three hours of knocking on doors, he had absolutely nothing to show for his efforts.

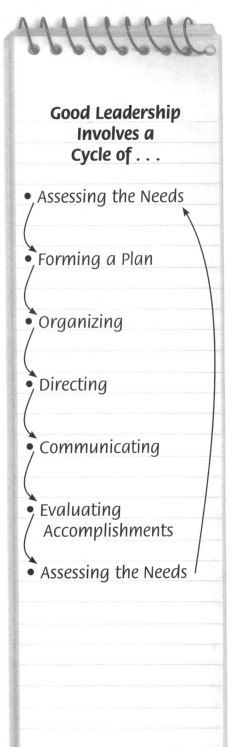

**Good Leadership
Involves a
Cycle of . . .**

- Assessing the Needs

- Forming a Plan

- Organizing

- Directing

- Communicating

- Evaluating
  Accomplishments

- Assessing the Needs

Traci knew the minute her husband entered their modest apartment that his visits had not gone well that afternoon. Trying to diffuse his obvious frustration, she teasingly said, "From the look on your face, I would guess that there will be at least 2000 people at Sunday's service."

Traci was always able to bring a smile to her husband's face. Her light-hearted humor helped him put things into perspective. Ted decided to play along. "Yes, it's been quite an afternoon. Office Systems is delivering 1500 chairs to the church this afternoon. You'll need to help me set them up before Sunday."

After they had a good laugh, the young pastor talked about the people he had met that afternoon. While many seemed interested in talking with him—and some had actually attended church when they were younger—none would make a commitment to attend Sunday's services. It was obvious to Traci that her husband was becoming discouraged.

After dinner, they headed to the mall for some shopping. Traci insisted that Ted go with her, knowing that he needed to get his mind off the events of the afternoon. At first he resisted, but then decided that it probably would be a good idea to get out for awhile. Besides, he always enjoyed browsing through the bookstores.

As the couple walked through the food court, Traci heard a familiar voice calling to her. Several tables away, she saw Pastor Bennett and his wife. She had met Mrs. Bennett at a recent luncheon but had never met her husband. Practically everyone in the city knew Pastor Bennett, who was considered the "elder statesman" among the pastors. He had been in the ministry over 40 years and was one of the most respected men in the city.

"It's good to see you again, Traci," Mrs. Bennett said as she welcomed Traci and Ted to the table. "We were just taking a little break from shopping for our grandson's birthday. Would you join us for a cup of coffee?"

The young couple appreciated the friendly gesture and accepted the offer. Pastor Bennett asked Ted how things were going for him. Ted said nothing about his disappointments from that afternoon. He focused instead on the exciting challenges at the church and their plans for the future. He also described how kind the congregation had been to them since their arrival.

"I'm pleased to hear that," Pastor Bennett responded. "They are a good group of people who have been waiting for an energetic young man like you to lead them."

Pastor Ted thanked him for the kind words. The conversation continued as the two couples became better acquainted. Soon Traci and Ted were ready to leave, but Pastor Bennett asked one last question that stopped both of them in their tracks. "How is your visitation going?" the pastor asked.

The young couple sat back down in their chairs, glancing at each other in disbelief. Before he could even think, Ted blurted out, "How did you know . . . ?"

Before Ted could finish his sentence, Pastor Bennett interrupted. "This isn't such a big town. I've been aware of your visitation efforts for weeks. I admire your hard work and tenacity. But I'm going to guess that your efforts haven't been too successful."

Leaders of the Church

- Overseer
  (Pastor, Bishop, Elder)

- Deacon
  (Elder, Servant)

They had to be godly, wise men, self-controlled, with a stable family life. They were responsible to teach and lead.

"And I also say to you that you are Peter, and on this rock I will build My church, and the gates of Hades shall not prevail against it." And the Lord added to the church daily those who were being saved.

Matthew 16:18 and Acts 2:47b

"You're right about that," Ted quickly responded. "As a matter of fact, one man I visited today told me that he didn't need the church and the church didn't need him."

Pastor Bennett replied almost immediately. "That doesn't surprise me at all. Most people have little idea what church is all about. Some view the church as the way to ensure they get into Heaven. Others see the church as a place to fulfill their religious obligations. And, of course, there are those who attend church for purely social reasons. Unfortunately, even most Christians misunderstand the purpose of the church in God's plan."

A puzzled look crosssed Traci's face. "I don't quite understand what you're saying. Isn't the church still relevant today?"

It was Mrs. Bennett's turn to join the conversation. "You probably don't know this, but my husband is considered quite an authority on the history and effectiveness of the church."

Pastor Bennett quickly interrupted with a smile, "I pay her for such exaggerations. Anyway, it's not all that important."

"Well, it is important that you've studied the subject extensively," Mrs. Bennett responded. "If you want to know something about churches today, Ted, he's the man to talk to."

"My wife is my best cheerleader," Pastor Bennett added, smiling at her affectionately. "Let me share some information with you that I'm sure you'll find interesting.

"Research indicates that Christians have had little influence on society. One of the reasons that may be true is because believers now think of themselves as individuals first. Truth for them is based on personal experience. Therefore, they accept that each individual can formulate different truths. Unless our priorities change, Christianity is just one more option among the numerous worldviews that people may choose. This should be a real wake-up call for the church.

"There is a second interesting fact that I've uncovered in my research. Believers tend to see the church experience as encompassing six practices: worship, evangelism, discipleship, fellowship, stewardship and service. Of these six, worship is the most important. However, their definition of worship relates to their own feelings—not giving due honor to God. They want to be entertained and inspired. My study indicates that the majority of those who attend church do not always feel that their expectations are fulfilled during the service."

"I believe true worship involves recognition and praise to God. It focuses on His nature and works," Pastor Ted explained.

"Exactly!" responded Pastor Bennett. "Worship means that He is the audience; we are there as participants in His presence."

"Are you saying that ministers are not concerned about providing a worshipful experience for their congregations?" the young pastor asked.

"No, I'm not saying that at all," Pastor Bennett assured him. "I'm sure that ministers devote considerable effort to providing a worshipful experience. But, have churches seriously tried to eliminate unnecessary distractions? For example, are late arrivals seated in a discreet manner? Is the service disrupted by constant program and event announcements? Are cell phones and beepers constantly going off during the service?"

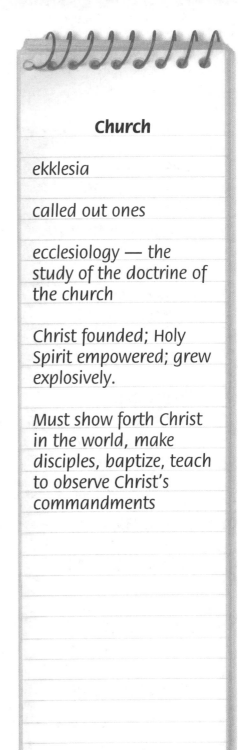

Church

ekklesia

called out ones

ecclesiology — the study of the doctrine of the church

Christ founded; Holy Spirit empowered; grew explosively.

Must show forth Christ in the world, make disciples, baptize, teach to observe Christ's commandments

Church involves . . .

- worship —
  Matthew 28:19;
  Romans 10:15-17; 2
  Corinthians 5:19-20

- evangelism —
  Mark 16:15-16;
  2 Timothy 4:2; 1
  Corinthians 1:17-18;
  Jude 3

- discipleship —
  Matthew 28:20; 1 John
  5:1-3; Philippians
  2:12-13

- fellowship —
  John 13:35; 1 John
  3:23 and 4:11, 20-21;
  Romans 12:10-13

- service —
  Matthew 5:13-16;
  25:44-45; Romans
  12:17-18, 21; 13:8-10;
  Philippians 2:14-16

"Now I understand," Pastor Ted replied. "Our congregation's need is to worship God, so we must do everything we can to ensure that true worship occurs."

"That's certainly true. Now, let me share with you what is probably the most shocking fact I've learned in my research. Do you realize that long-term church attendance has little effect on the theological beliefs of Americans? In other words, those adults who have consistently attended church and those who attend church only on special occasions hold similar views. And, many times, the views they hold are in direct conflict with what the Bible teaches."

Pastor Ted could hardly believe what he had just heard. "Do you mean that a person who has attended church all his life doesn't know any more about the Bible than those who only attend church sporadically?"

"That's not exactly what I said," Pastor Bennett replied. "People who regularly attend church may know more Bible facts. But they haven't developed a Biblical understanding of such key topics as the inspiration and accuracy of the Bible, the reality of Heaven and hell, and the path to salvation. Oftentimes, those who have attended many church services and those who seldom attend church think almost identically about these Biblical topics. Because their understanding and commitments are similar, the Bible seems to make little difference in the way people live."

Ted just had to ask, "Why hasn't the church had a greater influence on the Biblical understanding of believers? And why hasn't the church had a greater influence on our society?"

"Hold on, hold on, Ted. Just one question at a time." It was obvious that the elder pastor was enjoying the young man's enthusiasm. "Now you're starting to ask the important questions about the church. Let me ask you a question. How much do you know about God's plan for His church?"

"Well, until I met you, I thought I knew quite a lot about the church," Pastor Ted answered. "But now I'm not so sure."

Pastor Bennett appreciated the sincerity of Ted's response. This was a young man who had potential. So it just seemed natural to extend a special invitation.

"Why don't you and Traci join us Saturday afternoon for a refresher course on ecclesiology," Pastor Bennett said with a grin on his face.

Pastor Ted understood immediately. Although he was a recent seminary graduate, his education was far from over. He may have had a good theological understanding of the doctrine of the church, but now that he was "out in the trenches," he had a lot more questions than answers.

"Thank you," Ted replied. "I think a refresher course is exactly what I need."

Pastor Bennett was pleased with his response. "That's good. I suggest that between now and next Saturday, you read as much as you can about the role of the church in God's plan. We're going to start right from the beginning."

Ted and Traci got directions to the Bennetts' home before leaving. As the young couple resumed their shopping, they began reviewing what they had learned about the church. It was hard to believe that they already needed to go back to "school."

Truths about Baptism

- Christ's example
- Christ's command
- Early church practice
- To show forth the death, burial and resurrection of Christ
- Required for local church membership
- Responsibility of believers

Truths about the Lord's Supper

- Christ's command
- In remembrance of His death bringing atonement and right standing before God
- Privilege of all believers who are obedient to the Lord

QuestNote 25.1
Basic Questions about the Church

Summarize your study of each question related to the church.

Who ?

Church ?

When ?

What like ?

Head ?

Church vs. church ?

What day ?

Must attend ?

254

QuestNotes 25.2
Biblical Purposes of the Church

Summarize the purposes of the church based on Scripture.

1. Matthew 28:19; Romans 10:15–17; 2 Corinthians 5:19–20

2. Mark 16:15–16; 2 Timothy 4:2; 1 Corinthians 1:17–18; Jude 3

3. Matthew 28:20; 1 John 5:1–3; Philippians 2:12–13

4. John 13:35; 1 John 3:23 and 4:11, 20–21; Romans 12:10–13

5. Matthew 5:13–16; 25:44–45; Romans 12:17–18, 21; 13:8–10; Philippians 2:14–16

6. John 4:24; Romans 12:1–2; Hebrews 13:15

QuestNote 25.3
Governance and Leadership of the Church

Summarize the truths you have studied.

Why does the church need governance?

What kind of government do churches have?

Who are the leaders of the church?

QuestNotes 25.3
Governance and Leadership of the Church

What are the qualifications of leadership?

_____

_____

_____

_____

_____

_____

_____

_____

_____

What are the responsibilities of leadership?

_____

_____

_____

_____

_____

_____

_____

_____

_____

QuestNote 25.4
Ordinances of the Church

Summarize the essential truths related to two ordinances of the church.

1. Baptism *(history, purpose, when, what manner, believer's responsibility)*

_____

_____

_____

_____

_____

_____

_____

2. Lord's Supper *(history, purpose, when, what manner, believer's responsibility)*

_____

_____

_____

_____

_____

_____

_____

_____

The Believer's Participation

Pastor Ted kept his promise. He spent the entire week reading everything he could find about the church. Unlike his time in seminary, when his primary reason for reading was to complete assignments, this research was personal. Now that the responsibility for leading a congregation rested upon his shoulders, the "church" had become more than just another doctrine in his theology textbooks. He now saw the church as a body of believers who were seeking to follow the Lord in the midst of a culture that was antagonistic to God.

Throughout the week, he learned several fascinating facts about the early church. For instance, when two great plagues swept the Roman Empire in 165 and 251 A.D., mortality rates climbed higher than 30 percent. While pagans tried to avoid all contact with the sick, Christians tried to nurse the sick back to health. In many cases, these Christians contacted the plague and also died.

He learned that the early church had a high regard for women's rights, a fact certainly not true in the pagan community. Women greatly outnumbered men among early converts. However, in the Empire men vastly outnumbered women because of female infanticide. Unwanted girl babies were typically killed or discarded at birth. Christians, however, practiced neither abortion nor infanticide.

But probably the most interesting fact that Pastor Ted learned about the early church was its sense of community. Especially during the first few centuries, Greek and Roman cities were terribly overpopulated. Antioch in Syria, for example, had a population density of about 117 inhabitants per acre—more than three times that of New York City today. People lived in cubicles that were smoky, dark, often damp and always dirty. On the street, mud, open sewers and manure were commonplace. For a newcomer or stranger, these cities were extremely inhospitable.

> Let us hold fast the confession of our hope without wavering, for He who promised is faithful. And let us consider one another in order to stir up love and good works, not forsaking the assembling of ourselves together, as is the manner of some, but exhorting one another, and so much the more as you see the Day approaching.
>
> Hebrews 10:23–25

In the midst of these cities, the church stood out as a bright light in a dark room. This community of believers provided a strong sense of identity. To cities filled with the homeless, Christianity offered charity and hope. To newcomers and strangers, Christianity offered immediate friendship and fellowship. To orphans and widows, Christianity provided a new and caring family. The early church was a close-knit community.

Additionally, early churches had an amazing diversity. With converts of various descent (Hebrew, Roman, Greek, Arabic, African) and all levels of socio-economic strata, they unified to function as the body of Christ. There were landowners and slaves, politicians and jailers, men, women, old and young. The Gospel was extended to the world and the world responded.

While Pastor Ted enjoyed learning about life in the early church, his more immediate concern was the church today. His research soon led him to a series of articles describing the current conflict in church circles regarding worship and evangelism. The crux of the conflict was whether worship services should be designed to appeal to unbelievers, or unchurched people. Therefore, the style of the worship service should be more contemporary, with greater appeal to those immersed in cultural trends such as entertainment, MTV and pop psychology.

Of course, this conflict arose because many congregations were declining and large denominations were struggling to attract new members. Pastors, lay leaders and national church officers followed the advice of marketing gurus to throw out the traditions of their churches in order to appeal to the unchurched masses.

The result, Pastor Ted learned in his research, was a push for a worship style that lacks deep theological teaching and contemplation. Instead, it encourages an "easy-listening" consumerism. This was particularly evident in the music of these churches where neither the words of the songs, nor the actual music itself, encouraged worshipers to anchor themselves in Biblical teaching rather than personal feelings.

The "easy-listening" approach to church services also resulted in a failure to educate people concerning the true meaning and practice of worship, failure to understand the real influence of sin that keeps people from participating in the church, and the failure to equip the body of believers for outreach to the world. In an effort to attract new members, the church seems to have focused more on entertainment than worship.

Before the week was over, Pastor Ted had spent 30-plus hours conducting research about church practices. Although he had never spent that much time on any of his papers in seminary, he eagerly invested that time now. He knew that God had called him to pastor a local church. Thus, he had to know everything he could about the church and how to be successful in leading it.

By the time Saturday arrived, Pastor Ted felt well-prepared for his refresher course with Dr. Bennett. Traci was also looking forward to sharing an afternoon with the Bennetts. She had spent considerable time thinking about her role as a pastor's wife, and she had some questions for Mrs. Bennett.

"Welcome," the Bennetts said as they greeted them at the front door. "We're so glad to see you again. Come on

Gifts of the Spirit "for the common good"

1. Apostle
2. Prophecy
3. Evangelist
4. Pastor
5. Ministry
6. Teacher
7. Wisdom
8. Knowledge
9. Exhortation
10. Faith
11. Miracles
12. Healing
13. Discerning spirits
14. Giving
15. Helps
16. Mercy
17. Administration
18. Tongues
19. Interpreting

worship = worth-ship

True worship occurs only when that part of human beings, their spirit, which is akin to the divine nature, actually meets with God and finds itself praising Him for His love, wisdom, beauty, truth, holiness, compassion, mercy, grace, power and other attributes.

– Dr. James Boice

in and sit down." For the next half hour, the two couples became better acquainted over some light refreshments. Pastor Ted explained that he was the first member of his family to enter the ministry. Traci added that her brother was a pastor and that several other family members were involved in Christian organizations. The Bennetts shared stories from their first years in the ministry.

"Well, it's time to start class," Dr. Bennett announced as his wife went to the kitchen to make a new pot of coffee. "Tell me, what have you learned about the church this week?"

Pastor Ted reviewed his research while the elder statesman listened attentively. In conclusion, the young pastor described what concerned him the most. "I can't believe how the attitudes toward worship have changed. It seems to me that so many people are coming to church for reasons other than personally meeting with God."

"In many respects, you're exactly right," Dr. Bennett responded. "As pastors, our responsibility is to teach our congregations the true meaning of worship. This is a responsibility that we must take very seriously. But believers have responsibilities as well."

"What do you mean?" Traci asked.

"I'm sure that as part of your research you read Acts 2:42–47," Dr. Bennett began. "Now this might seem like a silly question, but do you want your church to be like God's church?"

Ted was surprised by the question but nodded in agreement.

"There is little question that Christianity, especially as it is represented through the local church, is losing influence in our country. It's not because God's Word is less powerful or that He has abandoned the church. It's because today's church has become less like the church God intended. Let me describe for you four characteristics of the church as described in Acts 2:42–47. I think you will quickly see that each characteristic places a responsibility on the believer."

Pastor Ted opened his notebook to write down the four characteristics. Now he truly did feel like he was back in class. As Dr. Bennett outlined the four characteristics, the young minister took notes.

Characteristic 1: God's church is committed.
("And they continued steadfastly . . . .")

"Steadfast" means to be firm in a position or to be constant in the exercise of duties. It involves consistent dedication, or faithfulness. The church is to be committed in its teaching, fellowship, the breaking of bread and prayer. The church is not to drift from one momentary emotional outburst to the next. It should not be blown around by every new wind of doctrine or fad in service styles. Instead, it must hold unswervingly to the principles of faith delivered to the early saints and passed to us through church leaders, sometimes at the cost of their life.

Characteristic 2: God's church is empowered by the Holy Spirit.
("Then fear came upon every soul . . . .")

The fear described in this verse is a godly, reverential awe much like the fear experienced by Moses as he approached the mountain of God in Exodus

The early church was. . .

- Committed

- Empowered

- Unselfish

- Unified

Giving should be done . . .

- after I give myself to the Lord

- based on God's blessing to me

- even out of poverty

- generously, cheerfully

- knowing God will bless the giver

20:20. The evidence of God's Spirit among them could be seen in signs, wonders, people being healed and changed lives. Paul explained that we worship by the Spirit of God (Philippians 3:3).

Characteristic 3: God's church is unselfish.
("Now all who believed were together, and had all things in common . . . .")

Early churches had an intense feeling of responsibility for each other. Some have mistakenly interpreted this verse to imply that the members of early churches lived together in some sort of commune. That is not accurate, for it is clear from other passages of Scripture that they had their own homes and possessions. What this verse teaches is that early Christians held their possessions "lightly." These believers possessed such a generous spirit that some sold their own possessions to provide money for those in need.

Characteristic 4: God's church is unified.
("So continuing daily in one accord . . . .")

The unifying factor of the early church was Jesus Christ. For the early believers, church was not a "Sunday only" activity and worship was not limited to a building. Their faith in Jesus Christ and obedience to His Word were daily experiences. Their single focus was to honor the Lord.

As the elder pastor completed his explanation of the fourth characteristic, Pastor Ted placed his pen and notebook on a table beside his chair. "As you described the four characteristics of the church," he said, "I began to see the responsibilities that believers have as church members. Two thousand years ago a church was viewed as a body of believers who daily practiced what Jesus taught. Today a church is viewed more as a building or a program of services and activities."

"That's a very good point," Pastor Bennett replied. He realized that the young pastor was now starting to understand the true nature of the church. It was time to further challenge his thinking. "I want you to consider two things before we get together again. First, identify the believer's responsibilities to the church based upon the four characteristics of the church I've described to you. Second, I want you to tell me your responsibilities as the pastor of your church."

Ted and Traci thanked the Bennetts for their kind hospitality and the opportunity to talk about their church's ministry. They also arranged a time to meet later that week. After saying goodbye, the young couple headed to their car.

As soon as the car doors were shut, Traci turned to her husband. "Do you realize what just happened?"

Ted looked at her with a puzzled expression. "What? Did I do or say something wrong?"

"No, of course not," Traci replied with a smile. "I just thought that it was funny for you to get a homework assignment."

Pastor Ted thought for a second. "I guess I did, didn't I?"

"Father Abraham, whom have you in Heaven? Any Episcopalians?"

"No!"

"Any Presbyterians?"

"No!"

"Any Independents and Methodists?"

"No, no, no!"

"Whom have you there?"

"We don't know those names here. All who are here are Christians."

"Oh, is this the case? Then God help us to forget party names and to become Christians in deed and truth."

– George Whitfield
Philadelphia, 1740

QuestNote 26.1
Basics of Worship

Answer the five basic questions related to worship.

Who ?

What ?

Where ?

How ?

Why ?

QuestNote 26.2
Spiritual Gifts Summary

Answer the questions as a summary on Spiritual gifts.

1. What are gifts of the Spirit? Name some of them. _____

_____

_____

2. Who gives these gifts? Who receives them? _____

_____

_____

3. Why are the gifts given? _____

_____

_____

4. What is the responsibility of believers to use their gift? _____

_____

_____

5. How does a church benefit from each member using his or her gift? _____

_____

_____

QuestNote 26.3
Church Financial Support Summary

1. What was the pattern of giving in the Old Testament?

2. Are New Testament believers commanded to tithe?

3. How should believers give?

4. What can be accomplished with these gifts?

5. What blessings accrue to a generous giver?

The Believer's Commitment

Ever since Pastor Ted knew God was calling him to the ministry, he had kept a journal. However, he had neglected to make entries during the past few weeks. That was very unusual, because he typically recorded his observations and thoughts at least a couple of times a week. His encounter with Pastor Bennett had disrupted his regular routine. Lately, the young pastor had spent every spare minute learning more about the church. Today, though, he would take the time to record in his journal. The last two weeks had given him lots to write about.

As was his custom, Ted did not try to structure his journal entries. Rather, he would write down random thoughts as they came to his mind. This morning, his mind was filled with more random thoughts than he could capture.

Actually serving as a pastor is a whole lot more difficult than learning how to be a pastor.

For a few minutes, Pastor Ted reflected on his seminary training. He had received a good education, but nothing could really have prepared him for the reality of leading a congregation. For the next few minutes, he recorded the many lessons he had already learned as a young pastor. At that point another thought came to his mind.

People hold many different views about the role of the church.

In Pastor Ted's mind, the role of the church was easy to define. But his first few months of ministry had been a rude awakening. Church had various meanings for different people. He found it very difficult to pastor a church, or even invite someone to church, when people hold such a variety of views about the purpose of churches. Ted wrote for quite a while before beginning another section.

Church-goers may know facts about the Bible, but that doesn't mean that they understand the Bible.

This was one of the important lessons that Dr. Bennett had tried to teach him over the past few weeks. Since he had only been in the pastorate a short time, it was not a lesson that he had learned from personal experience.

At that moment an idea occurred to him. Why not see just how much his congregation knew about the Bible? The majority of his church members had been Christians many years. They had certainly spent enough time in church to know more than just a bunch of Bible facts. He would learn for himself if Dr. Bennett's statements were true.

"Are you sure you want to do this?" Traci asked her husband upon first hearing his idea. "You haven't been their pastor very long. I'm not so sure that it's a good idea to try to trick them."

"I'm not trying to trick them," Pastor Ted responded. "Matter of fact, they're not even going to know that I'm conducting this little experiment. I want to know just how much my congregation understands the Bible. There's nothing wrong with that, is there?"

Traci thought about it for a moment. Then she replied, "I guess not. In a way, I'm kind of curious to know, myself."

Pastor Ted had recently preached two different series of sermons. One series was on the doctrine of the Holy Spirit. The other series—the one he had just completed the prior Sunday—focused on the believer's growth. This would be a good place to start. Surely his congregation would remember and understand what he had been preaching during the past two months.

And Jesus came and spoke to them, saying, "All authority has been given to Me in heaven and on earth. Go therefore and make disciples of all the nations, baptizing them in the name of the Father and of the Son and of the Holy Spirit, teaching them to observe all things that I have commanded you; and lo, I am with you always, even to the end of the age." Amen.

Matthew 28:18–20

In addition to asking the members about these two doctrines, Pastor Ted wanted to know how much they understood about the church. After all, it was Dr. Bennett's research about church members that had spurred him to conduct this experiment. He couldn't wait to get started!

Pastor Ted could have approached his research in various ways. But he ultimately decided on a plan that was both direct and personal. He selected three groups from his congregation that he believed would be a good representative sample of the entire congregation. He then interviewed each group separately in an attempt to learn what they understood about the three doctrines. To the first group, he posed questions related to the Holy Spirit.

He quickly realized that the group was a little skeptical of his motives. After all, he was still very new to the congregation. The members of the first group seemed reluctant to talk. Pastor Ted wasn't sure if they were uncomfortable in the group setting or if they were unsure of their responses. Afterward, he wrote a brief summary of his conclusions, noting specifically the following:

Clearly, the group does not understand how the ministry of the Holy Spirit differs from the ministries of God the Father and God the Son. Nor do they understand that the Holy Spirit is a Person. While the group does believe that the Holy Spirit abides in every believer, they do not seem to understand that He is a real Person in the same way that God the Father and Jesus Christ are real Persons. Finally, the group does seem to have a good understanding of the role the Holy Spirit played in the development of the early church. However, they aren't convinced that the Holy Spirit works in the same powerful way in the church today.

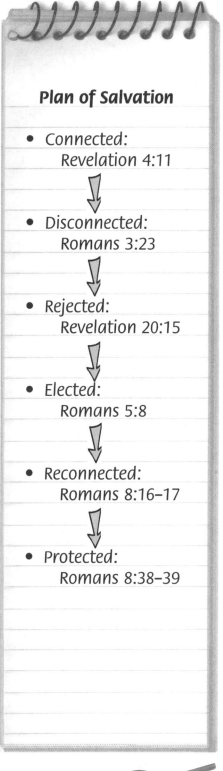

Plan of Salvation

- Connected:
  Revelation 4:11

- Disconnected:
  Romans 3:23

- Rejected:
  Revelation 20:15

- Elected:
  Romans 5:8

- Reconnected:
  Romans 8:16–17

- Protected:
  Romans 8:38–39

Evangelism —
    The process of sharing the message of God, especially the good news of Jesus Christ

Missions —
    Going to all people groups (especially to countries where exposure to the Gospel is limited) to evangelize

After completing his summary, Pastor Ted arranged to meet with the second group. The questions for this group would focus on the believer's growth.

This group seemed to be much more at ease with him than the first group. In fact, they were actually quite talkative. The reason might have been related to the age of the group members. They were considerably younger than the first group. Pastor Ted realized that he should have had a variety of ages represented in each group.

Once again, after the meeting concluded, he wrote a brief summary of what he had learned. His notes revealed that he was particularly concerned about the lack of "connection" between knowing and doing what was right.

Each member knows that they are to avoid gossip, to control their anger, avoid sinful pleasures, and pray regularly. Yet there seems to be little connection between what they know and what they actually practice in daily life. The group members do not seem to understand that growing in the grace and knowledge of the Lord is not optional—like a nice idea if you're in the mood. They do not understand that as believers, we are commanded to grow. Our growth is evidence of our faith!

The meeting with the second group had been an eye-opener. While each of the group's members seemed to know what a believer should do to grow in his relationship to the Lord, little commitment existed to actually live according to the faith they had professed. Pastor Ted now turned his attention to the third, and final, group. He had lots of questions about the church for this group.

Right from the beginning, the young pastor knew that this group was different from the others. For one thing, they had all sorts of questions about why he was meeting with groups of church members to ask them questions about the Bible. Obviously, the word had gotten around about what he was doing. Second, they wanted to know why they were the ones chosen to answer questions about the church.

After Pastor Ted answered their questions, he began to ask questions of his own. The meeting with this group lasted almost two hours. Unlike the other meetings, the information gathered from this group was the most difficult to summarize. The following excerpt from Pastor Ted's notes says it all.

It's amazing how little these members of our church understand the role of the church in God's overall plan. For them (and I am sure for many others), the church is just one more obligation to fulfill during the week. Their attendance at church, as well as their willingness to serve in some area of leadership, is dependent upon what else is going on in their life. In other words, the church is not a priority, but one option among many.

After conducting his research, the young pastor concluded that Dr. Bennett was correct. Church members know a lot of facts about the doctrines of the Bible, but they have very little understanding of these doctrines. Interestingly, using the same Bible facts, church members will arrive at different conclusions about what the Bible says. This obviously presents a formidable challenge for any pastor to overcome.

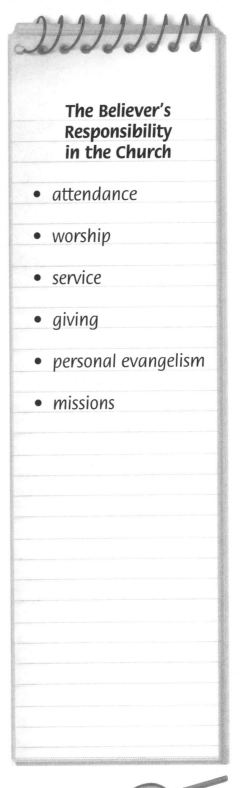

The Believer's Responsibility in the Church

- attendance
- worship
- service
- giving
- personal evangelism
- missions

Here Am I

Let none hear you idly
saying,
"There is nothing I can
do,"
While the souls of men
are dying,
And the Master calls for
you.
Take the task He gives
you gladly,
Let His work your
pleasure be;
Answer quickly when
He calleth,
"Here am I; send me,
send me!"

– J. Danson Smith

As planned, Ted and Traci met with the Bennetts for one last class. These had been enjoyable experiences for all of them. Ted and Traci had so many questions, and Pastor Bennett loved to share his thoughts from a lifetime of ministry.

Before the afternoon was over, Ted presented his findings from the research he had completed within his church. Although the facts were a bit disconcerting to the young pastor and his wife, the Bennetts were not at all surprised by what they heard.

"You know," Pastor Ted began, "It seems like things have changed so much from when I first attended church as a child. And it seems like church has changed dramatically in recent years. I guess I'm a little unsure as to how I should lead my congregation. I want to do things right and honor the Lord by the way I pastor this church."

Dr. Bennett nodded understandingly. "I know what you mean. I felt the same way many years ago when I began my ministry. But always remember this." Dr. Bennett drew from his pocket an envelope with Ted's name on it. "This will be a reminder of the time we've spent together. Go ahead and read it."

Pastor Ted opened the envelope and read the message aloud.

While there are so many changes in the world, it is the unique function of the church to declare by both word and deed that some things never change. One is the message that God—the supreme, unchanging, omnipotent Creator of the universe—loves humanity and wants us to know Him in a personal way. This message presents the truth that mankind has separated himself from God. It emphasizes the reality that God has taken the initiative—through Jesus Christ—to restore the relationship between Himself and people. It is the message that there is hope for the future. Jesus Christ has risen from the dead, and one day He will reign victorious over all the forces of evil, death and hell.

No matter what you face in the years ahead, remember that God will never change. That's why the preaching of the Gospel continues to be God's highest calling. The Gospel is still the power of God to salvation for everyone who believes. The Gospel compelled early Christians to go into their world, often paying the price for their commitment with their lives. It is that same message that must be the center of our ministry today.

Pastor Ted closed the card and returned it to its envelope. He was obviously touched by Dr. Bennett's message of challenge and encouragement.

It was very quiet for the next few moments. Finally, the young pastor looked at the elder statesman and simply said, "Thank you. I still have so much to learn and a lot of exciting challenges before me."

QuestNote 27.1
Personal Evangelism and Missions

Summarize four Biblical truths for personal evangelism and missions.

1. On what Biblical basis are believers responsible for personal evangelism and missions?

2. What are the similarities and contrasts between personal evangelism and missions?

3. What are five suggestions for a believer who wants to talk with someone about Christ?

4. How can a teen be involved in a church's missions program?

QuestNote 27.2
Essential Truths — The Doctrine of the Church

Review the QuestNotes you have completed for Weeks 25, 26 and 27. Summarize these into cohesive paragraphs that focus on 1) the church's founding, definition and mission, 2) its sacraments and leadership, and 3) believers' responsibility to their church in the areas of attendance, worship, service, giving, personal evangelism and missions.

QuestNote 27.3
Doctrinal Summaries

Write a statement of Biblical truth related to the areas listed. Each topic should have a short essay composed of about 12 sentences. An outline will be reviewed by your instructor.

1. The Doctrine of the Holy Spirit

QuestNote 27.3
Doctrinal Summaries

2. The Doctrine of Christian Living

QuestNote 27.3
Doctrinal Summaries

3. The Doctrine of the Church

Angels Among Us

"This really makes me feel creepy," Janet said as she pushed the book away. "Can't we watch a video or listen to some music instead?"

The other girls just laughed. They knew even before they had invited Janet to the weekend retreat that she would be uncomfortable with some of the things they had planned. But the girls liked her and hoped that she would fit in with the rest of them. They didn't want to make fun of her. They really wanted her to be a part of their group.

Janet wanted to be friends with the group; that's why she had accepted their invitation even though they had a reputation on campus for being interested in ESP and other unexplainable paranormal phenomena. She expected they would talk about the occult some time during the weekend, but she was taken aback to see a book explaining how to cast spells. The content and pictures made her feel very uneasy.

"What are you afraid of?" Melanie asked. "Don't take it so seriously. I don't really believe in this stuff. I just think it's kind of intriguing—you know, just for fun."

Amy was quick to challenge Melanie's statement. "I want all of you to know that I seriously believe in the occult. I've been studying it for a long time. It makes a lot of sense to me."

For over an hour the girls discussed the powers of the spirit world. The more Janet heard, the more uncomfortable she became. Finally, when it seemed that this discussion was putting a damper on their fun, the girls decided it was time to do something else. The rest of the evening went fine. Janet and the other girls enjoyed everything from discussing the new softball uniforms to the pizza that was delivered way past midnight.

The rest of the retreat went well. All too soon, it was Monday morning and time to start another week at school. Janet never could understand why weekends passed so fast. It always seemed as if Monday followed right behind Friday. She could hardly remember what she did during her two days off from school.

But this Monday morning was a little different. The discussion about the occult still disturbed her. She kept visualizing the grotesque pictures of Satan and his demons that she had seen in Amy's book. No matter how hard she tried, she couldn't get those images out of her mind.

Janet's class just before lunch was humanities. She would have never enrolled in the class if it had not been a requirement for graduation. However, it was a lot better than she had expected. In addition to learning about a culture's art and music, she learned its history and philosophy as well. Today the class was starting a unit covering the medieval era—one of her favorite periods of history.

But when she opened to the assigned chapter in her textbook, Janet almost fell out of her chair. Many of the paintings and sculptures pictured in her book depicted Satan and his demons. It was almost as if she were still at the retreat. There was extreme similarity between the pictures in her textbook and those she had seen in Amy's book.

Before the class ended, the professor explained that the students would be responsible to research a topic related to the medieval period. Each class member had to choose a topic and have it approved by the end of the week. Normally, Janet would think about a potential topic for a couple of days before making a decision. But this time was different; she knew exactly what she wanted to research.

As the students left the classroom, Janet stopped to talk to her professor. "Is it all right if I do my project on Satan and his demons? It's obvious from the pictures and discussion in our text that people were interested in the spirit world during the medieval period."

Dr. Johnston had taught the humanities class for years, but this was the first time that a student had chosen Satan and his demons as a topic. "Janet," Dr. Johnston began, "I'll approve your topic, but I am curious as to why you selected that subject. I didn't know that you had that much interest in Satan and his demons."

"In a way, I don't," Janet replied. "But some things have come up recently that bother me. This project will give me the opportunity to learn more about the spirit world. I have some questions that need answers."

Dr. Johnston was delighted with her student's positive attitude toward the project. "If I can be of any help, please let me know."

Janet wasted no time getting started with her research. She went straight to the library as soon as the school day ended. At church she had learned some basic facts about Satan and his demons, but she knew that her knowledge was very limited. When she saw the multitude of resources that were available, she knew that she had an important decision to make.

Janet scanned the library's large collection related to Satan and his demons. She quickly realized that the books could be grouped into two categories. All of the books in the first group used the Bible as the basis for an understanding of Satan and his demons, while the books in the second group referred to a variety of religions, as well as

Angels in the Life of Christ

- announced the birth of John the Baptist

- announced the birth of Christ to Mary

- announced birth of Christ to Joseph

- announced Christ's birth to the shepherds

- warned Joseph to flee to Egypt

- instructed Joseph to return to Nazareth

- ministered after Christ's temptation

- ministered to Christ in the Garden of Gethsemane

- appeared and announced Christ's resurrection

- appeared at Christ's ascension

- will appear at Christ's return

myths and legends, to explain the spirit world. Janet chose the books based on the Bible to begin her research.

She settled comfortably into a chair with the books she had chosen spread out on the table before her. Remembering what she had learned in her English classes, Janet began by identifying the question she would try to answer in her research. After a number of attempts, she finally wrote a question on the first page of her notebook.

Are angels, the devil and demons the result of ignorant superstition, or are they objective realities?

In Janet's mind, the answer to that question was fundamental to her research. If angels, the devil and demons are mere superstitions, then Amy's occult book was harmless. But if they are real, then their power to influence lives is real as well. Now that Janet's research question had been identified, it was time to go to work.

For the next two hours, she carefully read what each book said about the angelic world. There were seven facts upon which all of the books seemed to agree. So she decided to make a list of those facts to guide her research over the next few weeks.

Fact 1: Angels are mentioned in both the Old and the New Testament.

Fact 2: Angels are created beings.

Fact 3: Angels are more intelligent and powerful than mankind, but their knowledge, presence and strength are limited.

Fact 4: Angels stand in the very presence of God, ready to do His will.

Fact 5: There are both good and evil angels (demons).

Fact 6: Both Satan and demons are real.

Fact 7: Satan is a fallen angel, powerful but limited in authority.

It had been a long day, but Janet was pleased with how much she had learned. As she reviewed her notes, she realized that before she could do further research on Satan and his demons, she must first learn more about angels. After all, Satan was created by God just like the rest of the angels. Until she knew more about angels, she would not be able to fully understand Satan and his demons.

The following day after humanities class, Dr. Johnston indicated to Janet that she wanted to talk with her. "Have you started your research?" she asked.

"Yes," Janet replied. "I spent over two hours in the library yesterday. I've already gathered some information, although I have a lot more research to do."

Dr. Johnston smiled approvingly. "Would you mind stopping in after school and telling me what you've learned so far?"

Janet was pleased that Dr. Johnston was taking such an interest in her research. "Of course not," she answered.

Shortly after her last class, Janet knocked on the door of Dr. Johnston's office. "Do you still have time to talk about my research?" she asked.

Angel Facts

Fact 1: Angels are mentioned in both the Old and the New Testament.

Fact 2: Angels are created beings.

Fact 3: Angels are more intelligent and powerful than mankind, but their knowledge, presence and strength are limited.

Fact 4: Angels stand in the very presence of God, ready to do His will.

Fact 5: There are both good and evil angels (demons).

Fact 6: Both Satan and demons are real.

Fact 7: Satan is a fallen angel, powerful but limited in authority.

"Sure," Dr. Johnston replied, looking up from piles of books and papers on the desk. "I've been looking forward to meeting with you this afternoon. Take a seat and tell me what you've learned so far."

Janet explained that she was faced with a challenge right at the outset of her research. The books about Satan and his demons were either based on the Bible or based on a wide variety of religions, myths and legends. She had decided to begin her research by understanding what the Bible says.

Next, Janet stated the question that she had chosen to guide her research: Are angels, the devil and demons the result of ignorant superstition, or are they objective realities? Finally, Janet showed her teacher the seven "facts" that she had listed in her notes.

"My next step is to learn as much about angels as I can," Janet concluded. "Unless I know more about angels, I won't be able to fully understand Satan and his demons."

As they discussed her project, Janet was surprised at how much Dr. Johnston knew about the spirit world. Janet took notes as her professor talked.

"Remember, Janet," Dr. Johnston explained, "there are approximately 300 references to angels in the Bible. The Greek word translated 'angel' simply means 'messenger.' Angels are spirit beings, which means they do not have material bodies as people have. However, they have occasionally assumed human form. Of course, as you know, there are both good and evil angels. Many of the graphic depictions of angels present them as female; however, they are always presented as masculine in the Scriptures."

Once again, Janet was surprised at Dr. Johnston's knowledge. "How do you know so much about angels? Did you have to do a research paper too?" Janet asked half jokingly.

"Actually," Dr. Johnston responded, "I had quite an interest in the spirit world when I was in high school. To tell the truth, you might even call it an obsession. Throughout my college years, I continued to learn everything I could about angels, demons, witchcraft, and even the devil."

"You're kidding!" Janet responded in amazement. "You . . . you don't seem like the type."

Dr. Johnston laughed. "Well, it's true. Maybe I'll tell you later why I am no longer obsessed with the spirit world. But for now, you need to get back to your research."

Janet began collecting her books and papers, not knowing quite how to respond to what she had just heard. Dr. Johnston sensed Janet's uneasiness. The revelation had come as a surprise. It only took a moment for Dr. Johnston to decide to take the next step.

"I've got a few questions for you that will help guide your research," Dr. Johnston began. "Would you like to hear them?"

Janet's response was an immediate "Yes, sure!" Dr. Johnston motioned Janet to sit down again and get out a piece of paper. "I want you to find the answers to the following questions."

Angels spell out the tenderness of God's love, meet a desperate need, then they are gone. Angels never draw attention to themselves but ascribe glory to God and press His message upon the hearers as a delivering and sustaining word of the highest order. They are vigorous in delivering the heirs of salvation from the stratagems of evil.

— Billy Graham

QuestNote 28.1
Angels — Part 1

Summarize the truths you have discussed.

Origin:_____

_____

Number:_____

_____

Appearance:_____

_____

_____

_____

Four Classes, or Types:_____

_____

_____

_____

Organization:_____

_____

_____

_____

QuestNote 28.2
Angels — Part 2

Summarize the truths you have discussed.

Ministries:

1. _____

   _____

2. _____

   _____

3. _____

   _____

4. _____

   _____

5. _____

   _____

6. _____

   _____

7. _____

   _____

QuestNote 28.3
Angels — Part 3

Summarize the truths you have discussed.

How we should respond: _____

_____

_____

_____

_____

_____

_____

_____

_____

_____

_____

_____

_____

_____

_____

Satan and His Demons

As Janet continued her research, she wondered about Dr. Johnston's past. She had taught at the college for a long time. Janet knew that, because her older brother had taken Dr. Johnston's English course four years earlier. She was respected by the students and was considered to be one of the best instructors on campus. How could anyone imagine that her background included a serious interest in angels, demons and Satan?

The questions Dr. Johnston had assigned helped Janet prepare for the next phase of her research. She now felt comfortable with her general knowledge of the angelic world. It was time to move on to a more in-depth study of Satan and demons, the primary reason she had chosen this topic for her research in the first place. As a result of her professor's help, Janet knew exactly what to do next.

Dr. Johnston had suggested that Janet briefly review some of the misconceptions about Satan, at the same time cautioning, "Be careful that you don't spend too much time gathering information about Satan from books that misrepresent him. The Bible is the only source that provides accurate information on Satan and his followers. It is far better to know the truth about what Satan is like than to have a lot of misinformation based on what other people *think*."

It didn't take long for Janet to realize how right Dr. Johnston was. She couldn't believe how many different ways Satan had been represented throughout history. For example, in the tenth century it seemed that Satan was everywhere. Sermons recounted his plots and temptations to lure mankind into sin. Paintings and sculptures depicted him as both evil and powerful. Stories about Satan were told in taverns and in homes as bedtime stories.

Be sober, be vigilant; because your adversary the devil walks about like a roaring lion, seeking whom he may devour. Resist him, steadfast in the faith, knowing that the same sufferings are experienced by your brotherhood in the world.

1 Peter 5:8-9

It seemed like no part of life was immune from Satan's attacks. Matter of fact, people at that time believed Satan was always waiting, lurking, looking for an opportunity to enter an unprotected part of the body. That's why, to this day, we say "God bless you" when we hear someone sneeze. People believed that the opening of the nose was momentarily unguarded, thus providing an opportunity for Satan's minions to enter the body.

In contrast, it seems today as if Satan has become a fantasy figure, the anti-hero for movies, comic books and video games. While it may be true that 48% of Americans believe the devil exists, most people are light-hearted about the evil reality that is Satan.

Janet was intrigued by what she was learning. It seemed that theologians had been arguing for centuries about the person and power of Satan. Yet today, the average person on the street has no real theological understanding of who Satan really is. In fact, most people envision him as a sleek, dark-complexioned male figure, with black chin-whiskers, little horns and cloven hooves, charmingly handsome in his red suit or else clothed in darkness behind a black cape.

But these images of the devil are relatively recent ones. Through her research, Janet learned that artists, authors and poets had represented the devil very differently for centuries. Typically, he was portrayed in terrible, grotesque figures. This was meant to be both frightening and disgusting, thus demonstrating the horror and folly of sin. Devices like red-hot prongs were pictured being used by the devil to torture sinners down through the depths of hell. Interestingly, these were the same devices being used in Europe to torture those declared to be heretics by the established church hierarchy.

Janet looked at many artists' renderings of the devil. She was most interested in the two paintings by the Renaissance artist, Raphael. In 1505 he painted a traditional picture of Saint Michael forcing the devil out of Heaven. In the painting, Satan was portrayed as an over-sized, science-fiction insect with horns, wings and a madman's look on his face.

Thirteen years later, Raphael portrayed the devil in a very different way. He chose the same scene with Saint Michael, but this time the devil looked very human. The only unusual feature was a pair of bat wings growing out of his shoulders. In just 13 years, the painter's view of the devil had changed dramatically.

Janet looked at her watch and suddenly realized that she had spent more than two hours researching the mis-representations of the devil. She had done exactly what Dr. Johnston had warned against. It was time to turn her attention to what the Bible has to say about the devil. She drew two lines across the page of her notebook, indicating that her research was taking a new direction. However, before going any further, she wrote down the words of the seventeenth-century Englishman, Richard Greenham, as a reminder of the importance of her research.

> "... it is the policy of the Devil to persuade us that there is no Devil."

It seemed to Janet that people either do not believe in the devil or they distort the reality of his existence. Either way, the devil is then free to continue his efforts to disrupt God's plans.

The Doctrine of Satan

1. *His Existence*

2. *His Ultimate Desire*

3. *His Origin*

4. *His Nature (Character)*

5. *His Abilities (Works)*

6. *His Relation to God's People*

7. *His Relation to Demons*

8. *His Relation to Christ*

9. *His Destiny*

Three Reasons We Experience Evil

• We live in a world that is under the curse of death. Therefore, the natural order is decay, destruction, difficulty, turmoil and chaos.

• Our own sinful nature leads us to make wrong choices which, in turn, lead to suffering as a logical consequence.

• Satan cunningly entices, tempts and enslaves people to sin.

Taking Dr. Johnston's advice, Janet first looked at the many names given to the devil in the Bible. She quickly learned that "*Abbadon*" in the Old Testament and "*Apollyon*" in the New Testament were the words translated as "devil" in her English Bible. Both words were literally translated as "destroyer," an obvious indication of the character of the one described.

But what Janet found most interesting was the number of names ascribed to the devil in the Bible. In the New Testament alone she found 15 names in addition to the name "devil." Each name revealed something new about the character of this fallen angel. Janet took out a separate piece of paper to record the names and references she had found.

In Matthew 4:1, she noted one of the many times the name "devil" was used. She also found other names in Matthew—"tempter" (4:3), "Beelzebub" (12:24), "the wicked one" (13:19) and "enemy" (13:39). Mark used the name "Satan" (1:13), and John referred to him as a "murderer," "liar" and "father of lies" (8:44) as well as the "ruler of this world" (12:31).

Paul referred to him as the "god of this age" (2 Corinthians 4:4), "Belial" (2 Corinthians 6:15) and "tempter" (1 Thessalonians 3:5). The Apostle Peter described the devil as our "adversary" (1 Peter 5:8), like a roaring lion seeking anyone he can devour.

Janet was not surprised to learn that the book of Revelation added names that were unique to the theme of the book. In this book the devil was called the "angel of the bottomless pit" (9:11), the "great red dragon" (12:3) and the "accuser of our brethren" (12:10).

Janet recorded all of the names she found, then sat back in her chair to reflect on the meanings of the various names ascribed to the devil. Although she had seen most of these names before, she had never grouped them all together at the same time. She was amazed at the length of the list and the evil implications associated with each of the names.

Janet realized she was growing tired and decided to quit for the day. Gathering her notes and books, she headed for home. Tomorrow was a class day, and she had other homework to complete. She knew it would be hard to concentrate on her other work because of her intense interest in her research. She looked forward to giving an update on her research and possibly learning more about Dr. Johnston's prior involvement with the spirit world.

The trip to campus the next morning was a wet one. Thunderstorms had moved in during the night, and the rain and wind were intense. As Janet hurried from the student parking lot, it was all she could do to hold onto her books and umbrella. She stepped inside the building and finally relaxed. Closing her umbrella and looking up, she found Melanie standing right in front of her. The two had not said much to each other since the retreat.

Melanie initiated the conversation. "I hear that you're doing your research on demons."

"Well, that's not quite accurate," Janet responded hesitantly. She wasn't sure if Melanie was trying to make fun of her or was just interested in the topic. "I'm researching the entire angelic world. I want to know if angels, the devil and demons are the result of superstition or are objective realities."

The Doctrine of Demons

1. *Their Origin*

2. *Their Purpose*

3. *Their Number*

4. *Their Nature (Character)*

5. *Their Relation to Christ*

6. *Their Abilities (Works) Related to Unsaved People*

7. *Their Abilities Related to Believers*

8. *Their Destiny*

(a letter to a young demon from his uncle Screwtape)

Dear Wormwood,

You will say these are very small sins; and doubtless, like all young tempters, you are anxious to be able to report spectacular wickedness. But do remember, the only thing that matters is the extent to which you separate the man from the Enemy [God].

— C. S. Lewis
Screwtape Letters

"Is this because of what happened at the retreat?" Melanie asked. "I certainly wasn't trying to scare you or make fun of you. I didn't realize that you were going to take all that witchcraft stuff so seriously."

Janet sensed the sincerity in Melanie's words. "What happened that night really didn't scare me, but it did make me think. When I had the opportunity to research the topic for my humanities class, I took advantage of it. Would you like to know what I've learned so far?"

Since the first class wouldn't start for another 30 minutes, the two girls headed for the atrium, where they could sit and talk without being disturbed. Janet picked up the notebook containing her research notes.

After reviewing Janet's notes, Melanie was clearly impressed. But what piqued her interest most was Janet's conversation with Dr. Johnston.

"Do you really think Dr. Johnson was involved with spirits when she was younger?" Melanie asked. But before Janet could respond, someone else joined the conversation.

"Did I hear my name mentioned?" the newcomer asked with a smile. It was Dr. Johnston. Both girls sat silently as the veteran teacher walked toward them.

"Good morning Janet . . . Melanie. I was on my way to the resource center when I saw you sitting here. I'm sure I heard my name mentioned. Is there a problem?"

Janet explained to Dr. Johnston that they had come to the atrium to discuss her research. Of course, Dr. Johnston's name had come up because of the help she had provided.

Although Dr. Johnston was satisfied with Janet's response, she noticed a confused expression on Melanie's face. "What's the matter?" she asked.

Melanie was not known for her diplomacy. Before even thinking about how it would sound, she blurted out her question. "Did you ever practice witchcraft?"

If the question shocked Dr. Johnston, she didn't show it. But Janet felt like she wanted to crawl into a hole and hide for the rest of the day. As always, Dr. Johnston responded in a calm manner. "I guess my past is starting to get around," Dr. Johnston replied with a more serious look on her face.

Before Dr. Johnston could say anything else, Janet had to say something. "Please don't be upset. I really . . . ."

Dr. Johnston raised her hand, indicating that Janet did not need to explain further. "If I had been afraid to let anyone know about my past, I wouldn't have said anything to you in the first place. But it's probably time that I explain what happened in my life many years ago. Why don't you both come to my office after class today and we'll talk about it."

Both girls breathed a sigh of relief and immediately promised to meet with her. Still sensing the awkwardness of the situation, they picked up their books and started to leave. Both wondered what Dr. Johnston would reveal next.

QuestNote 29.1
The Doctrine of Satan

Summarize the truths you have discussed.

His existence: _____

_____

_____

His ultimate desire: _____

_____

_____

His origin: _____

_____

_____

His nature: _____

_____

_____

His abilities: _____

_____

_____

QuestNote 29.1
The Doctrine of Satan

His relation to God's people: _____

_____

_____

_____

His relation to demons: _____

_____

_____

_____

His relation to Christ: _____

_____

_____

_____

His destiny: _____

_____

_____

_____

QuestNote 29.2
The Doctrine of Demons

List some truths discussed in class regarding demons.

1.	*4.*
2.	*5.*
3.	*6.*

Standing for God

Neither Janet nor Melanie had been able to keep their minds focused on classwork. All they could think about was their upcoming meeting with Dr. Johnston. They couldn't begin to imagine the story that she would tell.

After their final class, the girls met at Melanie's car to drop off their backpacks. It was time for the meeting in Dr. Johnston's office. Needless to say, both girls were a little anxious.

"Are you ready for this?" Melanie asked as she closed her car door. "She is actually going to tell us that she practiced witchcraft."

"Stop it!" Janet insisted with a stern look. "Don't say things like that about Dr. Johnston. She has been at this college for years, and everyone knows she is a good person and a great teacher. Whatever happened in the past, is in the past. I'm sure there's a reason that she is willing to tell us about it now."

"Okay, just calm down," Melanie responded defensively.

As expected, Dr. Johnston was waiting for the two girls. They entered her office, and Janet noticed the stack of books on the corner of her desk. She also saw a variety of notebooks, papers and even a photo album.

"You are very observant," Dr. Johnston said as she watched Janet study the various items. "Yes, these will all play a part in our meeting today. I thought we would have a little Show and Tell. Let's get started."

Both of the girls quickly took a seat in front of the desk, and Dr. Johnston sat on the corner of it. Her first question to each of the girls was not at all what they expected to hear.

"What is the most serious mistake you've ever made in your life?"

At first the girls didn't know what to say, but Dr. Johnston obviously expected a response. After a few minutes of reflection, each girl admitted to a major mistake.

"The mistakes you both made don't hold a candle to the biggest mistake I ever made. During my freshman year in college, I attended a party where I met several very friendly people who were deeply involved in the occult. I decided to listen to what they had to say. By the time the party ended, I was hooked and wanted to know more. That was the beginning of a six-year journey that almost cost my life."

Dr. Johnston explained that the occult is generally associated with secret knowledge and practices dealing with the supernatural, or psychic phenomena, often for the purpose of obtaining personal power. Occultic prac- tices rely on demons, or evil spirits, to achieve their goals. She also noted that belief in the occult is rapidly increasing throughout the world. Presently, there are thousands of occultic books and magazines.

After answering the girls' questions about the occult, Dr. Johnston proceeded to describe the aspect of the occult that had intrigued her the most—channeling. She explained that channeling is a divination method that has been practiced throughout history. A channeler is someone who becomes a receptive agent for communications from the spirit world. Through a mildly altered state of consciousness, the channeler is able to psychically perceive spirit messages. At this point, Dr. Johnston picked up several books on her desk that were devoted solely to channeling.

"These were the books that I studied during those years," Dr. Johnston explained. "I don't remember how many hours I spent reading and studying these and many other books about the occult and channeling."

"So then what happened?" Melanie asked.

"Slow down," Dr. Johnston cautioned. "Before I tell you what happened next in my life, I want to make sure you understand something about the occult and channeling."

Replacing the two books, Dr. Johnston picked up her Bible. She reminded the students that channeling is a modern name for what the Bible refers to as mediums or spiritism. Seeking guidance from mediums or spirits was common among the many nations encountered by God's people. In fact, God warned the children of Israel about it just before they entered the Promised Land. The students listened as she read Deuteronomy 18:9–12.

Dr. Johnston explained that God knew mankind's curiosity and desire to know the future would cause them to seek knowledge from the spirit world. This practice was so dangerous that God forbade His people to use mediums or contact spirits. This time Dr. Johnston read from Leviticus 19:31.

"Give no regard to mediums and familiar spirits; do not seek after them, to be defiled by them: I am the Lord your God."

Reaching across the desk, Dr. Johnston picked up one of the notebooks. Thumbing through the pages, she obviously knew exactly what she was looking for. Janet realized that the notebook was actually a journal.

When you come into the land which the Lord your God is giving you, you shall not learn to follow the abominations of those nations. There shall not be found among you anyone who makes his son or his daughter pass through the fire, or one who practices witchcraft, or a soothsayer, or one who interprets omens, or a sorcerer, or one who conjures spells, or a medium, or a spiritist, or one who calls up the dead. For all who do these things are an abomination to the Lord, and because of these abominations the Lord your God drives them out from before you.

Deuteronomy 18:9–12

Satan Is . . .

- *prince of the power of the air (Ephesians 2:2; Luke 11:14–18)*

- *ruler of this world (John 12:31; 14:30; 16:11)*

- *the god of this age (2 Corinthians 4:4)*

- *very powerful (Ephesians 6:11–12; 2 Thessalonians 2:9–10)*

- *father of the unsaved (John 8:44; Acts 13:10; 26:18; 1 John 3:10; 5:19)*

- *extremely wicked (1 John 5:19; Matthew 5:37; 13:19; John 8:44; 13:2, 27; 1 John 2:13; 3:8)*

"Did you keep a record of what you were doing?" Janet asked.

"Of course," Dr. Johnston answered. "I made these entries over the six-year period that I was involved with the occult. Are you sure you want to hear this?"

Although Melanie was far more enthusiastic about what they were about to hear, Janet agreed as well.

Dr. Johnston sat in a chair between the two girls. "I want to read four excerpts from my journal. The first two entries were written during my first year with the occult. The last two entries were written during the sixth year of my journey. Just listen while I read all four entries."

Pointing to each of the entries, Dr. Johnston let the girls track along with her as she read each entry aloud.

"Although I don't understand everything I'm reading, I feel compelled to know more. The information and knowledge contained in these books have almost a hypnotic effect on my mind."

"This has been the greatest day of my life! I truly believe that I was in contact with some type of spirit being. I'm not sure yet what the information means. But I know that if I call on this spirit again, it will return and give me the guidance I seek."

The girls were shocked by what they were reading. Dr. Johnston actually believed that a spirit being had communicated with her. Both girls sat quietly as their professor turned to the final pages.

304

"I cannot escape them! Everywhere I turn I hear their voices. They've filled my mind with terrible, disgusting thoughts. I know now that these spirits are not my friends. But I can't get rid of them. Why won't they leave me alone?"

"The sun just came up, but I've been awake all night. I'm determined to enjoy this sunrise, because it will be my last."

Dr. Johnston closed her journal and looked at the two girls. "Do you understand what was happening?" she asked. "The only way I knew to rid myself of those controlling evil spirits was to take my own life."

Once again Dr. Johnston turned to her Bible to show the students the seriousness of seeking power and guidance from the spirit world. She first turned to 1 Samuel 28, where she read the story of King Saul seeking counsel from a medium called the Witch of Endor. King Saul's quest for knowledge ended in tragedy. Shortly after his visit to the witch, the king took his own life after he was wounded in battle.

Then Dr. Johnston showed the girls what was written about Saul in 1 Chronicles 10:13. "So Saul died for his unfaithfulness which he had committed against the Lord, because he did not keep the word of the Lord, and also because he consulted a medium for guidance."

After pointing out examples of other encounters with wicked spirits in the Bible, Dr. Johnston reminded the girls that the wicked spirits had once been part of God's angelic host. But when Satan rebelled against God, a portion of the angels joined him. Of these, some are reserved in chains until judgment (1 Corinthians 6:3; 2 Peter 2:4; Jude 6). Others, however, are allowed to remain free.

The Armor for Spiritual Warfare

- belt of truth

- breastplate of righteousness

- boots of the gospel of peace

- shield of faith

- helmet of salvation

- sword of the Word of God

Ephesians 6:14–17

The Believer's
Response to Satan and
His Demons

1. Be alert and watch-
ful. (1 Peter 5:8)

2. Don't give Satan
any room to work.
(Ephesians 4:27; 2
Corinthians 10:3-5)

3. Test and avoid evil
spirits. (1 John 4:1;
1 Thessalonians 5:22;
Deuteronomy 18:10-
11)

4. Resist Satan.
(James 4:7)

5. Stand. Don't give
in. Hold your ground.
(Ephesians 6:11, 14;
1 Peter 5:9)

6. Recognize the power
of God to keep you.
(1 John 5:18;
Colossians 1:13)

These are the ones referred to throughout the Bible as demons or devils (Mark 5:9, 15; Luke 8:30; 1 Timothy 4:1). They are Satan's servants and they will share his fate (Matthew 25:41; Revelation 20:10).

For the last fifteen minutes neither of the girls had said a word as Dr. Johnston discussed what the Bible taught about angels. Janet was the first to ask a question. "Why are you telling us all of this?"

"I don't want to see you girls start down the path that nearly cost me my life," she replied. "When I went to that party years ago, the furthest thing from my mind was get-ting involved with the occult. At first, it sounds so fascinating and mysterious. Then you find yourself want-ing to learn more and more. Before you know it, you are no longer able to control what's happening. That's why the Bible commands us to stay away from the occult."

It was Melanie's turn to ask a question. "Why are people so interested in the spirit world?"

"Everyone's different," Dr. Johnston began. "Some people are just curious. But I think that most people who turn to the spirit world are searching for a more meaning-ful life or for deeper spiritually. They are certainly not looking for an encounter with evil spirits."

"Dr. Johnston," Janet began, "what happened after you wrote that last entry in your journal?"

"I've been waiting for one of you to ask me that ques-tion," she replied. "Jesus Christ delivered me from being ensnared in the occult. Let me tell you what happened just a few hours after I wrote that last entry."

Slowly Dr. Johnston pulled out another journal and opened it to the first page.

QuestNote 30.1
The Believer's Response to Satan and His Demons

Summarize the principles you discussed in class.

1.	**4.**
2.	**5.**
3.	**6.**

QuestNote 30.2
Summary of the Doctrine of Spirit Beings

Angels (their existence, origin, kinds, purpose, ministry in Christ's life, ministry in a believer's life, eternal ministry) _____

_____

_____

_____

Satan (his origin, purpose, character [nature], how he works against God, how he works against believers, his final destiny)

_____

_____

_____

Demons (their origin, purpose, character, abilities, submission to Christ, harm to people, final doom) _____

_____

_____

The Believer's response to Satan and his demons _____

_____

_____

_____

Christ Is Coming Again

After the four college freshmen finished their coffee, the fortune teller emptied one of the cups then overturned it. A few minutes later, various shapes of coffee granules had dried on its sides, and the fortune teller began her predictions.

"A blind woman will visit you soon, and she will bring sadness and death to one of your relatives," the old woman said to Mark. "Your family will soon be grieving, but I can also see a bird, which means good news will follow."

Mark looked at his friends around the table. They were as surprised as he was to hear what the fortune teller had to say. Although he didn't believe a word of it, he acted as if everything she had just said would certainly come true.

Ashley held out her cup, motioning that she wanted to be next. The old woman took the cup and repeated the process. After a few minutes, the fortune teller made this prediction: "You have pain in your eye and in your leg, and you are now looking for a husband. Your eye and leg will soon get better. But you will have to be patient until you meet your husband."

It was all Ashley could do to keep a straight face. Jeff was next. Unlike Mark and Ashley, he took fortune telling a little more seriously. When he heard the fortune teller say that he might need to change his major, he nearly panicked.

Julie was the last of the foursome to have her fortune read. She was the one who had insisted that the others give up part of their Saturday afternoon to visit this fortune teller—not because she had any confidence in fortune tellers. On the contrary, she had no faith in them at all.

> "Let not your heart be troubled; you believe in God, believe also in Me. In My Father's house are many mansions; if it were not so, I would have told you. I go to prepare a place for you. And if I go and prepare a place for you, I will come again and receive you to Myself; that where I am, there you may be also. And where I go you know, and the way you know."
>
> John 14:1–4

It was all about Jeff. The two had been dating for almost a year, and they were starting to talk about marriage. He was a great guy in every way except one. He had an obsession about wanting to know the future. Jeff would do almost anything to gain insight about his future.

Although Jeff had never been to a fortune teller, Julie thought that this little "field trip" might just convince him once and for all that fortune tellers and other means of prognostication are nothing more than hoaxes. Like the others, the fortune teller had a prediction for Julie as well. She listened patiently but gave no other indication of approval or disapproval. All the time, she was keeping an eye on her boyfriend. It was his reaction that interested her the most.

Soon the group was back outside, discussing all they had heard and seen. Mark and Ashley were doing most of the talking—and laughing. They obviously didn't believe a word they had just heard. However, Jeff was uncharacteristically quiet. Julie wondered what he was thinking.

"Ashley and I have to get going," Mark explained after they walked back to the parking lot. "We promised that we would join her parents for dinner tonight. If we don't hit the road, we'll be late."

"You guys have a good time," Julie said. "Thanks for coming with us today. We'll talk more about it next week."

Jeff and Julie headed to his car for the short trip back to campus. Now that they were alone, Julie could learn his reaction to the fortune teller. "So, what did you think?" she asked, not quite knowing how to open the conversation. "Does she have the power to see into the future?"

"I don't know what I think anymore," Jeff began. "Her predictions about Mark and Ashley were kind of stupid. I could tell that they weren't impressed. But she might be right about my major. You know that I'm still not sure what I want to do when I get out of college. I would give anything to know what the future holds for me and you."

Julie was noticeably frustrated with her boyfriend. Rather than helping him see the silliness of trying to predict the future, the visit to the fortune teller had only confused him more. She couldn't understand why he was so obsessed with knowing the future. Her emotions finally got the best of her.

"What is your problem, Jeff?" she asked, unable to conceal her irritation. "What is so important about the future? Why can't you just be happy with what's going on in your life right now?"

Jeff was taken off guard by her reaction. He hadn't realized that his concern about the future was a problem, but maybe it was. Her question was a good one. Why was it so important for him to know the future?

"I think we need some time apart," he replied slowly. "I need to do some serious research on my own. I don't know why I'm obsessing about the future, but I know I am. I've got to find some answers."

Julie hadn't expected the afternoon to end this way. But some time apart might be a good idea. Their relationship was obviously at a standstill until Jeff could resolve this issue in his life. Julie expressed her love for Jeff and encouraged him to take all the time he needed. She didn't know what else to say or do.

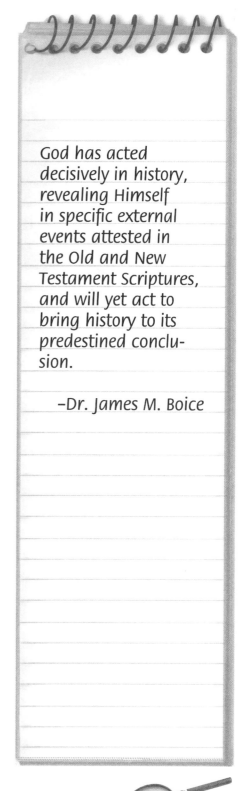

God has acted decisively in history, revealing Himself in specific external events attested in the Old and New Testament Scriptures, and will yet act to bring history to its predestined conclusion.

–Dr. James M. Boice

Maranatha!

The Lord Returns!

Almost two weeks later, Jeff was still struggling to find the right direction for his research. He had analyzed the claims of astrology, studied writings by such people as Nostradamus, Edgar Cayce and Jeanne Dixon, and even visited other fortune tellers to compare their predictions about his future. But he still did not have answers to the two questions that bothered him most: *Why am I so concerned about the future?* and *What is going to happen to me in the future?*

Although they saw little of each other during the two weeks, Julie asked Jeff to attend a celebration party hosted by her parents at a local restaurant. Her uncle had just been selected as dean of the seminary where he had been teaching for the last 20 years.

Even though Julie did not know her uncle very well and didn't consider herself really religious, this was an important occasion for her family. She wanted Jeff to be with her to celebrate this special time. Jeff eagerly accepted the invitation—not only as a diversion from his frustrating research, but also because he welcomed the opportunity to spend time with Julie.

The evening could not have gone better. The food was great and the young couple had the opportunity to talk about the difficult time they'd had during the past few weeks. Jeff even admitted that it was time to set aside his obsession about knowing the future so they could get on with their relationship. From Julie's perspective, it looked as if things were returning to normal. That is, until her father decided he wanted Uncle Rob—actually the eminent Dr. Robert Parker—to say a few words to the guests.

Julie's uncle, a tall and stately man, rose slowly from his place at the table. Strangely, though he often spoke to large groups of people, he was a little uncomfortable, not knowing exactly what to say on this occasion. However, he never turned down the opportunity to testify to the goodness of God in his life.

"As you all know," he began, "I'm a bit of a history buff. So I hope you don't mind if I tell a little story that I believe will help me express how I feel tonight.

In 1974 Malcolm Muggeridge, one of Britain's most interesting and controversial journalists, spoke to over 4000 delegates at the International Congress on World Evangelization in Lusanne, Switzerland. During his address, he traced his experiences in public life for over half a century, beginning with World War I. He was convinced that the war, and the subsequent establishment of the League of Nations, would ensure peace in the world. In every column and article he wrote, he would praise the war effort and the formation of the League of Nations. But when World War II broke out, his dreams of world peace vanished.

Mr. Muggeridge then decided to devote all of his efforts to supporting Britain's Labor Party. He had been brought up to believe that the welfare state policies of the Labor Party would bring Jesus' kingdom to earth. When the Labor Party finally took control of England's government, to Muggeridge's surprise Jesus' kingdom failed to appear.

Disillusioned, Muggeridge turned his hopes for a better world toward the Soviet Union. He moved to Moscow to serve as a correspondent so that he could watch, firsthand, the formation of a new society. But it took only a few years for him to realize

End Times

- Normal life to continue—eating, drinking, marrying

- Increase of natural disasters, incurable diseases, unusual weather and catastrophes

- Mankind practicing extreme evil

- Mankind rejecting truths of God for human thinking

- Rejection of God leading to increased persecution of Christians

Jesus
Matthew 24

Timeline of Future Events

Christ's First Coming
  Crucifixion
  Resurrection
  Ascension

Church Age

Christ's Second Coming

Judgment

Time on Earth Ends

Eternity:
  Heaven
  or Hell

that the Soviet regime was rapidly turning into one of the most absolutist tyrannies of history. Finally, Muggeridge realized that mankind is incapable of shaping his own destiny.

Although Jeff was not familiar with the details of England's history, he was curious as to where Julie's uncle was going with his story. In just a matter of moments, he would find out.

Now that his audience had been introduced to Malcolm Muggeridge, Julie's uncle explained the connection between their two lives.

Who would think of blaming Muggeridge for his pursuit of history's meaning? Throughout his life he sought to understand his future and the future of the human race. It was late in his life when he finally realized that mankind is incapable of shaping his own destiny. When Muggeridge became a Christian, he realized the true meaning of life and how the future would unfold.

Uncle Rob had Jeff's full attention as he continued.

Like Mr. Muggeridge, I spent many years searching for the meaning to life. Although I came to know Jesus Christ as my Savior at an early age, it took lots of years for me to understand that history is simply the unfolding plan of God. In Him it's possible to understand mankind's past, present and future. Since then I have devoted my life to helping others find the answers they seek. Remember, the same God who created and sustains all things also directs the affairs of individuals and nations. He is more than an idle spectator of the human drama; He guides human events according to His purpose and plan.

Jeff was amazed at what he heard. It was as if Julie's uncle was talking directly to him. Here was someone else who shared his passion to understand the future.

"Julie," Jeff whispered as he leaned toward her, "do you think your uncle would mind if I asked him a couple of questions?"

"Not at all," she responded. "I'll go see if he can meet with you after the party's over."

While other guests were leaving, Julie approached her uncle. "Uncle Rob, my boyfriend would like to talk with you. Do you have a few minutes to meet with him?"

"Of course, Julie," he answered. "Jeff seems like such a nice fellow. I would like the opportunity to know him better. Any idea what's on his mind?"

Julie hesitated at first, but then decided to tell her uncle about Jeff's obsession with knowing the future. "I'm not quite sure what he'll ask you," she concluded, "but you must have said something that got his attention."

After listening to Julie's explanation, Uncle Rob was even more interested in talking with Jeff. "Remember what I said earlier? God is more than an idle spectator of the human drama—He guides human events according to His purpose and plan. There is no doubt in my mind that God has brought the three of us together this evening. Let's meet on the veranda in about 30 minutes."

With her mission accomplished, Julie returned to their table to tell Jeff the news.

QuestNote 31.1
Christ Will Return!

Summarize five truths for each of the four topics studied this week.

1. **The fact that Christ will return**

2. **The Day of the Lord**

QuestNote 31.1
Christ Will Return!

3. **End Times**

4. **The place of Israel in God's plans**

Personal QuestNotes

The Coming Tribulation

The meeting on the veranda of the restaurant lasted for over an hour. Jeff was impressed with Dr. Parker's ability to calmly and confidently answer his questions. It seemed as if Julie's uncle knew exactly what was on his mind.

"Would you two like to come by the seminary sometime next week?" Dr. Parker asked. "I would be happy to discuss your questions in more detail then."

Jeff responded immediately, "I would love that, sir."

They compared calendars and agreed to meet the following Thursday. As Julie and Jeff drove back to campus, she could sense Jeff's excitement about meeting with her uncle.

Thursday rolled around quickly, and Jeff and Julie appeared at her Uncle Rob's office right on schedule. This was the first time that either of them had been on the seminary campus.

"Welcome," Dr. Parker said with a warm smile. It was obvious that he was expecting them. Light refreshments were on a small table near some very comfortable looking chairs. Dr. Parker motioned them toward the chairs. "Choose a seat and feel free to have something to eat and drink."

After a few minutes of pleasantries, Julie thanked her uncle for meeting with them. "I know you're busy, Uncle Rob, and we appreciate your making time for us to visit. Jeff's questions about the future are very important to him." Julie paused for a moment, and then continued, "Knowing what's going to happen in the future is important to me too."

> For the Lord Himself will descend with the voice of an archangel, and with the trumpet of God. And the dead in Christ will rise first. Then we who are alive and remain shall be caught up together with them in the clouds to meet the Lord in the air. And thus we shall always be with the Lord. Therefore comfort one another with these words.
>
> 1 Thessalonians 4:16-18

Jeff opened his notebook and pulled a small recorder from his pocket. "Do you mind if I record our conversation?" he asked.

"Not at all," Dr. Parker replied. "Nowadays, over half the students in my classes record my lectures. I guess it's their way of making sure they don't miss any information that I might include on their exam."

Both Julie and Jeff smiled at his observation. He understood college students all too well.

Jeff turned on his recorder and Dr. Parker began his private tutorial session. "Does God have a plan that includes the earth and the human race? If so, can people know it? The answer to both questions is an emphatic YES! God does have a plan, and that plan is clearly outlined in His Word, the Bible.

"Mankind can know God's plan clearly if he seeks to understand the Bible and allows God's Holy Spirit to teach him. Unfortunately, in today's society many deliberately refuse to consult Scripture about the future. People are willing to consult astrology, taro cards, tea leaves, the psychic channel and even fortune tellers in an attempt to learn about the future. Yet, all the while, God's divine plan is plainly set forth in the Bible."

Dr. Parker caught Jeff's attention when he mentioned fortune tellers. He had already quit taking notes, trusting his recorder to do the work for him.

Turning to Isaiah in his Bible, Dr. Parker read the following words:

"Remember the former things of old, for I am God, and there is no other; I am God, and there is none

like Me, declaring the end from the beginning, and from ancient times things that are not yet done, saying, My counsel shall stand, and I will do all My pleasure, calling a bird of prey from the east, the man who executes My counsel, from a far country. Indeed I have spoken it; I will also bring it to pass. I have purposed it; I will also do it.

"Listen to Me, you stubborn-hearted, who are far from righteousness: I bring My righteousness near, it shall not be far off; My salvation shall not linger. And I will place salvation in Zion, for Israel my Glory." (Isaiah 46:9–13)

"Do you understand what God is saying here?" Julie's uncle asked. "Nowhere in the writings of mortal man can anything like it be found. The claims are supernatural, applying to none other than God Himself. In this passage God declares Himself to be self-existent, eternal, sovereign and uncreated. He alone 'declares the end from the beginning.'"

Settling into his teacher mode, Dr. Parker continued. "And where has He made this declaration? He has revealed the end from the beginning in the Bible. Holy men of God, guided by the Holy Spirit, wrote of great world events centuries before they were to occur. Since it is mankind's nature to want to know the future, God chose to reveal certain aspects of it."

Jeff started to raise his hand, but quickly realized that he was not in class. However, he did have a question. "Are you saying that the reason God wrote the Bible was to tell us about the future?"

"Well, that's partially true," Dr. Parker replied. "The Bible reveals God's Plan—past, present and future. Prophecy constitutes a large part of the Scriptures. If

Christ Calls Up His Church

1. The Lord will descend from Heaven.

2. A shout sounds with the voice of the archangel.

3. The trumpet of God sounds.

4. The resurrected bodies of all dead believers will rise first.

5. Christians who are alive on earth will be caught up into the clouds with those being brought up from graves, all given immortal bodies.

6. All believers will thus meet the Lord in the air and forever be with Him.

Events of the Tribulation

1. John observes the throne room of God.

2. John witnesses the opening of the scroll in Heaven.

3. Six Seal Judgments are unleashed.

4. The Antichrist rises to world power.

5. The Antichrist is joined by false religions and the false prophet.

6. The Antichrist establishes a peace agreement with Israel.

7. Jews will return in mass to Israel.

8. 144,000 Jewish evangelists will convert to Christ and carry His message to the world.

the prophecies in the Bible were not being fulfilled, the remainder of the Book would be meaningless.

"The first prophecy was given right after the fall of man. It was the promise of a Redeemer (Genesis 3:15). This first prediction is the pivotal prophecy of the entire Word of God. If you go all the way through the Bible, you will discover that Jesus Christ is the grand theme of the Scriptures. Listen to the words of Jesus in John 5:46: 'For if you believed Moses, you would believe Me; for he wrote about Me.'"

Dr. Parker handed Bibles to both Julie and Jeff and invited them to read the verses as he explained how Jesus Christ was the unifying point of all prophecy.

- To Adam and Eve, Jesus Christ was the Seed who would crush the serpent's head (Genesis 3:15).

- To Abraham, God said that in Christ all the nations of the earth would be blessed (Genesis 22:18; Galatians 3:14–16).

- To Israel, the Passover lamb foreshadowed the Lamb of God who takes away the sin of the world (Exodus 12; John 1:29; 1 Corinthians 5:7).

- To Israel in the wilderness, the serpent of brass lifted up on a pole (Numbers 21: 8–9) looked forward to the time when Christ would be lifted up on the cross (John 3:14).

- To Philip, Jesus Christ was the One promised by the Law and the prophets (John 1:45).

The new dean of the seminary then reminded the young couple that the closing words of the Bible declare that "the testimony of Jesus is the spirit of prophecy" (Revelation 19:10). Jesus is the key to prophecy. The person and work of Jesus Christ unify the prophetic Scriptures. Bible prophecies, Bible analogies and Bible types are so closely related to Jesus Christ that He alone explains them.

Once again, Jeff had something he wanted to say. "Dr. Parker, when I started my research to try to better understand the future, I noticed that a lot of sources either ignored what the Bible has to say or dismissed the Bible's teachings as myth. Why is that?"

It was obvious that Dr. Parker had been asked that question before. "Many people refuse to accept prophetic Scriptures because the prophecies of the Bible shatter the illusion that mankind's own efforts—his religion, science, psychology, philosophy or government—can produce universal peace. Do you remember the story about Malcolm Muggeridge that I told at the restaurant the other night? He is a perfect example of why individuals resist the teachings of the Bible. He was convinced that mankind, through his own accomplishments, could establish a peaceful world."

Turning to Mark 8, he paused then spoke again, "The Scriptures teach, however, that the very things in which mankind is placing his hope must be abandoned. The human heart is by nature proud and will not readily admit that its confidence is misplaced. Even professing Christians have made idols of church organizations, a denomination, or personal achievements only to be faced with the reality that they are inadequate to bring peace or answer the real questions of life.

"For centuries, men and women in all walks of life have asked, 'Where are we going? What's next? When

9. Two powerful witnesses will appear.

10. The Temple in Jerusalem will be rebuilt.

11. Armies to the north and south will invade Israel but be defeated by God.

12. The Antichrist becomes more powerful, is wounded, but arises from the dead. He is declared "god" and his statue must be worshiped. Those who refuse his mark are persecuted and killed.

13. A ferocious campaign is launched to annihilate the Jews, but God preserves a remnant. The 144,000 evangelists and two witnesses are martyred.

14. God continues to pour out the trumpet and bowl judgments that include great destruction—earthquakes, death, diseases, hail, etc.

15. Both the false religious system and the economic systems of Babylon are destroyed.

16. The armies of the Antichrist assemble to fight against God in the Battle of Armageddon. They are defeated by Christ and His angelic army.

17. Antichrist and false prophet are cast into the lake of fire.

will the end come?' Thousands of authors, scientists and philosophers have tried to address man's uncertainty and concern about the future. But it is only through the prophetic Scriptures that God provides a light on the pathway of our tomorrows. Listen to the words of 2 Peter 1:19: 'And so we have the prophetic word confirmed, which you do well to heed as a light that shines in a dark place, until the day dawns and the morning star rises in your hearts.'

"The Apostle had just related what he had seen and heard while on the Mount of Transfiguration (verses 16–18). There he saw a vision and heard a voice from Heaven testifying to the glory of the Lord Jesus Christ. Yet Peter says that the prophetic Word is even a surer confirmation of God's plans than what he had experienced on the Mount. For Peter, the certainty of the prophecies were more reliable than what he had personally seen and heard."

It was Julie's turn to interrupt this time. "So you're saying that the future can be known, but only as it is revealed in the Bible. How do we know that the Bible's explanation of the future is the true version?"

Dr. Parker couldn't help but smile at her question. "You're asking me to explain in a few minutes what our seminarians spend years learning. I suggest that you look at the hundreds of Bible prophecies that have already come true exactly as the writers of the Bible predicted. Can you point to any other book that can make such a claim?"

Julie had no response. She was determined to take a closer look at some Bible prophecies. However, what he said next really caught the young couple's attention.

"Generally three different attitudes toward the future can exist," he began. "The first is indifference, the second is fear and the third is hope. I don't think any intelligent person wants to be indifferent about what the future holds. And it is my firm conviction that no one needs to fear the future. According to the Bible, there is comfort and hope for all who believe. Paul makes this point in Romans 15:4 when he writes, 'For whatever things were written before were written for our learning, that we through the patience and comfort of the Scriptures might have hope.'"

Dr. Parker looked directly at Jeff as he continued. "One of the greatest fears facing mankind is his fear of the future. Many people cannot be happy unless they have some idea of what the next day may bring. This uncertainty robs many people of happiness and joy in life. They hesitate to make plans or pursue goals. The Bible word 'lost' aptly describes their inability to set direction and to get on with life.

"In contrast, those who have accepted Christ as Savior, and who understand that He sovereignly holds the future, are able to face each tomorrow with confidence and comfort. That is the first and most important step. Once we receive Him as personal Savior, we are ready to understand what the future holds."

Over the next 45 minutes, Julie and Jeff realized that though they saw themselves as religious, they had never committed themselves to Jesus Christ. Before the afternoon was over, Dr. Parker had the privilege of leading them to the Lord.

As the young couple, hand in hand, left Dr. Parker's office, they promised to meet with him again the following week. During this next meeting, Julie's uncle would explain what the Bible has to say about the end of history.

Charles G. Finney

"Finney, what are you going to do when you finish law school?"
"Put out a shingle and practice law."
"Then what?"
"Get rich."
"Then what?"
"Retire."
"Then what?"
"Die."
"Then what?"
And the words came trembling, "The judgment."
He ran for the woods a half mile away. All day he prayed, and vowed that he would never leave until he had made his peace with God.
Finney came out of the woods that evening, after a long struggle, with the high purpose of living henceforth to the glory of God and of enjoying Him forever.

QuestNote 32.1
The Rapture

Summarize the future event known as the Rapture of the Church.

1. Briefly describe the six events related to Christ calling up the members of His Church.

2. Why can we not know exactly when this event will take place?

3. Why should the study of these events give comfort to believers?

QuestNote 32.2
The Tribulation

Answer key questions about the period of time known as the Tribulation.

1. In general, what is meant by the term "the Tribulation"? _____

_____

_____

2. What would you say to counter the claim that these events will never happen as described—that they were just John's dream? _____

_____

_____

_____

3. List and describe ten events that will occur during this seven-year period.

1) _____

_____

2) _____

_____

3) _____

_____

4) _____

_____

5) _____

_____

6) _____

_____

7) _____

_____

8) _____

_____

9) _____

_____

10) _____

_____

4. Should a Christian fear these events? Why or why not? _____

_____

The Coming King

Another week had passed, and Jeff and Julie were on their way back to Dr. Parker's office. It had been a great week as the young couple reflected on their new faith in Christ and found opportunity to share with many of their friends what had happened. In preparation for their meeting with Julie's uncle, they both read the book of Revelation. It was this book, they were told, in which God revealed His plan for the future.

As they approached the seminary, they realized that they were quite early for their meeting. "Why don't we stop and get something to drink?" Julie suggested, looking at her watch. "We don't want to show up too early—my uncle might have another appointment. I wouldn't want to rush him."

"Good idea," Jeff agreed. "I know a good restaurant that's close to the campus."

At the restaurant, they chose a booth by the window to enjoy the bright, sunny day. Both decided on a soft drink, and Jeff ordered a piece of chocolate pie. Julie was well aware of her boyfriend's weakness for chocolate. When the waitress reappeared with their order, Jeff wasted no time taking his first bite.

"Did you hear what my uncle said as we were leaving his office last week?" Julie asked.

It seemed that Julie always asked Jeff a question when his mouth was full of food. He didn't know whether to swallow it quickly or to just take his time and enjoy the flavor. Fortunately, Julie didn't bother waiting for an answer.

Believers —
Here, there or in the air—they're with the Lord forever!

Judgment Seat of Christ—
Judged for use of talents entrusted to them (not to determine salvation).

Marriage Supper of the Lamb —
Presented to Christ as His bride.

"He said that this week he would explain to us what the Bible has to say about the end of history. I've never thought about it that way. It's kind of scary to think about history coming to an end. Do you think that's what he really meant to say?"

By now Jeff was ready to join the conversation. "Knowing your uncle, he knew exactly what he was saying."

Soon they were back in Dr. Parker's office, seated in the same chairs as before. Both Julie and Jeff anxiously anticipated what her uncle would have to say. After asking for permission, Jeff once again took out his recorder.

Sitting back in his chair, Dr. Parker began by asking the same question they had discussed in the restaurant. "How will history end? While all Christians believe in the Second Coming of Jesus Christ, I would not say that all Christians agree as to the details of His coming. Didn't you mention a few minutes ago that you had both read the book of Revelation this past week?"

They nodded in agreement, and Dr. Parker continued. "The coming of Jesus Christ is the theme of Revelation. Originally known as the Apocalypse, meaning 'unveiling' or 'disclosure,' this book pulls the curtain back to reveal the end of history as we know it. While the book is written in highly symbolic language, its ultimate end is easily understood. Jesus Christ is the Lord of history. He is, according to the eighth verse of the first chapter, 'the Alpha and the Omega, the Beginning and the End . . . who is and who was and who is to come.'"

Julie spoke before her uncle went any further. "Both Jeff and I had a lot of trouble understanding the language in Revelation. Is the book really that difficult?"

"Yes, it is," he replied. "Revelation is perhaps the most difficult book in the Bible to understand. Throughout history Bible scholars have offered many different interpretations to try to explain its meaning. Some believe that the book is best understood from an allegorical perspective. Others have taken it more literally and tried to link it to actual historical events.

"It is important for anyone who reads the book to know that it is written in a style known as apocalyptic. Apocalyptic literature seeks to reveal divine mysteries that would otherwise remain hidden. However, in the communication of its message, the book often speaks in figurative rather than literal terms. It is sometimes difficult to know when one ends and another begins. Revelation is the only New Testament book of apocalyptic writing, although Jesus' teachings, such as Matthew 13 and 24, fit the category. There are many examples in the Old Testament, especially the books of Daniel, Ezekiel and Zechariah."

Jeff couldn't help but ask several questions. "If apocalyptic books are supposed to reveal divine mysteries, then why is Revelation so difficult to understand? Why did John use symbolism rather than plain, simple language?"

"There are at least two reasons," Dr. Parker explained. "Apocalyptic literature is often written during times of danger. As a result, the author may find it safer to hide his meaning in symbols and images that his readers will understand, but his enemies will not.

"We know that the book of Revelation was written during the reign of the Roman Emperor Domitian (81–96 A.D.). It was Domitian who demanded that the entire empire honor him as both Lord and God. According to Revelation 1:9, John had been exiled to the Isle of Patmos under Domitian. It may be that John was trying to con-

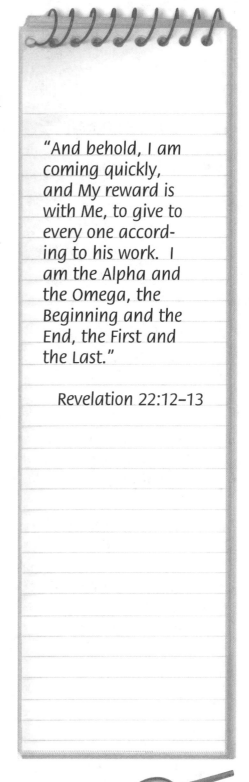

"And behold, I am coming quickly, and My reward is with Me, to give to every one according to his work. I am the Alpha and the Omega, the Beginning and the End, the First and the Last."

Revelation 22:12–13

Christ Comes!

- Armies gather in Israel under Antichrist

- Christ appears in the heavens with angelic hosts

- Touches earth on Mount of Olives

- Defeats armies

- Casts Antichrist and false prophet into lake of fire

- Casts Satan into pit for 1000 years

- Reigns on earth as Messiah

ceal the message of his book from Domitian. John was confident that believers would understand what he wrote.

"A second reason is related to the nature of what John was trying to communicate. Remember, John's task was to explain Heavenly realities in earthly terms. Words were not always adequate to describe what he saw. He used images and symbols familiar to the readers of his time in an effort to convey these Heavenly realities."

"Then how do we even begin to interpret the book?" Jeff asked.

"First of all," Dr. Parker responded, "we accept the book of Revelation as real. It is not a tale of fantasy or myth. John's vision was not a figment of his imagination. Jesus did appear to John just as he records in the opening verse of the book.

"Second, we must never lose sight of the overall focus of the book. History is coming to its fulfillment in Jesus Christ. It is Jesus who will triumph over Satan, his demons and death. It is Jesus who will usher in the new Heaven and new earth. And it is Jesus who will reign eternally. This is the ultimate message of the book of Revelation."

Both Jeff and Julie agreed that they now had a better understanding of the book. But they still had many questions. They didn't realize that their lack of general knowledge about the Bible made it even more difficult for them to understand Revelation. However, as they continued their discussion with Julie's uncle, they began to realize that God's plan for the end of history was not limited to the last book of the Bible. There are many places in the Bible where God talks about the end of history.

"I think we've covered just about all we have time for today," Dr. Parker said as he checked his watch. "I have a meeting with my faculty in an hour, and I need to prepare for it. Before we get together again, would you mind if I gave you another homework assignment?"

As college students, Jeff and Julie had plenty of homework to keep them busy. But they didn't see this as real homework. They were happy to complete whatever he assigned before their next meeting.

"Let me list, with some brief explanation, some of the key events that the Bible says will occur at the end of history," Dr. Parker began. "I would like for you to learn as much as possible about these events before we meet again.

"First, there is the event described in 1 Thessalonians 4:13–18 that is known as the Rapture of the Church. The Bible teaches that this is one of the end-time events.

"Next, I want you to learn all you can about the Tribulation. You might want to take a look at what is recorded in Revelation 3:10. Be sure that you give careful thought to the rationale for the Tribulation. In other words, why is God allowing the period of the Tribulation to take place?

"Then, explain what happens at the Second Coming of Christ, sometimes called the revelation of Christ. While you're at it, tell me when the first coming of Christ occurred. Also, how is the Rapture different from either the first or second coming of our Lord?

"I'm sure you've heard of the Battle of Armageddon. Read Revelation 20:7–10 and tell me what the Bible says about that battle.

Topics to Study

- Rapture of the Church

- Tribulation

- Battle of Armageddon

- Second Coming

- Millennial Reign

- Satan's Final Battle

- Great White Throne Judgment

- Hell

- Heaven

Ever since the first days of the Christian church, evangelicals have been "looking for that blessed hope, and the glorious appearing of the great God and Savior Jesus Christ." They may have disagreed as to its timing and to the events on the eschatological calendar. They may have differed as to a pre-tribulation or post-tribulation rapture—the pre- or post- or non-millennial coming. They may have been divided as to a literal rebirth of Israel. However, all are agreed that the final solution to the problems of this world is in the hands of the King of kings who will someday make the kingdoms of this world His very own.

– Arnold T. Olsen

"I suppose the next event you should study is the Millennium. Like the Tribulation, explain the rationale for the Millennium. Also explain how perspectives vary even among conscientious believers.

"Finally, learn all you can about Satan's final battle, the Great White Throne Judgment, and the new Heaven and new earth. These events mark the end of history as we know it."

The young couple thanked Dr. Parker for meeting with them and assured him that they would be well prepared for their next meeting. However, before they left, the seminary dean felt compelled to share a story he had read long ago.

"In one of his books," Dr. Parker began, "the New Testament scholar A. M. Hunter relates the story of a dying man who asked his Christian doctor to tell him something about the place where he was going. As the doctor struggled for an appropriate reply to the question, he heard a scratching at the door. Immediately, he knew how to answer the man.

"Do you hear that?" he asked his patient. "It's my dog. I left him downstairs, but he has grown impatient and has come up because he hears my voice. He has no notion what is inside this door, but he knows that I am here. Isn't it the same with you? You don't know what lies beyond the Door, but you know that your Master is there."

"While we may not always have answers to our questions about the future, as Christians we can always be confident about our future. Never forget the words of Hebrews 13:8, 'Jesus Christ is the same yesterday, today, and forever.'

"See you next week."

QuestNote 33.1
Christ Returns to the Earth

Describe the following details involved in Christ actually returning to earth.

1. When will it occur in relation to the Tribulation?

2. What occurs in relation to the armies of the world?

3. What occurs in relation to Christ the King?

4. What occurs in relation to the Mount of Olives?

5. What occurs in relation to the Battle of Armageddon?

6. What occurs in relation to the Antichrist, false prophet and Satan with his demons?

7. What occurs in relation to Christ being received as Messiah?

QuestNote 33.2
Believers' Death, Judgment and Celebration

Summarize the truths regarding the following three topics.

A believer's death and resurrection

The Judgment Seat of Christ

The Marriage Supper of the Lamb

QuestNote 33.3
The Millennial Reign of Christ

Complete brief descriptions for each section of the outline.

1. *Definition:* _____

_____

_____

2. *Different Views:* _____

_____

_____

_____

3. *Leadership:*

A. *Who?* _____

_____

B. *From where?* _____

_____

4. *Characteristics:* _____

_____

_____

_____

_____

QuestNote 33.3
The Millennial Reign of Christ

5. *Events at the End:*

Be Ready!

Over the course of several months, Julie and Jeff grew in their faith as a result of their meetings with Dr. Parker. He never failed to challenge their thinking and send them searching for Biblical answers to their questions. The subject of conversation this time would be the doctrine of hell.

Jeff had to admit that he had never really given a whole lot of thought to the subject of hell. Matter of fact, when the thought did cross his mind he would immediately try to think of something else. And yet, Dr. Parker had assigned this as their topic of discussion.

Once again, the couple arrived at her uncle's office a few minutes ahead of schedule. They took seats and Jeff picked up the latest copy of *Theology Today* from the center table. Although not normally readers of such religious magazines, they had become familiar with the journal during their research on future events. Some of the back issues contained some excellent articles, although challenging to new students of the subject.

Thumbing through the journal, Jeff stopped in amazement at the article on page 68. It never occurred to him that this newest edition of the journal might also address the subject of hell. But here it was—in black and white—an article entitled "Many Faiths, Many Hells." The opening sentence of the article was enough to capture his attention:

> *"The threat of painful punishment in the hereafter has its counterparts in almost every major world religion."*

At that moment, Dr. Parker opened the door. "Good afternoon," he said as he invited Jeff and Julie into his office. "It's good to see you again."

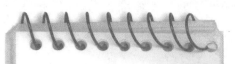

Therefore, since all these things will be dissolved, what manner of persons ought you to be in holy conduct and godliness. Nevertheless we, according to His promise, look for new heavens and a new earth in which righteousness dwells. Therefore, beloved, looking forward to these things, be diligent to be found by Him in peace, without spot and blameless.

2 Peter 3:11, 13–14

"Thank you, Uncle Rob, for your willingness to meet with us again," Julie replied.

"Have you seen this article?" Jeff asked, pointing to the magazine. "I was just starting to read it when . . ."

Dr. Parker interrupted, "Actually, I read the article several days ago. It contains a lot of very interesting information. Have a seat and we'll talk about some of the salient points."

Dr. Parker agreed with the article's author that most major religions have their own concept of hell. For example, in Islam hell is depicted as a huge crater of fire beneath a narrow bridge that all souls must pass over to go to paradise. Those who are judged by Allah as unworthy fall from the bridge and suffer endless physical torments in one of seven levels of hell. The Quran, Islam's holy book, uses much of the same imagery as the Bible to describe hell's fiery attributes. For example, hell is referred to as a "lake of fire" and a burning "bed of misery" where the wicked and the infidel suffer endlessly, apart from God.

In Hinduism, with its belief in reincarnation, hell is merely one stage in the continuum of a soul as it passes from one life to the next. Twenty-one Hindu hells serve as temporary places where bad karma, the evil that one commits during a lifetime, is burned away. Once purged, the soul is recycled to a higher state in the next life. In the hierarchy of Hindu hells, some are more terrible than others. These various hells are described in the ancient Hindu writings called *Puranas*.

Dr. Parker explained that a Hindu believes the soul of someone whose karma is not so bad may simply be reborn as an animal. Those who steal meat may return as vultures, while those who steal grain may return as rats. Worse sinners may come back as grass, shrubs or some inanimate object. Those who are extremely wicked face condemnation to the lower hells, where they may be scorched in hot sand, boiled in jars or devoured by ravens.

"Buddhism," Dr. Parker explained, "also teaches the concept of multiple hells. The Buddhist believes that these hells are temporary stops in a person's journey toward nirvana, a sort of blissful nonexistence. Most Buddhists believe that there are at least seven 'hot hells' that await those who commit evil. Each of these hells is surrounded by four torture chambers that include a fiery pit and a quagmire. However, Tibetan Buddhists also believe that there are eight 'cold hells' and certain 'frontier hells' for those guilty of lesser sins."

The threesome discussed the article for almost half an hour. Finally, Dr. Parker summarized the article. "All views of hell seem to have in common a sense that some evils are so great that there is no punishment in this life that can be adequate. As a result, people generally accept the belief that there must be some type of punishment beyond the grave. It is the God-given sense of justice that leads mankind to understand the necessity of punishment. Therefore, we find these beliefs in religions throughout the world."

"I thought that hell was something that only Christians believed in," Julie responded. "I had no idea that such a belief was universal."

"I only wish that Christians took hell more seriously," Dr. Parker noted.

"What do you mean?" Julie asked.

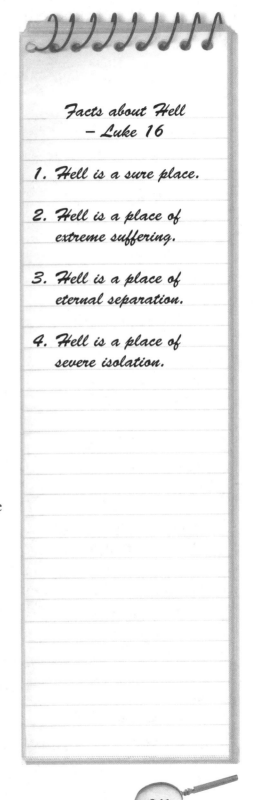

Facts about Hell
– Luke 16

1. Hell is a sure place.

2. Hell is a place of extreme suffering.

3. Hell is a place of eternal separation.

4. Hell is a place of severe isolation.

In light of His coming, what manner of person should I be?

- love others
  1 Thessalonians 3:12–13

- do not judge (don't criticize others)
  1 Corinthians 4:5

- comfort others
  1 Thessalonians 4:16, 18

- be patient and persevere
  James 5:8

- live a pure life
  1 John 2:28; 3:2–3; Titus 2:12–13

- set your heart and mind on things of God
  Colossians 3:1–4

- fellowship and support work of local congregation
  Hebrews 10:25

"The doctrine of hell is one of the most neglected doctrines in all of Scripture. Other than a curse, the idea of hell is generally ridiculed. It's as if the whole idea of hell were so old-fashioned that only the naive and ignorant would really believe such a place actually exists. People hate the idea of being held accountable for their words and actions by a holy God. They offer all sorts of reasons why hell could not possibly exist. Even religious leaders are now attacking the existence of hell. It's not unusual to hear someone say, 'I can't believe that a loving God would send anyone to hell.'"

Julie couldn't help but ask, "What kind of arguments do people use to counter the existence of hell?"

"Actually," Dr. Parker began, "people hold several different views. Probably one of the most popular is what I call the 'second chance' view. They believe that after death, God will still provide a way to escape hell."

"So these people actually do believe in hell," Jeff observed, "just not as it's taught in the Bible."

"Yes," Dr. Parker responded. "But these folks forget what Jesus taught in the story of the rich man and Lazarus in Luke 16. There is no indication that unbelievers will have a second chance after they die and enter hell. In addition to this story, we have the clear teaching of Hebrews 9:27: 'It is appointed for men to die once, but after this the judgment.' Again, there is no indication of a 'second chance' in that passage."

Julie was amazed at her uncle's comments. "I never thought that unbelievers would actually have a second chance if they ended up in hell. But I can understand why people might wish it could happen."

"Certainly, not all people believe that," he reminded Julie. "Many others believe that all people who go to hell will be totally annihilated. While they believe that Heaven is real, they refuse to believe that hell is an actual place. They believe that when people die and go to hell, their spirits simply cease to exist. Interestingly, they do believe that people who go to Heaven will exist forever. Of course, many others believe that all souls will be annihilated when they die—that physical death is the end of their existence."

"What sources of truth do these people use to defend this position?" Jeff asked. "It sounds more like wishful thinking than a logically developed argument."

"You're right, Jeff. I'm not aware of any rational argument for this position. It denies the resurrection of the unsaved that is clearly taught in John 5:28. It also denies the fact of conscious torment that is taught in John 3:16 and 36."

Before going any further, Dr. Parker opened his Bible and showed Jeff and Julie the passages from the gospel of John. He wanted to make sure that they saw for themselves exactly what the Bible teaches.

Dr. Parker continued, "As I mentioned, another popular objection to hell proposes that a loving God would not send people to such a horrific destiny. They cannot seem to reconcile that a loving God would create an eternal place of torment. However, these people fail to realize that a holy God cannot overlook evil. If God is holy as described in the Bible, and humans are truly free, there must be a place of judgment for those who freely turn away from God. If hell is not real, then either God is not holy, or humans are not truly free."

- *participate in the Lord's Supper*
  1 Corinthians 11:26

- *preach the Word of God*
  1 Timothy 4:1–2;
  1 Peter 5:2, 4

- *bring people to Christ*
  Jude 21–23

Evangelist Mordecai Ham tells about visiting a teenage girl on her deathbed:

Bending over her right at the end, he asked, "What is it like? What is it like?"

The lost girl's lips barely moved as she replied, "It's dark, oh, so dark! I'm lost! Lost! Forever, I'm lost!"

With those pathetic words as her dying testimony, she went out to a Christless eternity.

"I'm not quite sure I understand what you're saying," Julie responded.

Dr. Parker thought for a moment then explained his point from a different perspective. "I don't think anyone would deny that the world is full of injustice. People are killed for no reason at all; children are abandoned or beaten; tyrants rule over helpless people; the rich exploit the poor. While some criminals are punished on earth for their wicked deeds, the vast majority of evildoers goes unpunished.

"Yet, in spite of all of this, the instinct of justice remains strong in our thinking. In fact, one of the first sentences a child learns to say is 'That's not fair!' All of us want to see wickedness punished and righteousness rewarded. While we know, in the final analysis, that life is not fair, we still long for ultimate justice."

Julie nodded her head, indicating that she was beginning to understand the point her uncle was trying to make. He continued to present his argument.

"How can a God who is both all-powerful and totally good allow injustice to continue? If He does nothing to correct wrong, then He is either not all-powerful, or He doesn't really care about righteous behavior. But if He is all-powerful and good, as the Bible teaches, then He will ensure that justice prevails."

"Based upon everything you've explained," Jeff began, "it seems to me that God doesn't send people to hell—they choose it through their own decision to reject Christ."

"That's exactly the point the Apostle Paul made in Romans 1:18–25," Dr. Parker answered. "God created us as free individuals. We can choose to either honor Him or reject Him. As much as people may try to deny the existence of hell, our God-given sense of justice demands its existence. Additionally, the Scriptures confirm that such a place does exist. In Matthew 25:32 Jesus described a judgment in terms of a shepherd separating the sheep from the goats. Jesus clearly taught that in the future life, there would be people excluded from the presence of God—people who would experience a second death of eternal punishment."

As the discussion continued, the conversation turned in a different direction. In considering the reality of hell, all three participants were reminded of the importance of sharing the Gospel with a lost and dying world—a world where people are making choices every day that affect their eternity.

No excuse is good enough to miss Heaven!

QuestNote 34.1
Judgment for Evildoers

Use the following terms in a paragraph that explains the Great White Throne Judgment: the rest of the dead raised, second resurrection, Satan's final end, God on a white throne, books, the Book of Life, according to their works, second death, lake of fire.

QuestNote 34.2
Hell—Not the Place to Be

Summarize Jesus' teachings regarding the rich man and Lazarus in Luke 16.

Verses 19–21: _____

_____

_____

Verse 22: _____

_____

Verses 23–26:

1. Hell is a sure place. _____

_____

2. Hell is a place of extreme suffering. _____

_____

3. Hell is a place of eternal separation. _____

_____

4. Hell is a place of severe isolation. _____

_____

Verses 27–31: _____

QuestNote 34.3
Our Response to Jesus' Teachings

List five admonitions from the Bible as we consider the coming of Christ, judgment and our eternal future.

1. _____

   _____

   _____

2. _____

   _____

   _____

3. _____

   _____

   _____

4. _____

   _____

   _____

5. _____

   _____

   _____

Heaven: Our Home Awaits

Julie and the nurses sat around the break-room table enjoying a few minutes of peace and quiet. The emergency room had been especially busy this evening. But that's part of what causes ER nurses to choose this area of specialty. The emergency room is totally unpredictable; you never know what kind of trauma will come through the door next.

Julie was enjoying the down time with her coworkers. As part of her bachelor of science degree in nursing, she was required to complete a 13-week practicum in various disciplines. She had already successfully completed practicums in the geriatric and psychiatric units. Although the emergency room was not a required practicum for her program, Julie found it intriguing. That's why she requested permission to spend the next 13 weeks in the ER.

"Have you seen the new issue of *ER Nursing*?" the nursing supervisor asked. "I think you'll find the article 'Near Death—Back from Beyond' pretty interesting. Some of the testimonials sound just like some of the people we've treated here."

Remembering all the discussions she and Jeff had had about life beyond the grave, Julie's eyes grew wide. "Have you actually talked to people who have died and then come back to life?" she asked, not sure if she really wanted to hear the answer. "I thought near-death experiences were a hoax."

Paul, one of the more experienced ER nurses, was the first to offer his thoughts. "Well, that all depends on who you talk to. I have been working in emergency rooms for almost 18 years. I've certainly seen my share of people who we thought would never make it. Many of these survivors had pretty interesting stories to tell when they regained consciousness. I'll have to admit that there may be some truth to what they experienced."

And there shall be no more curse, but the throne of God and of the Lamb shall be in it, and His servants shall serve Him. They shall see His face, and His name shall be on their fore-heads. There shall be no night there: They need no lamp nor light of the sun, for the Lord God gives them light. And they shall reign forever and ever.

Revelation 22:3–5

"What kind of stories?" Julie asked.

Paul was more than happy to tell about some of his experiences. "Well, I remember one guy who had been struck by lightning. We thought he was a goner when he got here. But the docs were able to revive him. When he was finally able to talk, he said that he met this 'Being of Light' who granted him forgiveness for all the bad things he had done in his life."

Julie was fascinated by the story. "Did you believe him?"

"I don't know whether or not it really happened," Paul answered, "but I do believe that he was convinced of what he saw."

For the next few minutes, the nurses took turns telling about patients who had described near-death experiences. It was obvious that the nurses were not quite sure how much to believe of what they had heard. The mood around the table was pretty somber. That is, until the nursing supervisor told her story.

"I remember a school teacher who came into the ER in full cardiac arrest. She was on the operating table for a really long time. Nobody thought she would survive, but she did. After she came out of the recovery room, she told us that she had traveled down a long tunnel to a place filled with love and a beautiful bright white light. We were all convinced that what she was telling us was true. Until . . . she told us that Elvis Presley took her hand and guided her back."

Everyone in the room burst into laughter. For the rest of the shift, the nursing supervisor's story was the topic of conversation.

As Julie drove home that evening, the discussions about near-death experiences were still on her mind. All sorts of questions crowded her thinking. Had these people actually died? Were they hallucinating? Was the bright light the entrance to Heaven? As soon as Julie got to the dorm, she called Jeff and shared the stories. He was just as fascinated as Julie. It was surely something they wanted to learn more about. They agreed to meet at the library the following day.

Julie arrived shortly after the doors opened. After just a few minutes on the computer, she knew exactly which books she wanted to look at first. Soon she was sitting in a comfortable chair with a short stack of books next to her notebook.

The first book she opened explained that reports of strange events in the borderland between life and death were hardly new. Over 2000 years ago, in *The Republic*, Plato told the story of a gravely wounded soldier's journey toward "a straight light like a pillar, most nearly resembling a rainbow, but brighter and purer." A 13th-century monk wrote of a farmer who returned from the edge with tales of corridors of fire and icy paths to the afterlife. Although Julie was fascinated by the various stories, she was looking for more specific answers to her questions.

About an hour later, Jeff arrived. After a quick hug he picked up Dr. Raymond Moody's *Life After Life*. Until the publication of his book in 1975, many people had been hesitant to describe their experiences for fear of being labeled crazy. But the medical community's perception changed dramatically after the publication of Dr. Moody's research. His book contained the results of interviews he had conducted with 150 patients who reported these hard-to-define phenomena. In fact, it was Dr. Moody who coined the term "near-death experience" (NDE) in his book.

Terms to Know

Alpha, Antichrist, apocalyptic, Battle of Armageddon, beast, books, Bride of Christ, Daniel's prophecy of 70 weeks of years, Day of the Lord, end times, eschatology, eternal, false prophet, first resurrection, Great White Throne Judgment, Heaven, hell, Judgment of Nations, Judgment Seat of Christ, Kingdom of God/ Heaven, lake of fire, Lamb's Book of Life, man of sin, Marriage Supper of the Lamb, Millennial Reign, New Jerusalem, Omega, outer darkness, prophecy, Rapture, revelation, Satan's final battle, Second Coming, second death, second resurrection, Tribulation

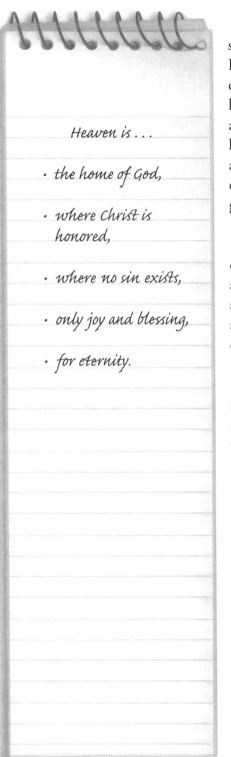

Heaven is . . .

· the home of God,

· where Christ is honored,

· where no sin exists,

· only joy and blessing,

· for eternity.

Scores of psychiatrists and neuroscientists have since sought to uncover the roots of these powerful experiences. But serious research into the phenomena has been difficult. Julie and Jeff learned that physiological findings have led many researchers to view NDEs not as glimpses into a world beyond, but as insights into the world within the human mind. Dr. Sherwin Nuland believes that NDEs are the result of opiate-like neuro-chemicals known as endorphins, which are released by the brain at times of great physical stress to deaden pain and alleviate fear.

However, Dr. Daniel Alkon says anoxia (oxygen deprivation in the brain) lies at the root of all NDEs. He argues that when death appears certain, the body will often shut down and "play dead" as a last course of action. His skepticism is significant because many years ago, as a result of a hemorrhage, he had his own near-death experience.

As Julie continued to review the research, she was struck by the fact that a "vision of Heaven" occured in so many of the reports. And, much to her surprise, these visions were seen by people throughout the world, both religious and non-religious. These people were convinced that they had seen Heaven and, in many cases, that they had even seen God Himself.

The morning passed quickly, but the couple hardly noticed the time. Their research had taken a slightly different direction since starting three hours earlier. The repeated mention of Heaven by those reporting near-death experiences caused them to start thinking about the afterlife. Of course, they remembered sermons about Heaven from time to time in church, but they had never really paid a whole lot of attention. This was the topic they wanted to discuss during their next appointment with Julie's uncle after lunch.

Always punctual, Jeff and Julie arrived at Dr. Parker's office just minutes before their scheduled appointment. "Hello, it's good to see you again. Come on in," Dr. Parker said as he held the door for them.

They entered and sat in the two chairs facing his desk. For the next few minutes, Jeff and Julie summarized their research and discussions about near-death experiences. Julie concluded that since so many people believed they had experienced Heaven, or at least some place that they thought was Heaven, she needed to know more about it.

"You've had quite an interesting few days," her uncle observed as he leaned back in his chair. "Let me ask both of you a question. Do you believe that Heaven is a real, actual place?"

Jeff was taken back by the question but responded first. "Well . . . yes, I do. Isn't that what the Bible teaches?"

"Yes, that is what the Bible teaches," Dr. Parker answered. "But I heard a little hesitancy in your voice. Did you know that most people say they believe in Heaven, but they don't believe that Heaven is an actual place?"

"How can you believe in Heaven and not believe that it's a real place?" Julie asked.

"When Heaven comes up in public debate these days, it is often used as a metaphor for man's ability to achieve a perfect society here on earth. Most people do not think of Heaven in the same terms as it is described in the Bible. In fact, I read an article the other day in which the writer refused to speculate about the architecture or geography associated with Heaven.

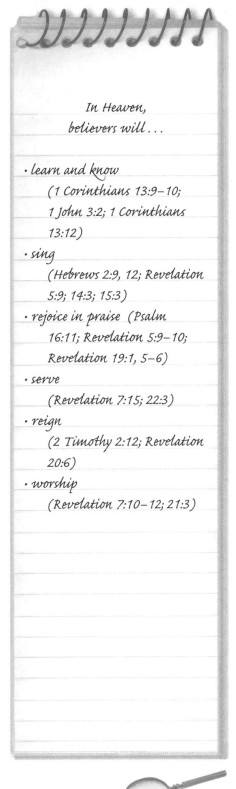

In Heaven, believers will . . .

- learn and know (1 Corinthians 13:9–10; 1 John 3:2; 1 Corinthians 13:12)
- sing (Hebrews 2:9, 12; Revelation 5:9; 14:3; 15:3)
- rejoice in praise (Psalm 16:11; Revelation 5:9–10; Revelation 19:1, 5–6)
- serve (Revelation 7:15; 22:3)
- reign (2 Timothy 2:12; Revelation 20:6)
- worship (Revelation 7:10–12; 21:3)

The Surety of the Future

• *Christ will return.*

• *Believers will meet Him in the air, never to be separated again.*

• *The earth will experience great tribulation, ending in Christ's triumphant return.*

• *Christ will establish His kingdom.*

• *All beings will be judged.*

• *Eternal punishment in hell awaits Satan, demons and unbelievers.*

• *Eternal life in Heaven awaits believers.*

"You see, many people view Heaven as a state of mind rather than an actual place as taught in Scripture. They have a vague and fuzzy idea of what Heaven is like. Their beliefs about Heaven are shaped by their own ideas, feelings and hopes."

"So, if people do not believe that Heaven is an actual place, they probably don't believe that hell is real either," Jeff observed.

"That's a pretty accurate statement," Dr. Parker responded. "I know that you came here to ask questions about Heaven, especially since we talked about hell last week. Believe it or not, some people say that they believe in Heaven but refuse to believe that there is a hell. Of course, the Bible teaches the reality of both places."

Dr. Parker paused for a moment before continuing. "So, let's talk about Heaven. I'd like to ask you another important question."

Julie could tell by looking at her uncle's face that the question he was about to ask was one they would have to seriously think about.

Right on cue, Dr. Parker asked Jeff and Julie a question they had never been asked before. "Is Heaven a place where you really want to be?"

354

QuestNotes 35.1
Heaven: God's Home

Take notes during class discussions regarding Heaven.

1. How does the Bible describe Heaven?

2. Where is Heaven located?

3. Is Heaven a real place?

4. Why is there a place called Heaven?

5. How long will it take for a believer to get to Heaven?

QuestNote 35.2
Experiencing Heaven

1. Who are the inhabitants of Heaven? _____

_____

_____

2. What is the position of God in Heaven? _____

_____

_____

3. What is the position of Christ in Heaven? _____

_____

_____

4. Write a description of Heaven based on the New Jerusalem. _____

_____

_____

5. What will characterize the new existence of believers in Heaven? _____

_____

_____

6. What will believers do in Heaven? _____

_____

_____

QuestNotes 35.3
Summary of Future Events

Review your summary statements in Week 33 and add statements for hell and Heaven as you summarize the Doctrine of Future Events (eschatology). You can use the listing of topics to guide your writing, but remember that there are overlapping timelines.

Christ will return for believers.

Believers will be raptured and appear before the Judgment Seat of Christ.

The earth will experience tribulation (judgments from Heaven, rise of the Antichrist and false prophet, Jewish evangelists and martyrs, the Battle of Armageddon).

QuestNote 35.3

Christ will return and establish His rule on earth.

Individuals will be judged (Satan and demons, all unbelievers).

Hell exists as a place of eternal punishment.

Heaven exists as a place of eternal blessing. The New Jerusalem is the beginning of believers' eternal home with God.

Review of Truths
130 Answers You Should Know

The Doctrine of the Holy Spirit

1.1   Who is the Holy Spirit?
1.2   What is the Trinity?
1.3   What is the Holy Spirit like?
1.4   What was the work of the Holy Spirit in relation to Creation?
1.5   What was the work of the Holy Spirit in relation to Old Testament believers?
1.6   What was the work of the Holy Spirit in relation to the Bible?
1.7   What was the work of the Holy Spirit in relation to Christ?
1.8   What did Jesus teach regarding the Holy Spirit?
1.9   What happened when the Holy Spirit came at Pentecost?
1.10 What is the baptism of the Holy Spirit?
1.11 What is the work of the Holy Spirit in relation to the Church?
1.12 What is the work of the Holy Spirit in relation to believers?
1.13 What is the fruit of the Holy Spirit?
1.14 What are the gifts of the Spirit?
1.15 What is blasphemy against the Holy Spirit?
1.16 What offenses can be committed against the Holy Spirit?
1.17 What is the believer's responsibility to the Holy Spirit?

The Doctrine of Christian Living

2.1   What event initiates the Christian life?
2.2   What is sanctification?
2.3   What is the believer's responsibility regarding the work of the Holy Spirit?
2.4   Why is Bible study critical for a believer?

2.5   Why is prayer critical for a believer?

2.6   How should believers pray?

2.7   How does God answer prayer?

2.8   Why is obedience critical for believers?

2.9   What happens to a believer who sins?

2.10   How can a believer avoid sin?

2.11   How does God chastise believers?

2.12   What does Scripture teach about the "old man" vs. the "new man"?

2.13   What is the relation between faith and works?

2.14   How can a believer walk worthy of the Lord?

2.15   How can a believer's mind be transformed?

2.16   Why must a believer be committed to personal purity?

2.17   What should characterize believers' relationships with each other?

2.18   How should believers resolve conflicts?

2.19   What should characterize believers' relationships with unbelievers?

2.20   How does the Christian life attract unbelievers to God?

2.21   What does it mean to live in submission to authority?

2.22   Why is the Christian life difficult?

2.23   How can believers be victorious in the Christian life?

The Doctrine of the Church

3.1   What is the definition of the Church?

3.2   What is the definition of a church?

3.3   How was the Church originally established?

3.4   What are some characteristics of the early church?

3.5   What are some purposes of a church?

3.6   What are church sacraments?

3.7   What is baptism?

3.8   Why do believers participate in water baptism?

3.9   What is the Lord's Supper?

3.10   How should believers participate in the Lord's Supper?

3.11   What leaders should a church have?

3.12   What qualifications should church leaders have?

3.13   Why are believers responsible to attend a local church?

3.14   Why should believers be involved in worship?

3.15   How should believers serve within a local church?

3.16 Why should believers financially support their local church?
3.17 Should believers still practice tithing today?
3.18 Should believers still observe the Sabbath today?
3.19 Why should believers be involved in personal evangelism?
3.20 What responsibility do believers have regarding missions?

The Doctrine of Spirit Beings

ANGELS

4.1   What are angels?
4.2   What are angels like?
4.3   What different kinds of angels are there?
4.4   How many angels are there?
4.5   What service do angels perform in relation to God?
4.6   What is meant by the Old Testament phrase "Angel of the Lord"?
4.7   What service did angels perform in relation to the nation of Israel?
4.8   What service did angels perform in relation to Jesus?
4.9   What service do angels perform in relation to believers?
4.10 What will angels do in the future?

SATAN

4.11 Who is Satan?
4.12 What is the origin of Satan?
4.13 What is Satan's ultimate goal?
4.14 What is Satan like (his nature)?
4.15 What does Satan do (his abilities)?
4.16 What was Satan's relationship to Christ?
4.17 How did sin (evil) enter the world?
4.18 What is temptation?
4.19 Where does temptation come from?
4.20 How should believers respond to Satan?
4.21 What role will Satan have during the Tribulation?
4.22 What is the eventual destiny of Satan?

DEMONS

4.23   What are demons?

4.24   What are demons like?

4.25   What did demons do in relation to Christ's ministry?

4.26   What can demons do in relation to unbelievers?

4.27   What can demons do in relation to believers?

4.28   What cautions should believers exercise in relation to demons?

4.29   What is the eventual destiny of demons?

The Doctrine of Future Events

THE SECOND COMING OF CHRIST

5.1   Why do Christians believe that Christ will some day return to earth?

5.2   What will be the purpose of Christ coming again?

5.3   How did early believers feel about Christ's return?

5.4   How do believers respond to the truth that Christ will come again?

5.5   When will Christ return?

5.6   What happens to unsaved people when they die?

5.7   What happens to saved people when they die?

5.8   What is meant by the "End Times"?

5.9   What is meant by the "Rapture"?

5.10   What events will occur in the Rapture?

5.11   When will the Rapture occur?

5.12   What is meant by the "Great Tribulation"?

5.13   What is the timing of the Tribulation in relation to Jewish history?

5.14   What events will occur on earth during the first half of the Tribulation?

5.15   Who is the Antichrist?

5.16   Who is the false prophet?

5.17   Will people be saved during the Tribulation?

5.18   What events will occur on earth during the second half of the Tribulation?

5.19   What is happening in Heaven during the Tribulation on earth?

5.20   What is the "Judgment Seat of Christ"?

5.21   What is the "Marriage Supper of the Lamb"?

5.22   What is the "Battle of Armageddon"?

HELL AND HEAVEN

QuestNote 36.1
Review of Doctrines

Succinctly state the essential truths related to the doctrines studied this semester.

1. **The Doctrine of the Holy Spirit**

2. **The Doctrine of Christian Living**

QuestNote 36.1
Review of Doctrines

3. The Doctrine of the Church

4. The Doctrine of Spirit Beings

Angels

Satan

Demons

QuestNote 36.1
Review of Doctrines

5. **The Doctrine of Future Events**

The Second Coming of Christ

Hell

Heaven

QuestNote 36.2
Review of RealityQuest

On the basis of the doctrines studied, describe the three top commitments you need to make in your life.

1. _____

_____

_____

_____

2. _____

_____

_____

_____

3. _____

_____

_____

_____

Describe how you feel this course has helped you so far.

_____

_____

_____

_____

_____

Commitment to Life
Based on the Truths of God

Accepting the challenges presented in this course, I am willing to commit myself to a life based on the truths of God. I understand that this includes my commitment to mature choices, a right attitude and conscientious actions.

We give thanks to the God and Father of our Lord Jesus Christ, praying always for you, since we heard of your faith in Christ Jesus and of your love for all the saints; because of the hope which is laid up for you in heaven, of which you heard before in the word of the truth of the gospel, which has come to you, as it has also to the world, and is bringing forth fruit, as it is also among you since the day you heard and knew the grace of God in truth.

Colossians 1:3–6

Signed _____

Dated _____